PART TWO

THE WINDOW OF THE

LORD'S

RETURN

2012 – 2020

THE UNFOLDING SIGNS OF THE END TIMES

—JOHN SHOREY—

For more information go to
www.tribulationtruth.com

Window of the Lord's Return Part Two, 2012 - 2020
By John Shorey

ISBN-978-0-578-14086-5

Cover Design: David Whitlock
Printed in the United States of America
Copyright© April 2015

First Printing May 2015

TABLE OF CONTENTS

Letters From the Pulpits to the Pews 1

Pre-Introduction. 5

Introduction 7

1. Could We be Wrong About A Pre-Tribulation Rapture? 17

2. A Needed Second Look at the Rapture 26

3. The Sealing of the 144,000 and Other Pre-Rapture Events 36

4. How Does the United States Fit into the Prophetic Picture? 45

5. God's "No Man Left Behind" 49

6. Can Gentiles be Saved After the Rapture? 54

7. Other Bible Teachers' Perspectives Concerning the Rapture 58

8. The Coming Antichrist 75

9. Pre-vs.-Mid-Tribulation View of the Rapture 87

10. Post Tribulation View of the Rapture 111

11. Mid-Tribulation Rapture? I Make my Case. 126

12. A Warning to Those Who Add or Subtract from God's Word. 146

13. Can We Know When the Lord is Actually Coming? 152

14. The Window of the Lord's Return. 159

15. The Night of the Blood Moon. 179

16. God's Warning of Coming Judgement. 186

17. There Will be Signs in the Sun, Moon and the Stars 199

18. The Five End Times Wars. 222

19. A Possible Scenario Story Leading up to the Rapture. 238

20. How to Prepare for the End Times. 256

21. Closing Thoughts About the Lord's Return. .274

Appendix. 280

ACKNOWLEDGMENTS

I would like to thank a few of those who have continued with me as I have worked on this study. Those who gave me their opinions and encouragement were:

My wife Shawnette, Betty Bransford, and Lottie Holland.

My biggest thanks to Jim Bakker who has so generosuly shared his platform to allow me to spread the message the Holy Spirit has revealed to me.

LETTERS FROM THE
PULPITS TO THE PEWS

I have known John Shorey since 1974 and have always observed his very careful and considerate study of the Word of God. Therefore, I feel sure that this venture into the subject of the prophetic future is accompanied by much prayer and careful study of God's Word. It is a task most men would try to avoid, for the task is awesome, and the message often is rejected by the rank and file of Christianity.

Based upon the serious situations simmering in our world, his writings make the reader determine to be all God would have him to be as the time-clock moves closer to midnight.

May we determine to have oil in our lamps, trimmed and shining brightly, until that day.
Reverend Jack and Betty Bransford
Retired pastors and former Alaska District Superintendent of the Assembly of God

---

Dear Brother John,

I am an Assembly of God pastor, I grew up in the Assemblies from a child, and we have always believed and were taught that the church would not have to go through the seven year tribulation period. We would be caught up in the air with Christ and escape this period. After reading your book and searching the scriptures, I am convinced that we will not be pre-raptured before this period of time. It looks like the scriptures are saying the Rapture will occur somewhere around the sealing on the 144,000 Jewish missionaries. Wow, what an eye-opener. Thank you so much for all your hard work. Now mine is just beginning!

Thanks for laboring and putting the scriptures together where even a man, who from childhood was taught differently, can make sense of it all.

I will be ordering five books to start because I must get some key people on my side here in the church. You know what I mean I'm sure.

In Jesus Christ's Service,
~Pastor Bill

John,

As I told you at the onset of our recent phone conversation, I had come to a place several years ago, to see more of a "mid-trib" rapture as a result of a series of sermons I preached on the book of Revelation.

Your book brought all of that back to me, but with many more of the "blanks" filled in. How significant is the instruction God gave to Daniel clearly telling him that certain details of the end were to be "sealed up" until the end was near, which is obviously the time we are presently living in. I know how difficult it will be for mainstream Pentecostals to even "open" their hearts and minds to the possibility of a change in their theology concerning the Rapture. I know, our movement (A/G) has prided themselves on being doctrinally pure in this area, having never altered their pre-trib position in almost 100 years, or since the inception of the Assemblies of God fellowship. They guard and protect all our doctrines – 16 Fundamental Truths—with a vengeance. I am praying, along with you, that the Holy Spirit will get through to some of our key leaders, and your book will "fall" into their hands and into their hearts. How significant it is that Jim Bakker has received your message. He certainly does have an international reach. I have always felt a mandate from God to preach Christ's coming to the church and urge them to be "ready" and "prepared" to meet the Lord VERY SOON. I will continue to do that with even more urgency and conviction.

Blessings!

~Pastor Cal

Hi Brother John Shorey,

I received your book last Saturday. I have a "Bible Institute" degree from Liberty University, and I have studied prophecy since 1994.

Thanks be to God that he used you to write this book! I believe the Holy Spirit has used you to write this book and do surgery in detail to the Book of Revelation and events soon to occur. I have already read to page 128, and it is hard to put it down!

You make a compelling case for the mid-tribulation rapture as I have not ever read before! And you prove it by using and allowing the Bible to interpret it by the Old Testament, giving meaning to the New Testament and vice-versa which I believe is the right method of interpretation. The Window of the Lord's Return is a masterpiece for the End Times.

Glory to God!

~Antonio

John,

I obtained this book about a month ago. I started reading it one night and literally couldn't put it down until I had finished it. I have always had so many questions about the timing of the rapture--even after attending Bible School, hearing many sermons and teachings, and studying the Word myself over the years. I believe the Lord has really blessed John with fresh understanding on this subject. After being so inspired, I called him and ordered 40 copies and have been handing them out to my pastor friends and to anyone who has an open mind. I really have had some positive feedback. This to me is a real must read. Thanks, John, for being obedient and taking the time and effort to write this book.

*~*Jerry

If you are a born again Christian, you have often heard about the Rapture and you probably believe it will happen before the Great Tribulation. That has been my belief for over 35 years, but not anymore. John Shorey in his thorough study of end time events has helped me to see the truth that we will not be living in heaven during the first half of this earth-shaking seven year period. I recommend you read this book, check every Bible verse, make spiritual and physical preparations, and share it with your family, pastor and friends.

We need not be surprised as these near future events begin to happen. If we heed Jesus' words to watch, be not deceived, beware, be ready and hear what the Spirit says to the churches. I pray that you will give John Shorey the opportunity to help you take a second look at the timing of the Rapture, have a more accurate understanding of the scriptures, and seriously consider the warning signs of our times.

*~*Charles

This is one of the most riveting books I have ever read. I read all the scriptures in the Bible, and they back up everything John Shorey says. For the many of us who have been taught and believed in the pre-trib theology, this book will open our hearts and minds to a different belief. God bless John Shorey for writing this book in obedience to God's urging.

*~*Bonnie

Since watching John Shorey on the Jim Bakker show I had to have this book. It has changed my view of the last days. I am happy that John has opened my eyes to what the Bible really says about the End Times.

*~*Joseph

Hi John,

Your book has opened up a new avenue for study. I have enjoyed reading your book and studying with a whole new outlook on the timing of the end time events.

The thing I like most about your book is that it does not tell us how to believe, or that we should believe in Mid-Tribulation. It gives us "Food for Thought" that we can study for ourselves. It leaves me wondering where we went wrong in our study to start with. Why, with all the well-educated and highly respected ministers that are preaching today, have we not heard more preaching about this?

I have to say, John, You have done a very good job putting this book together. I can tell that you have spent a lot of time in prayer and did a great deal of time studying to do this. I thank God for godly men like you who are willing to share your thoughts and put them into a book for all to read. That gives us a chance to study and make our own minds up as to what we believe for ourselves.

I pray that your book will reach many readers all over the world and give them "Food for Thought." You have made a believer of me!

Thank you and may God richly bless you and your family,

-Lois

Part Two

The Window of the Lord's Return

Some will ask, "Why did you write a part two, too, The Window of the Lord's Return, and How is it different from part one?" It has been two years since I last updated, The Window of the Lord's Return. In these last two years, so much revelation concerning the Last Days has come to light. In fact I believe we have seen more Last Days revelation come to light in the last two to three years then what we have seen in the last twenty to thirty years. The thought recently hit me, that the Lord has personally revealed many important revelations to me in the last two years and this information is important and it should be put into a book. At first, I thought the Lord was prompting me to write a new book but after prayer and listening to the inner voice of the Holy Spirit, I heard loud and clear that this material completes my book, The Window of the Lord's Return. I realized that if this material went into a new book and the reader had not read the "Part One", they would not have all the information God has assigned me to deliver to the Body of Christ. So what I have done is placed a new book within the covers of my first book, The Window of the Lord's Return, and called it "Part Two".

The Core of this new information is found in five chapters and the Appendix.

15. The Night of the Blood Moon, A Revelation Revealed.

16. God's Warning of Coming judgment.

17. There will be Signs in the Sun Moon and the Stars.

18. The Five End Times Wars.

19. A Possible Scenario Story Leading up to the Rapture.

These five chapters were all written separately but they fit so well together that I believe the Holy Spirit was helping me write this new book, one piece to a time. Almost every chapter in this new edition has been touched with new studies and revelations. I will list just a few below.

Added to the Introduction is the "Mystery of the Fig Tree"

Added to Chapter Eight, "New Clues to the Coming Antichrist."

Added to Chapter Ten, "Is the Day of the Lord", The Rapture?

Added to Chapter Eleven, "The Matthew 24 study".

The Appendix has about forty pages of great prepper advice, much that cannot be found anywhere. Also included here is a section called, "Words from God's Prophets" This section includes many must read prophecies that are current and of the utmost importance that we receive this information, Now.

For those of you who enjoy reading this book and want to dig deeper, to have a greater understanding of the book of Revelation and the End-Times. My second book called Unlocking the Mystery of the Book of Revelation, is a must read book. The Holy Spirit opened my eyes to see why the book of Revelation is so hard to understand. It seems so hard to believe but I believe I was allowed to see the key to unlocking the Mystery of the Book of Revelation. This book and other teaching materials can be found on my website, www.tribulationtruth.com.

May God Bless You, As You Search God's Word for Truth. **John Shorey**

INTRODUCTION

For centuries Christians have asked the question, "When will the Lord return?" I have written this book, *The Window of the Lord's Return*, because I believe I can present evidence from scripture and from the signs of the times that the Lord could return during this coming window of time between 2012 - 2020. Please allow me to introduce my thoughts here.

It is my conviction that when Israel became a nation in 1948, a time-clock was started, and this generation will not pass away until the return of the Lord Jesus. Recently, I heard Reverend John Hagee say that we are the "Terminal Generation." I believe he meant that this generation will live to see the coming of the Lord. Since 1948, sixty-four years of this generation have expired. In chapter Thirteen of this book, I will present a strong argument for my position that seventy years is the length of a generation.

Some will ask, "Where do you see the Bible teach that Israel would be restored as a nation in the last days?" First, we need to look at Ezekiel 36:24 (KJV), *"For I will take you from among the heathen, and gather you out of all countries, and will bring you into your own land."*

Then look at Matthew 24:32-34. *Learn this lesson from the fig tree: As soon as its twigs get tender and its leaves come out, you know that summer is near. Even so, when you see all these things, you know that it is near, right at the door.* **I tell you the truth; this generation will certainly not pass away until all these things have happened**.

The reference to the fig tree is referring to the nation of Israel, and figs refer to the people of Israel. I will show Bible references to support this teaching. The following verses in Joel 1:6-7 (KJV) show that Israel, the land that belongs to God, will be laid waste. This land is described as the fig tree, a fig tree that died. *For a nation is come upon my land, strong and without number, whose teeth are the teeth of a lion, and he hath the cheek teeth of a great lion. He hath laid my vine waste and barked my fig tree: he hath made it clean bare, and cast it away: the branches thereof are made white.*

The next verse I will use will show that the people of Israel were referred to as figs. They would be judged and removed from their land and dispersed around the world in judgment from God. Jeremiah 24:8-9 (KJV), *"And as the evil figs, which cannot be eaten, they are so evil; surely thus saith the LORD, So will I give Zedekiah the king of Judah, and his princes, and the residue of Jerusalem, that remain in this land, and them that dwell in the land of Egypt: And I will deliver them to be removed into all the kingdoms of the earth for their hurt, to be a reproach and a proverb, a taunt and a curse, in all the places whither I shall drive them."*

In 1948, the Children of Israel were allowed to return to the land of Israel. Note in Matthew 24:32: *When you see the branches get tender and its leaves come out …*, this is referring to life coming back to the fig tree or Israel, which was fulfilled in 1948. When you look at Joel 1:6-7 (above), you see that when the nation of Israel was brought back to life, it was referred to as the fig tree. This "land" is also referred to as the land that belongs to God, also called Israel.

The Mystery of the Fig Tree Unveiled

It was in January, 2015 when I was studying the topic of the Fig tree from Matthew 24, for a program to air on the Jim Bakker show that I spotted something in a verse found in Amos 9 that made me do a double-take. What I saw made me realize that our calculations of a generation from the rebirth of Israel in 1948 may have been off by one year. When I saw this it excited me because it made the pieces of the puzzle fit together. I knew that before I could share this, I had to study and prove in my own mind that this was a revelation from God as opposed to some thoughts coming out of my own mind.

First, what I will do is go back and share what I was studying and bring this new revelation into my study in its proper context and time. I was preparing to share a study from my first book, *The Window of the Lord's Return* on the rebirth of Israel as described in Matthew 24, where this rebirth of Israel is described as the budding of the Fig Tree.

The Key point I wanted to make was that this prophecy of the fig tree was fulfilled in 1948 and why we cannot kick the ball down the road for another seven years, as some have asserted. I will show that the land of Israel is the Fig Tree and that the Bible clearly states in the following prophetic verses that Israel would be planted in their **own land**. Without reference to the Jews going back to Jerusalem or occupying this city as a condition of the fulfillment of the rebirth of Israel as stated in Matthew 24 and other Old Testament Scriptures.

The following verses will establish that the nation of Israel is the fig tree that is destroyed. Then I will show that the future restoration of Israel will reference the Jews returning to their **own land**.

Joel 1:6-7 (KJV) shows that Israel is the Land that belongs to God and will be laid waste. This land is described as the fig tree. (A fig tree that died.) *"For a nation is come upon my land. strong and without number, whose teeth are the teeth of a lion, and hath the cheek teeth of a great lion. He hath laid my vine waste and barked my fig tree: he hath made it clean bare, and cast it away: the branches thereof are made white."* (When a fig tree dies, its branches turn white.)

Ezekiel 36:24 (KJV) *"For I will take you from among the heathen, and gather you out of all countries, and will bring you into **your own land**."*

Jeremiah 30:3 (NIV) *"The days are coming, declares the Lord, 'When I will bring my people Israel and Judah back from captivity and restore them to **the land I gave to their forefathers** to possess,' says the Lord."*

Amos 9:14,15 (NIV) *"I will bring back my exiled people Israel. They will rebuild the ruined cities and live in them. They will plant vineyards and drink their wine. They will make gardens and eat their fruit. **I will plant Israel in their own land**, never again to be uprooted from **the land I have given them**, says the Lord your God."* This verse in Amos 9 is the key to understanding what the Lord has shown me. If you will look at this verse, it says, **"I will plant Israel in their own land."** This event happened in May of 1948.

This event established the beginning of the generation of promise. "This generation will not pass away until the coming of the Son of Man." The Fig tree that would come back to life was planted in 1948, but we need to look at the Prophecy in Matthew a bit closer because this promise is connected to the twigs getting tender (This is the shooting forth of buds), and new leaves are coming out.

Matthew 24:32-33 (NIV) *"Learn this lesson from the fig tree: **As soon as its twigs get tender and its leaves come out**, you know that summer is near. Even so, when you see all these things, you know that it is near, right at the door. I tell you the truth; this generation will certainly not pass away until all these things have happened."*

When you plant a tree, which entails disturbing its roots, it goes into a kind of shock that sets back new growth for a while. When Israel was transplanted back into **its own land** in May of 1948, it was immediately attacked by its enemies. This was a shock; Israel's enemies tried to uproot this newly planted nation. This war went on for several months until the Armistice was signed on February 24, 1949. This peace agreement went into full force on March 23, 1949. This agreement that would allow Israel to flourish as a nation went into full effect three days after the beginning of spring in 1949. It was at this time that the prophecy in Matthew 24 was fulfilled. It was the beginning of spring 1949 that the fig tree of Israel budded and shot forth new leaves. This was the beginning moment of the last generation that would not pass away until the coming of the Son of Man. This revelation shifts the timing of Christ's coming by one year. The seventy year window is now shifted to conclude in 2019.

In my book, *The Window of the Lord's Return*, it clearly shows from my study of key scripture verses found in Revelation 13: 5-7, Daniel 7: 25, Daniel 9:27, and Daniel chapter 12, that the saints will go through three and a half years of what is described as Daniels Seventieth Week or what I call the seven year Great Tribulation. These verses establish the Rapture as an event that will happen three and a half years after the antichrist signs a new Armistice agreement with Israel.

This is referenced in Daniel 9:27, (NIV) *"He will confirm a covenant with many for one 'seven', but in the middle of that seven he will put an end to sacrifice and offering. And the one who causes desolations will place abominations on a wing of the temple until the end that is decreed is poured out on him."*

When you factor in this new revelation, that Israel budded and shot forth new leaves and started to thrive as a nation in 1949, this one year shift in the time-line of coming events brings these future events into better focus. Seventy years later from 1949 is 2019. These seventy years are the time of a generation, as established in Psalms 90:10.

Many Bible teachers are in agreement that the Rapture will happen during the Feast of Trumpets, which is a fall harvest festival occurring in September. With a mid-tribulation rapture occurring in September of 2019, and with three and a half years of tribulation leading up to the Rapture, this would require that the tribulation period would need to start in March of 2016.

Below, I will share my thoughts on how I see coming events and dates coming into focus. What I am now seeing are three dates as reference points to build the time line that will lead us to the beginning of the Great Tribulation and the Coming of the Lord.

1. March 20, 2015 with the solar eclipse marking the judgment of the gentile nations, I believe the instrument of judgment God will use will be earthquakes and financial reckoning.

2. The fourth blood moon in September, 2015 follows by two weeks the end of the seven year Shemittah cycle. I see this as the time of financial reckoning that will manifest in America as well as globally. The global collapse will lead to the need for a global solution, thus paving the way for the coming One World Government and the coming antichrist.

3. March, 2016 may be the beginning of the Great Tribulation that will last for three and a half years and conclude on the Feast of Trumpets in September of 2019.

The first step in the timeline leading to the beginning of the Great Tribulation from my list above concerns the coming solar eclipse this March 20 2015. Jewish Rabbis have said this event will be a time for judgment of the gentile nations. David Wilkerson, in his book "*Racing Toward Judgment*", says that one of the Instruments of judgment that God uses to judge nations is earthquakes. It is a scary thought to hear prophecies coming from many different men of God who are warning us of mega earthquakes coming to America and the world.

I have held to a conviction that the next domino to fall, that will trigger the other dominoes leading to the beginning of the Great Tribulation and the Coming of

the Lord, will be Financial reckoning and I fear that a great earthquake could be tied to this first domino. In fact, I believe a possible strong candidate for this coming earthquake will be the Cascadia fault off the coast of the Northwest. David Wilkerson, in his book, *"Racing Toward Judgment"* on page 67, says, "Judgment begins on the coasts". The Cascadia fault is sixty to eighty miles off the coast of the Northwest.

In May of 2013, I had a dream of a great earthquake coming to the Northwest. In this dream, I was talking to people I knew from the Northwest about this quake, and it was as if it had already happened. In this conversation, we knew this quake was the same size as what hit Alaska in 1964. That quake was a 9.2 on the Richter scale. Since that time more than one scientific report has been published concerning the Cascadia fault and this coming earthquake. They have said it is overdue, and it will produce an earthquake in the Seattle area of 9.2 on the Richter scale, (confirming my dream). I will go into greater detail in a later chapter concerning this dream.

A few days after I shared this dream with a large group of contacts, I received a link to prophecies from Jonathan Hansen concerning a vision God gave him that predicted this same Northwest quake with greater detail. **One of the things God showed Him was a coming collapse of the stock market following this quake.**

Then in the spring of 2014, God led me to revelations God gave David Wilkerson concerning the biggest earthquake in history that would come to America. What was interesting is that even though he did not say it would be in the Northwest, how he described it geographically sounds like the Northwest. **In his vision, he also saw a coming collapse of the stock market and economic confusion following this event.**

David Wilkerson, Jonathan Hansen and I have seen the coming of the greatest earthquake in history, hitting the Northwest portion of the United States. Jim Bakker and John Paul Jackson have seen a soon coming quake in California that John Paul Jackson predicted would be so bad that it would change the shape of the state of California on the maps. What is interesting about his vision is, in 2011, he came out with this prophecy but said it would not happen until there would be a devastating storm, a storm of the century event. This storm hit California in November 2014, and did vast damage all the way to the Northwest.

The third fault on the watch list is the New Madrid fault that goes from the Great lakes down the Mississippi river to the Gulf of Mexico. There have been numerous prophetic voices predicting that this event will happen soon. John Kilpatrick, for one, has said God told him that if America supports the dividing of Israel that God will split America apart.

What I am seeing as a frightening possibility is that at some point between the solar eclipse on March 20, 2015, and the coming fourth Blood Moon in September 2015, we could see all three of these major quakes happening at the same time as David Wilkerson alluded to in his book *"The Vision"* This combined earthquake event would certainly be the worst earthquake disaster in world history. As I was saying, above, I see these coming mega quakes coming sometime close to the spring of 2015 and no later than around the end of September. I really hope and pray I am wrong. I see what I have explained above as the first major domino that will trigger all the coming dominoes leading to the beginning of the Great Tribulation and the Coming of the Lord.

I listed three dates to watch above; the second date to watch will be the date of September 28, 2015, the date of the fourth Blood Moon. Jonathan Cahn has pointed out that we could very well see economic chaos along with the collapse of the Stock Market at this time at the end of the Shemittah Year cycle that falls just two weeks before the fourth Blood Moon.

It makes sense that the first domino of earthquakes will be followed by the stock market collapse and the coming economic collapse that will topple nations. The order of these events makes a lot of sense to me. With an economic collapse following closely after the fourth Blood Moon, it is easy for me to see the collapse of global economies and the collapse of nations that will make the world ripe for the rise of the antichrist.

I did not go into great detail about what the effects these coming earthquakes would have on America and the world. On the West coast, hydroelectric dams would collapse causing the whole electric grid from Washington to California to shut down. The destruction of these dams would cause great loss of life. Transportation in and out of the west coast would be destroyed. This would include collapsing bridges, covered mountain passes and a tsunami that would take out west coast ports. This would lead to famine, starvation, anarchy and martial law. The damage to transportation and the east coast electric grid from the effects of the New Madrid earthquake would be unimaginable. The panic on Wall Street and Main Street America would be impossible to control.

If David Wilkerson is correct, then what we will witness in America will be happening around the world. Again I will copy a quote from his book that I shared earlier above. **"The earth is actually going to shake, and there will be numerous other earthquakes in various places throughout the world."**

I do not take pleasure or satisfaction in connecting the dots of coming events for 2015 and 2016. I am calling it as I see it. I would rather be wrong in giving a warning too early then to be wrong and give the warning too late.

I truly believe these earthquakes are coming, and it makes so much sense that they will happen this coming year as appointed judgments on the nations. So as we approach the last of the Blood Moons, it again makes sense that the economic chaos following the judgment of God on the nations in 2015 will make the world ripe for a global solution to what will appear as insurmountable problems. I see a global solution to these problems being rolled out in early 2016 in time for a new One World Government to be put in place. Then the man of sin will arise, and we will see the beginning of the Great Tribulation starting by March of 2016.

It has taken the sharing of many thoughts to finally pull this study all together, but as I shared in the beginning of this study, the unveiling of the mystery of the fig tree points to the last generation starting in the spring of 1949 with the budding of the newly planted fig tree of the nation of Israel. If the coming of the Lord is to take place during The Feast of Trumpets in September of 2019,(seventy years from the budding of the fig tree of Israel), then, as I have pointed out above, I see the beginning of the Great Tribulation starting in the spring of 2016. This math adds up to the saints going through three and a half years, or forty-two months, of War on the Saints as is described in both Daniel and the book of Revelation.

My greatest fear is for all those who are holding to the hope of a pre-tribulation Rapture. They are being taught that the Rapture will occur and the Great Tribulation will be starting this next September of 2015 at the timing of the fourth Blood Moon.

(Those who hold to the pre-tribulation teaching do not see the need to prepare.) Earthquakes, major calamities and disruptions in critical infrastructure may be rampart before we reach the fourth Blood Moon. When it is realized that the Rapture is not happening as soon as was thought, it will be too late to prepare for what the saints will be going through. Will this lead to a great falling away? I believe it will.

John Shorey

In this study, I will be looking at this narrowing window of time and attempt to show how close we could be to the Lord's return. I will also be sharing an in-depth study on the Rapture and other related end-time subjects. One of the subjects that I will be covering is the timing of the Rapture in relation to the Great Tribulation. I realize that this is a sensitive subject for many. Please realize that the timing of the Rapture has no bearing on our salvation, but it is important that we get it right.

I was reared mostly in the Catholic church (my mother's choice) where I never heard anything about end time doctrines. My father came from a large Protestant Christian family. It was from his family that I was first exposed to end-times doctrines. When I became a Christian in 1974, the church was all abuzz about the Rapture and imminent return of Jesus Christ. So, early in my new Christian walk, the Rapture doctrine and the book of Revelation caught my attention and have been an area of interest throughout my Christian life. I have heard some great preaching on the subject, mostly years ago. It is interesting, now that we are so close to the return of Christ, that we do not seem to hear as much preaching on the subject. Why is that? Could it be that many prophets of our time have been wrong, and sayings like, "You are as slow as the Second Coming," have made some steer away from this important end-time teaching? Could it be that some think that end-time events are too negative a subject and that the church is so caught up in the things of the world and keeping up with the Joneses that we do not want to hear this message that would disrupt our lives? I was recently told by an evangelist friend of mine that he was told by some churches that preaching on the End Times is off limits. They want feel-good messages and messages on prosperity.

I have studied this subject intently over the years, and have come up with some interesting thoughts. This book is presented to you as a journey. You will find some questions presented in the first few chapters are answered later in the book. When I combine my study in the Word of God with current events as they are, I am seeing so many of the parts of the mystery of the Lord's return coming together. I feel God's direction to share them with others; I believe God is trying to tell us something. I am convinced that we do not want to get caught unprepared for these coming events.

I have separated these thoughts into a few individual, separate discussions, and you can decide if they all fit together.

The question that each of us needs to ask ourselves is this—do we really *want* to know the truth about the biblical timetable for the Rapture and the End Times? Allow me to illustrate.

Let us consider that the Bible admonishes us in 2 Timothy 2:15 (KJV) to *Study to show thyself approved unto God, a workman that needeth not to be ashamed, rightly dividing the word of truth.* It is interesting what is said in Daniel, *"...the truth of this prophecy would be sealed until the time of the end...* So since we have been trying to explain the return of Christ for hundreds of years, could it be possible that we have made some mistakes? Is studying and rightly dividing the word of truth concerning the biblical prophecies of the End Times important enough to take a serious second look at from time to time? I believe it is.

— CHAPTER ONE —

COULD WE BE WRONG ABOUT A PRE-TRIBULATION RAPTURE?

C ould it be possible that many mainstream churches have taken an incorrect doctrinal position on the End Times for their churches? Is there a chance that a doctrine on the Rapture and the imminent return of Christ is based on incomplete information and poor interpretation of scripture?

I do not understand why it is so hard for us to accept the fact that we do not always get our theology right. Throughout church history, time has had a way of revealing the truth and correcting our errors. Based on what Jesus said about John, Jesus' disciples thought that Jesus would return in their lifetime. All but one of Jesus' disciples were martyred, and they were wrong about the timing of Christ's return.

Then replacement theology came along, which teaches that the nation of Israel was rejected by God and was replaced by the church; therefore, Israel did not have to be reborn as a nation. Again, they were wrong.

Then almost two hundred years ago, John Darby had a revelation that said that Christ would return for His bride before the seven year Great Tribulation started. His teaching, along with the dream of a teenage girl, switched the church from a mid-tribulation view of the Rapture to a pre-tribulation view. If you research and study the history of the pre-tribulation view of the Rapture, you will see it was cloaked in confusion and disagreement. Over time, this change in doctrine was accepted because it sounded good and made people feel comfortable. Just because a doctrine sounds good does not make it right.

What I have discovered in sharing the first printing of this book with pastors is that pastors are not generally open to the possibility that they have taught a doctrine on Christ's coming that could be flawed. Sid Roth wrote a book called *They Thought for Themselves.* This book is about Jews who have discovered Jesus as their Lord because they thought for themselves. It is interesting the reaction I get from lay Christians who are students of the Word and have an open mind to read this study. I hear comments like the following all the time: "I read it twice, I looked up the Bible verses, I believe you are right, and I just cannot believe we didn't see it." A friend with whom I attended college told me, "John, when I saw where you were going with the mid-tribulation view of the Rapture, I did not want you to be right, but after I studied your position, I have to say, I believe you are right." **One Christian leader told me. "If anyone will read your book with an open mind, they will get it. The case for the mid-tribulation Rapture is so plain in your book."**

When I went to Northwest Bible College, one of the top doctrinal professors told us that the rapture doctrine is most popular in America. In many parts of the world, Christians have suffered and are suffering persecution, hunger, and martyrdom on a daily basis. It is interesting that American Christians believe so strongly that God would never allow His people to suffer and go through tribulation. We have lost sight of the fact that in the early church, many of Christ's disciples were martyred. We should all read the book *Foxe's Book of Martyrs.* We would realize that when the church was standing up to persecution, the fruit of their lives was the salvation of souls.

Could the church be wrong about the timing of the Rapture? If so, what would be the ramifications of this mistake? Please do not be offended if my conclusions fly totally contrary to what most Christian churches believe. I have been exploring this question from the beginning of this study, and I am seeing too many scriptures that do not add up, building a strong case that we will not see a pre-tribulation Rapture.

In all sincerity, I really would like someone to show me why I am wrong in my interpretation because I would much rather see a pre-tribulation rapture as opposed to going through part of the Great Tribulation. One question has to be asked: "Is it possible to misread God's Word and have a belief system based on the poor interpretation of God's Word?"

Here is an example from John 14:2-3 (KJV): *In my Father's house are many mansions; if it were not so, I would have told you. I go to prepare a place for you and if I go and prepare a place for you, I will come again and receive you to myself, that where I am, there you may be also.*

Many Christians read this and believe that we will all have a mansion in heaven. In fact, hymns and songs have been written enforcing this belief. If you read this verse carefully, you will see that this verse does not say that we will all have a mansion. What it says is, *"In my Father's house are MANY mansions..."* Many mansions does not mean that all places in heaven are mansions. In Hollywood, there are many mansions, but all homes in that area are not mansions. The Word goes on to say, *"I go to prepare a place for you . . ."* The key word here is "PLACE." A place could be a tent and a cot. Does not God's Word teach us that we can lay up treasures in heaven? It is similar to having a heavenly bank account. Does not the Word say that only what is done for Christ will last? If your place in heaven is based on your heavenly bank account, do you believe you will have a mansion or a tent waiting for you?

If you are still not convinced that we will not all have a mansion in heaven you should read 1 Corinthians 3:12-15: *For no one can lay any foundation other than the one already laid, which is Jesus Christ. If any man builds on this foundation using gold, silver, costly stones, wood, hay, or straw, his work will be shown for what it is, because the Day will bring it to light. It will be revealed with fire, and the fire will test the quality of each man's work. If what he has built survives, he will receive his reward. If it is burned up, he will suffer loss, he himself will be saved, but only as one escaping through the flames.*

I have received some comments, saying that I should not burst people's bubbles, but I should only teach words of comfort. I am sorry, but I disagree. I feel too many preachers have watered down their preaching instead of being honest with their flocks. When we arrive in eternity, would you want to be found guilty of holding back the truth? People need to realize that only what is done for Christ will count. Life is short, and we need to be sure we are burning our candle for God

I believe the most important book we should ever read is the Bible, inspired and breathed into his chosen writers to deliver the Word of God to man. I believe a mistake we can make is to take the writings and teachings of man as gospel-truth, instead of checking these teachings against the Word of God. In the New Testament, during the time of Paul, when he was preaching to the Bereans, Paul gave us a good example to follow. Acts 17:11: *Now the Bereans were of more noble character than the Thessalonians, for they received the message with great eagerness and examined the Scriptures every day to see if what Paul said was true.*

A book I recently read is a good example of why we need to examine what we read against what God's Word says. This book was about the Rapture and the End Times, written by a well-known teacher and preacher, a man I highly respect. In his chapter on the Rapture of the church, he says that 2 Thessalonians assures its readers that no saint will experience the seven-year Great Tribulation. The author does not quote chapter and verse to back up this statement. After reading 2 Thessalonians, I could not find any verse to back up this statement. We need to be like the Bereans, who search the scriptures to see if the Word of God backs up what our Bible teachers are telling us. Please do not question my motives for using real examples. The author of that book is a great teacher, but I am finding that even great teachers can be wrong in their interpretations of the Bible. I am sure that I will have mistakes pointed out to me as well.

As I mentioned at the beginning of these writings, I have always had a keen interest in prophecy and end-time teachings, much of which have come from the book of Revelation. I have always enjoyed reading Revelation, and I am spurred on to read more of Revelation from the admonition given in Revelation 1:3, *Blessed is the one who reads the words of this prophecy, and blessed are those who hear it and take to heart what is written in it, because the time is near.*

As I read the book of Revelation from my early years as a Christian, sometimes my reading generated more questions than answers. I have always believed that as we approach the time of the Lord's coming, the answers to our questions would be made plain to us. Over the years, I have read many of the classic books on the End Times. But as I look at Revelation in light of what has been happening in the last few years, I am seeing events coming together that make total sense. These events were never thought about thirty years ago when I was only a few years old in the Lord. Thirty years ago, who would have imagined the problems we are having with the Muslim nations and terrorists today? How could we have thought that the Muslim countries would hate America and want to see us destroyed, so that we would not stand in the way of the radical Muslims' ultimate goal of destroying Israel? Today, things are becoming so clear that I believe we need to revisit how we connect the dots to help us understand how the end-times' puzzle fits together.

To start off, I will examine the question: "Could we be wrong about a pre-Tribulation Rapture?" The first thought being: "When does the Great Tribulation start?" This is easy for my discussion, as it seems that many are in agreement that the Great Tribulation begins with the antichrist establishing a seven-year peace treaty with Israel and the Muslim nations, as mentioned in the book of Daniel. This event cannot happen until the antichrist is revealed. I believe the antichrist is revealed close to the opening of the first seal of the seven seals found in chapter six of the book of Revelation.

THE FIRST SIX SEALS IN REVELATION

The opening of the first seal reveals events that will take place close to the beginning of the Great Tribulation. I will show you from God's Word why the events that mark the beginning of the wrath of God will not occur until the trumpet judgments and the bowls of God's wrath later in the Great Tribulation. As I studied for this book, I learned that many believe that the wrath of God starts with the four horses at the opening of the seals. I will address this in greater detail later in this study, showing why I believe that the seals are not part of God's wrath. So for the sake of setting up my later discussion, I will bring you through the opening of the seals.

One reason, which points to the seals as representing events happening during the Great Tribulation that are not the outpouring of God's wrath, is that the fifth seal is the martyrdom of the saints. It is not God doing this to His saints.

A second reason why I do not believe that the opening of the seals represents the wrath of God is that God promised his saints that we would not be accounted for the wrath to come. If you carefully read Revelation 5:2, it says, *And I saw a mighty angel proclaiming in a loud voice, Who is worthy to break the seals and open the scroll? But no one in heaven or on earth or under the earth could open the scroll or even look inside it.* As you read this, you see there was a message in the opening of each seal, but it is inside the scroll that the wrath of God is found. The seals are only the locks that are opened by the Lamb to reveal what is contained inside the scroll.

The Lamb opened the first seal in Revelation 6:1. Here, it talks of a white horse and its rider who held a bow. This is seen as a false Christ coming. I believe this is the revealing of the antichrist. We have seen false Christs for generations, but this one is riding a white horse, imitating Christ. He has a bow, and no arrows are mentioned, for he is only an imitator without the power. My chapter on the coming antichrist is very insightful and will help in understanding this seal.

The second seal is a red horse whose rider is to take peace from the earth. Wars will be happening all over the earth. This will be far worse than wars and rumors of wars. I believe we will see many wars breaking out throughout the earth to mark this event; yet these wars are not the ones to come at the end of the seven-year time of the Great Tribulation. Later, I will discuss some thoughts I have on which nations I believe will be part of this seal.

The third seal talks about a black horse. Its rider will hold a pair of scales and say, *A quart of wheat for a day's wages.* This is talking about global famine, and this famine will result in the starvation of millions. Economists are saying that hyper-inflation and a global economic collapse are coming. It is no longer a question of *if,* but *when* it will hit. It has been said that 2009 was a year of many crop failures in America. In America we are used to having all the food we need just a few minutes away at the local grocery store. In America, we have had our silos full of wheat and other food commodities for years. What I have recently learned is that our back-up reserves have been disappearing, much being sold to China and Russia. China, a country that was once content to live on a bowl of rice, is now expanding their diet as their economy has expanded.

The year 2010 brought even more crop and food failures. A drought in Russia destroyed twenty-five percent of their wheat crops, and they cut off all exports of wheat in 2010. Russia is the world's largest exporter of wheat. When the seals start to open, and food shortages start to emerge, it will cause food panics unlike anything we have ever seen in America. This will lead to rapid inflation and rationing to try to keep food on store shelves. Ultimately, this will lead to a system of rationing that will require us to accept the antichrist's system in order to buy our food.

The fourth seal is Death followed by Hades, revealed as a rider on a pale horse. *And I looked, and behold a pale horse: and his name that sat on him was Death, and Hell followed with him. And power was given unto them over the fourth part of the earth, to kill with sword, and with hunger, and with death, and with the beasts of the earth.* Revelation 6:8 (KJV). I believe that the plagues mentioned here could be the work of terrorists using biological weapons to bring plagues and death to those whom this event is describing. It may also be possible that the plagues could be epidemics from viruses like SARS (severe acute respiratory system) or the swine flu. I have heard some say that this seal will lead to the death of one-quarter of the inhabitants on earth, but if we read this carefully, we realize it is saying that it will affect one-quarter of the earth geographically. It does not say that all will die in this one-quarter of the earth. Later, I will explain which countries could be involved. Three of these countries comprise about one-quarter of the earth's geopraphic area.

The fifth seal talks about Christians who are slain for their testimony of Christ during this part of the Great Tribulation. Read the following from Revelation 6:9-11, "*When he opened the Fifth Seal, I saw under the altar, the souls of those who had been slain because of the word of God and the testimony they had maintained. They called out in a loud voice, How long, Sovereign Lord, holy and true, until you judge the inhabitants of the earth and avenge our blood? Then each of them was given a white robe, and they were told to wait a little longer, until the number of their fellow servants and brothers who were to be killed as they had been, was completed.*" Currently the vilest of muslim terrorists groups, called ISIS are purging all christians out of Iraq and other muslim countries. Even the beheading little children who profess Christ. I believe the Fifth Seal is describing what we are currently seeing today.

These are interesting verses to think about. These verses reveal that Christians will be killed for staying true to God under the rule of the antichrist. One point to note is that they are under the altar, not at the throne. They are being told to wait for others who are to be killed, for they were to join them. Remember this phrase, "under the altar." It will be important later in this study. Also, note that those who are being killed for their testimony for Christ are asking God, *How long, Sovereign Lord, holy and true, until you judge the inhabitants of the earth and avenge our blood?* They could only ask this question if the wrath of God had not yet started. I will be showing more reasons later that add evidence to why the wrath of God does not start until

Revelation, chapter eight.

The sixth seal describes events happening in the heavens with the sun and the moon being affected. Revelation 6:12-17 (KJV) says, *And I beheld when he had opened the sixth seal, and, lo, there was a great earthquake; and the sun became black as sackcloth of hair, and the moon became as blood; And the stars of heaven fell unto the earth, even as a fig tree casteth her untimely figs, when she is shaken of a mighty wind. And the heaven departed as a scroll when it is rolled together; and every mountain and island were moved out of their places. And the kings of the earth, and the great men, and the rich men, and the chief captains, and the mighty men, and every bondman, and every free man, hid themselves in the dens and in the rocks of the mountains; And said to the mountains and rocks, Fall on us, and hide us from the face of him that sitteth on the throne, and from the wrath of the Lamb: For the great day of his wrath is come; and who shall be able to stand?*

This passage explains that the sun will be turned black and the moon will be blood-red. It talks about great earthquakes affecting the whole earth. I will cover this seal in greater detail later in this study. I believe that a cataclysmic event has been waiting to happen that could fulfill this seal.

Now something interesting happens during a break before the seventh seal is opened. In fact, all of chapter seven takes place and it is not until chapter eight that the seventh seal is opened. When the seventh seal is opened at the beginning of chapter eight, it says that when he opened the seal, there was silence in heaven for about half an hour, and the seventh seal was left a mystery.

What I want to do is go back and look at what happened in chapter seven. I have read other writers of prophecy discourse about this being an interlude during which millions of souls would be reached with the Gospel. This is the time the 144,000 Jews will be sealed to go out and take the Gospel and salvation knowledge of Christ to the Jews. I have heard over the years that eventually the time of the Gentiles would be over, and the dispensation for the revealing of Christ to the Jews would begin. At this time, I want to show you some events that are happening in Revelation 7.

The first observation I have made about the events of this chapter is that, if this is the time of the sealing of the 144,000 Jewish evangelists, then would it not make sense this is the beginning of the dispensation of the salvation of the Jews? And would it also make sense that this would be the end of the time of the Gentiles? As I discuss later in this study, I believe a great ingathering of Jews will occur at this time, just before the Rapture of God's elect.

Of course, there can be no credible study of the Rapture or the End Times unless we first thoroughly examine the scriptures. In the next chapter, I want to show you the scriptures that talk about the Rapture. Look at those scriptures from every angle possible, and decide what the Bible really says about the time of the return of Jesus Christ to rapture His saints.

— CHAPTER TWO —
A NEEDED SECOND LOOK
AT THE RAPTURE

B efore we offer any thoughts on the time of the Rapture, let's take a look at scripture verses that talk about the Rapture of the believers. It seems to be a consensus among prophetic teachers in the pre-tribulation camp that Revelation 4:1 describes the Rapture.

Revelation 4:1: *After this I looked, and there before me was a door standing open in heaven. And the voice I had first heard speaking to me like a trumpet said, "Come up here, and I will show you what must take place after this."*

Jack Van Impe and many other teachers of a pre-tribulation rapture use this verse to denote the Rapture of the church. Before we look at this verse in depth, I want to show you an event that happens in chapter seven after the sealing of the 144,000 Jews.

Revelation 7:9-12, *After this I looked and there before me was a great multitude that no one could count, from every nation, tribe, people and language, standing before the throne and in front of the Lamb. They were wearing white robes and were holding palm branches in their hands. And they cried out in a loud voice: "Salvation belongs to our God, who sits on the throne, and to the Lamb." All the angels were standing around the throne and around the elders and the four living creatures. They fell down on their faces before the throne and worshiped God, saying, "Amen! Praise and glory and wisdom and thanks and honor and power and strength be to our God for ever and ever, Amen!"*

Look at verse nine. It says, *A great multitude from every nation, tribe, people and language, standing before the throne.* Now go down to verse thirteen and hear what one of the elders who was at the throne has to say. *Then one of the elders asked me, "These in white robes -- who are they, and where did they come from?"*

Now, get the picture? One of the elders, who day and night is around the throne of God, suddenly notices a great multitude of uncountable Christians in white robes standing around the throne worshiping God. He acts as if he did not know where they came from. Then he answers his own question. Listen to the answer in verse fourteen. *I answered, "Sir, you know." And he said, "These are they who have come out of the Great Tribulation; they have washed their robes and made them white in the blood of the Lamb."*

My question is, "If this great multitude just now showed up in heaven after the sixth seal, and the Rapture happened in Revelation 4:1 before the Great Tribulation started, then who are these who just showed up?" Is there a second rapture for the tribulation saints? I do not see that as scriptural. To me, what we are seeing here is the church going through part of the Great Tribulation until it gets to the part where the 144,000 Jews are sealed to be God's chosen messengers to start preaching and revealing the love of Christ to the Jewish nation. I believe the 144,000 Jewish evangelists will bring many Jews to Christ, just in time for the Rapture of the bride of Christ.

One argument I have heard against what I just said is that this is a second rapture for the Jews. A big problem with this explanation is, "Why would you have a separate rapture of the Jews when all Jews who accept Christ will go up in the Rapture anyway?" Besides, the two witnesses who play a part in God's dealing with the Jews are not even yet mentioned. They are to witness to the Jewish nation for three and a half years during the second half of the Great Tribulation. So how can Revelation 7:14 be about a second rapture of the Jews? Also, when you read Revelation 7:9, it says these people who have just appeared in heaven came from every nation, tribe, people, and language.

The same argument is used that these are Jews who are living in every nation and speaking in every language. However, this verse says, "Every people, nation and language." This verse ties into another, and the result is very exciting. Look at Revelation 5:9. This scripture reveals that only Jesus was qualified to open the seals. *You are worthy to take the scroll and to open its seals, because you were slain, and with your blood you purchased men for God from every tribe, language, people, and nation.* THIS IS ME AND YOU! THIS IS THE CHURCH THAT CHRIST REDEEMED WITH HIS BLOOD. Now look at Revelation 7:9 and you will see Christ collecting in the Rapture what he has already purchased! *After this I looked, and there before me was a great multitude that no one could count, from every NATION, TRIBE, PEOPLE, and LANGUAGE, standing before the throne and in front of the Lamb.*

Please pay close attention to what I am going to show you.

I want to take you back to an event that lies between Revelation 4:1 and Revelation 7:11-14. Remember, Revelation 4:1 is the pre-tribulation verse for the occurrence of the Rapture. Look at Revelation 5:11-12 (KJV): *And I beheld, and I heard the voice of many angels around the throne and the beasts and the elders: and the number of them was ten thousand times ten thousand and thousands of thousands; Saying with a loud voice, "Worthy is the Lamb that was slain to receive power and riches and wisdom and strength, and honor and glory and blessing."* **Look at who are described as being around the throne. It is angels, beasts, and elders, but there is no mention of <u>saints</u> around the throne. If the saints were raptured in Revelation 4:1, they would be around the throne in white robes in this passage.**

Now when you read Revelation 7:11-14, you hear the elder, who is always around the throne, asking, "Who are these multitudes that no one can number in white robes...?" Who are these people that have suddenly shown up? The elder then reflects, and he says that they are those who have come out of the Great Tribulation. **Now stop right here and think about this. If the Rapture had already happened pre-tribulation in Revelation 4:1, then the millions of pre-tribulation Christians would have been in white robes around the throne in both Revelation chapter five and chapter seven. They would have blended in with the multitude that the elder was asking about in Revelation 7:11-14. Do you think there are two raptures? No. I do not see this in the Word of God. These verses show the Rapture just did not happen until Revelation 7:9.**

Next, I would like to go to 1 Thessalonians 4:15-18. This scripture shows why the Rapture could not have happened until after Revelation 5:11-12. Read 1 Thessalonians 4:15-18 (KJV*): For this we say unto you by the word of the Lord, that we which are alive and remain unto the coming of the Lord shall not prevent them which are asleep. For the*

Lord himself shall descend from heaven with a shout, with the voice of the archangel, and
with the trump of God: and the dead in Christ will rise first: Then we which are alive and
remain shall be caught up together with them in the clouds, to meet the Lord in the air:
and so shall we ever be with the Lord. *Wherefore comfort one another with these words.*

This scripture shows why the Rapture could not have happened until after Revelation
5:11-12. Read 1 Thessalonians 4:17 again. It says that both the dead in Christ and
those who are alive will both be raptured together to meet the Lord in the air, and
then it says that we shall ever be with the Lord. If, from the point of the Rapture,
we will forever be with the Lord, then think about this. If we will be with the Lord,
then we would have been with the Lord in Revelation 5:11-12 around the throne.
But if there is no mention of saints in white robes around the throne in Revelation
5:11-12, the Rapture has not yet happened. So when the elder in Revelation 7:9 and
13 asks who the multitudes in white robes are, whom no man can number, he is told
that they are the saints who have come out of the Great Tribulation. Revelation 7:9,
After this I looked and there before me was a great multitude that no one could count,
from every nation, tribe, people, and language standing before the throne and in front of
the Lamb. They were holding palm branches in their hands. Can it be any clearer? The
Rapture, the only Rapture, has just taken place according to Revelation 7:9.

MARTYRED SAINTS SHOW THE
TIMING OF THE RAPTURE

One argument I get is that these saints who suddenly appeared around the throne are
martyred saints who are coming out of the Great Tribulation as they are being killed
for refusing to take the mark of the beast. I want you to think about this as I share
why this could not be the case. To begin with, this event around the throne happens
in an instant, proven by the fact that the elder who is asking the question is always
at the throne. It is like he blinked, and suddenly there were millions in white robes
around the throne. This would mean, if they were the Great Tribulation martyred
saints, they would have had to be killed at the same time. I do not think this is
possible. Also, there is a second problem with this opinion. When the saints are being
martyred, as described in the fifth seal in Revelation 6:9, it says the martyred saints

are under the altar and not at the throne. Also, they are asking in, Revelation 6:10-11, *"How long, Sovereign Lord, holy and true, until you judge the inhabitants of the earth and avenge our blood?" Then each of them was given a white robe, and they were told to wait a little longer, until the number of their fellow servants and brothers who were to be killed as they had been was completed.*

The next scripture says they were each given a white robe. Notice, they are still under the altar, not at the throne! If these martyred saints were at the throne in Revelation 6:10, in the white robes that they were given while under the altar, then the elder in Revelation 7 would not have even noticed a second multitude showing up. For over 2000 years, millions of Christians have been martyred. At the point of the Rapture, they would all have <u>been</u> at the throne. **Now think about this: if all the martyred saints of all time do not show up at the throne until Revelation 7:9, then how can we say the Rapture happened in Revelation 4:1?**

Now let us go back and look at Revelation 4:1, which is considered the pre-tribulation rapture verse. *After this I looked, and there before me was a door standing open in heaven. And the voice I had first heard speaking to me like a trumpet said, "Come up here, and I will show you what must take place after this." At once I was in the Spirit, and there before me was the throne in heaven with someone sitting on it.*

I just do not see the Rapture in Revelation 4:1. What I do see is John, the Revelator, being taken to heaven to the very throne of God where God tells him, *...I will show you what must take place after this.* Paul had a similar experience when Christ was disclosing revelations to him. Then, if you will go to Revelation 19:11, you will see the heavens opened up again, just like what happened in Revelation 4:1. Read Revelation 19:11: *I saw heaven standing open, and there before me was a white horse, whose rider is called Faithful and True. With justice he judges and makes war.* This is a revelation of Christ after the battles have been won, and the marriage supper of the Lamb is about to take place. This heaven standing open does not mean a gateway is open for a rapture event because, if you will go back to Revelation 19:6-8, you will see that the saints are already <u>in</u> heaven about to celebrate with Christ at the marriage supper of the Lamb. Read Revelation 19:6-8, *Then I heard what sounded like a great multitude, like the roar of rushing waters, and like loud peals of thunder, shouting: "Hallelujah! For our Lord God Almighty reigns. Let us rejoice and be glad and give him* *glory! For the wedding of the Lamb has come, and his bride has made herself ready. Fine linen, bright and clean, was given her to wear."*

I would like to know where there is a second or third scripture that shows the timing of the Rapture as being pre-tribulation. I was taught in Bible school that doctrine has to be backed with the witness of two or three scriptures. You might ask where I see two or more scriptures to support the Rapture as happening after the opening of the six seals in Revelation 6. I have already shown you a number of verses in Revelation that show the Rapture happening after the opening of the seals during the Great Tribulation. Now I want to show you from the Gospels where I see three places that describe almost verbatim what is happening in the opening of the seven seals of Revelation 6. All three describe what I believe is the Rapture, happening after the opening of the sixth seal.

Please read the following verses:

Matthew 24:4-5: *Jesus answered: "Watch out that no one deceives you. For many will come in my name claiming, 'I am the Christ', and will deceive many."* This verse coincides with the first seal about false christs.

Matthew 24:7a: *Nation will rise against nation, and kingdom against kingdom.* This coincides with the second seal.

Matthew 24:7b: *There will be famines and earthquakes in various places.* This coincides with the third seal.

Matthew 24:9: *Then you will be handed over to be persecuted and put to death, and you will be hated by all nations because of me.* This coincides with the fifth seal.

Matthew 24:29: *The sun will be darkened, and the moon will not give its light, the stars will fall from the sky, and the heavenly bodies will be shaken.* This coincides with the sixth seal.

Now read Matthew 24:30-31, ***At that time***, *the sign of the Son of Man will appear in the sky, and all the nations of the earth will mourn. They will see the Son of Man coming on the clouds of the sky, with power and great glory. And he will send his angels with a loud trumpet call, and they will gather his elect from the four winds, from one end of the heavens to the other.* Am I taking this wrong? I do not think so. This sounds like the

Rapture. Look at Mark 13:6-27, and you will see a similar parallel. Then look at Luke 21:8-27, and you will see another.

One of the established arguments for the pre-tribulation rapture is conjecture from Revelation 4:1. Some teachers are saying that the church is not mentioned after Revelation 4:1. I do not see this as true, for it says the saints would be martyred during the fifth seal of the Great Tribulation in Revelation 6. Again, Revelation 14:11-13 is about those who are taking the mark of the beast and the necessity of patience for the saints. During this time, it goes on to say, many saints will be martyred. Now I know there are some who teach that these are tribulation saints. Tell me, where are the words "tribulation saints" found in the Bible?

Realize, we are setting the time of the Rapture as a pre-tribulation event, not based on scripture verses, but based on the omission of the word "church" after Revelation 4:1. As I see it, the timing of the Rapture is too important to establish this doctrine without scripture, chapter, and verse to back up this position. **Plus, think about this: what is the church? It is the saints that make the church, so if the saints are mentioned after Revelation 4:1, then the church is mentioned. Later in chapter nine, I did a study on the church, and what I found really strengthens what I am saying here.**

In closing, I want to pose the question that some will ask, "Is it really that important when the Rapture happens? Shouldn't we just be ready?" This is a good question. The problem I see is, if the churches are teaching that the Rapture will come before the Great Tribulation, then this gives the church a false sense of security. I have heard pastors say God would not allow His church to go through suffering. Yet as I mentioned above in Revelation 14:11-13, it says that the saints will have to have patient endurance during the Great Tribulation when the antichrist is pushing his system of the mark of the beast. If the saints who have expected the pre-tribulation Rapture are suddenly seeing themselves in the Great Tribulation without warning and no time to get ready for this turbulent time, I believe it will cause many Christians to turn away from God. They may start believing that they have been abandoned by God, and I believe it will lead to many accepting the system of the antichrist rather than starve to death. I believe that the events happening today, with the world economies on the verge of collapse, are setting the stage to cause the world populations to look for a savior in the form of the antichrist. We, as believers, need to be the ones who are looking for the signs of Christ's coming and preparing for the tribulation of these times as Joseph did in his time. When the hard times come, we will be able to take care of the needs of our families and others. We will be in a position to be used by God for the greatest revival the world has ever seen.

Before moving to the next section, I want to add some thoughts that will answer questions I often hear when this Bible verse is referenced: 1 Thessalonians 1:10 (KJV): *Even Jesus, which delivered us from the wrath to come.* This text is often taken to mean that the Rapture of the church will be a pre-tribulation event in order to spare the church from the wrath of the Great Tribulation, but the Bible calls the time period leading up to the return of Christ "the Great Tribulation," a seven-year period that will become more and more intense as we get closer to Christ's return.

If you look at the beginning of the Great Tribulation and the opening of the seven seals, you will see events that are similar to what has happened for all of time: wars, earthquakes, and famine, and even the martyrdom of the saints, which is the fifth seal. Just like a woman's labor pains grow in intensity as the time of the delivery of her child approaches, it will be the same growth of intensity when the seals are opened at the beginning of the Great Tribulation. The intensity of wars will be higher, earthquakes will be more devastating, and famines will be more widespread.

Most Christians, who hold to the pre-tribulation Rapture believe we will miss out on the seals and all of the Great Tribulation. Many people refer to 1 Thessalonians 1:10 (KJV): *And to wait for his Son from heaven, whom he raised from the dead, even Jesus, which delivered us from the wrath to come.* If you look closely at this verse, it says that we will be delivered from the wrath to come. This means the "wrath of God." This verse does not say that we will be delivered from tribulation to come. In fact, think about it, the Great Tribulation is not called the Great Wrath of God. When the seals are being opened, I do not see the evidence in God's Word that shows the seals are the wrath of God. God does not start wars, create famine, or martyr His saints as described in the fifth seal. The wrath of God does not start until Revelation 8-9, and then it picks up again in chapter fifteen.

We need to understand what the Bible teaches about tribulation. The Bible says tribulation works patience. It is interesting that during the Great Tribulation when the saints are battling with the antichrist, God's Word tells us in Revelation 13:10, *If anyone is to go into captivity, into captivity he will go. If anyone is to be killed with the sword, he will be killed. This calls for patient endurance on the part of the saints.* I believe this passage is teaching us that the saints will be going through a period of tribulation that will lead to a great revival and at the same time bring about a purification of the church. Does the Bible not teach us that Christ is coming back for a pure bride worthy of being called the bride of Christ?

Many churches today are caught up in entertaining both the saved and the lost, believing that great performances will make people feel good and so draw them closer to God. I believe if we would put more effort into ministering to the needs of the hurting, we would see a greater maturity in our churches and a greater harvest of the lost.

I have been reading a book on the Azusa Street Revival called *Azusa Street, They Told Me Their Stories.* I believe this was the greatest revival in the last hundred years. It was a 24/7 prayer meeting. It did not have great entertainers. It didn't even have great preachers. But the Glory of God was there. A cloud, like what appeared in the Old Testament called the Shekinah Glory, would appear. Witnesses said it was like basking in the breath of God, or like being swallowed in God's presence. Miracles were happening as God's servants reached out and prayed for those in need of a miracle. Arms grew back, legs grew back. I don't mean adding a couple of inches; I mean whole arms and legs grew back all the way to the finger nails. One man could hardly make enough of a living to buy food, but when God grew back his arm, his boss rehired him, and this man came back to the revival with two hundred people. Many received miracles that night. A crowd from a deaf school came, and they were all healed. In 1910, it was prophesied by two of the leaders, William Seymour and Charles Parham, that the Shekinah Glory would return and a revival greater then Azusa would come in about one hundred years. This prophecy was made at the end of the Azusa Street Revival in 1910. This revival is due; I believe the revival will come when the time of Christ's coming brings the church back to its knees.

The Bible teaches us that in these last days we will see the birth pains increasing preceding Christ's coming. His coming will turn people's lives upside down. As God allows economic and natural disasters on the earth, Christians may ask, "What are you doing, God?" I imagine God's answer to this question would be, "I'm not trying to make you feel good. I'm trying to wake you up and draw you closer to Me."

I was recently reading a book, *The Best of A. W. Tozer*. He was a great preacher of a previous generation, and he made a profound statement in the chapter, "Why We are Lukewarm About Christ's Return":

"History reveals that times of suffering for the church have also been times of looking upward. Tribulation has always sobered God's people and encouraged them to look for and yearn after the return of the Lord. Our present preoccupation with this world may be a warning of bitter days to come. God will wean us from the earth someway—the easy way if possible, the hard way if necessary. It's up to us."

— CHAPTER THREE —

THE SEALING OF THE 144,000 AND OTHER PRE-RAPTURE EVENTS

As I studied the book of Revelation, I noticed that the 144,000 Jews were mentioned in chapter seven and again in chapter fourteen. In chapter seven, the sealing of these Jews happens just before what I am convinced is the time of the Rapture of the church. As it says in Revelation 7:9, *After this, I looked and there before me was a great multitude that no one could count...* In Revelation 14, the 144,000 are mentioned again, and as we continue reading Revelation 14:14-19, we see what appears to be Jesus Christ in the clouds. Then in Revelation 14:15, the angel tells Jesus Christ to take his sickle and reap the harvest, for he says that the harvest of the earth is ripe. Read on in Revelation 14:16. It says that the earth was harvested. When I read this, it sounded like another description of the Rapture that happened in Revelation 7:9-10.

Matthew 24:30-31 gives another description of the Rapture that sounds very similar to Revelation 14:16. The Matthew passage says, *At that time the sign of the Son of Man will appear in the sky and all the nations of the earth will mourn. They will see the Son of Man coming on the clouds of the sky, with power and great glory. And he will send his angels with a loud trumpet call, and they will gather his elect from the four winds, from one end of the heavens to the other.* Continuing to read in Revelation 14:17-19, the scripture mentions a second harvest of the earth, harvested and thrown into the winepress of God's wrath. When we go back to the time of the Rapture as described in Revelation 7, we will see that the wrath of God starts in Revelation 8 and 9. When I first discovered this, I figured that Revelation 7 and 14 were two places in

Revelation that covered the same event, basically showing that not all of Revelation is in chronological order. This thought made sense to me until I pondered further and eventually got stumped as I studied the 144,000 mentioned in Revelation 14.

As I read Revelation 14:3, *And they sang a new song before the throne,* this really confused me, for this was showing that the 144,000 were with Christ around the throne, <u>before</u> the Rapture described in Revelation 14:14. It really did not seem possible that these Jews would be with Christ around the throne before the Rapture because this would contradict Revelation 9:4!

The Revelation 9:4 passage describes the fifth trumpet of God's wrath when the scorpion-like locusts are instructed not to harm the grass or trees but only those who did not have the mark of God on their foreheads. This passage shows the 144,000 Jews on the earth during the wrath of God, but they are not being harmed by God's wrath. So, you see why I was confused to see these Jews at the throne before the Rapture as described in Revelation 14:14.

I asked God in prayer to please show me why this seemed so confusing. I reread Revelation chapters 7-14 several times. On the third reading, it was like a light bulb came on, and I saw two separate verses that opened these chapters to a much clearer understanding. In fact, I was so excited I could hardly contain it.

If we go back and read about the seven seals, beginning in Revelation 6, we will notice an interlude between the sixth and seventh seals. This interlude in chapter seven is where the 144,000 are sealed, and then the Rapture is described. Next, when we read Revelation 8, the seventh seal is opened, and the seven trumpets of God's wrath start to sound.

These trumpets continue through the sounding of the sixth trumpet of God's wrath at the end of Revelation 9. Then there is another interruption just before the sounding of the seventh trumpet of God's wrath. During this interruption, a few different events in Revelation 10 and the first half of Revelation 11 are described. It is in this section I saw the first key to understanding why I was confused with the second description of the 144,000 Jews in Revelation 14.

If you read Revelation 10, you will see that during this interruption, a second, smaller scroll is opened and read by John the Revelator. After John read the scroll, he was told in Revelation 10:11, *Then I was told, "You must prophesy again about many peoples, nations, languages, and kings."* What is happening here is John, the writer of Revelation, is being told to prophesy again about the people who suddenly appear around the throne in Revelation 7:9. These are the same ones who, I believe, were the raptured and martyred saints which the elder was asking about in Revelation 7. So from Revelation 10:11 until the second description of the Rapture that is referred to as the harvest of the earth in Revelation 14:9, John is given further insights into a number of events.

These chapters, Revelation 10:11-14:2, contain some events that are pre-rapture events and show that this section of Revelation is not chronologically in order. Shortly, I will go into more detail about some of the events mentioned here. These chapters contain some exciting events that will take place before the Rapture, as described in both Revelation 7 and 14.

First, I want to show you how I understood there is no contradiction concerning the 144,000 Jews who were described as being around the throne with Jesus in Revelation 14. Revelation 14:1 says, *Then I looked and there before me was the Lamb, standing on Mount Zion and with him 144,000 who had his name and his Father's name written on their foreheads.* The key is that the Lamb is standing on Mount Zion. This event does not take place until Jesus returns to the earth at the end of the Great Tribulation. These verses confirm that some of these events in Revelation 10:11 through Revelation 14 are not in chronological order.

While meditating on these verses describing the 144,000, I noticed a verse that posed another dilemma. Revelation 14:4 says, *They were purchased from among men and offered as first-fruits to God and the Lamb.* The problem I noticed in this verse was that they are described as being offered to God and the Lamb as first-fruits. This term, first-fruits, is often seen as a reference to the first-fruits of the resurrection. How can the 144,000 Jews sealed in Revelation 7 be the first-fruits of the resurrection when the saints are raptured before these Jews get resurrected bodies at the end of the Great Tribulation? One logical explanation I see is when the 144,000 are sealed to do God's mission on earth throughout the time of God's wrath, they could be given their resurrected bodies. When they are sealed and receive resurrected bodies in Revelation 7, they would be the first-fruits of the resurrection <u>before</u> the Rapture of the saints takes place in Revelation 7:9. This explanation answers many questions about the 144,000 Jews who are chosen to do a special mission for God.

When you read Revelation 9:4, about how the scorpion locusts are unable to harm the 144,000, it would make sense they could not be harmed if they have resurrected bodies. Many teachers say the mission of the 144,000 is to be evangelists to the Jews around the world and to point the Jews to Jesus as the Messiah who first came 2,000 years ago. The Jews did not recognize Christ the first time. Think about this: these 144,000 Jews appear on the scene just before the Rapture as described in Revelation 7:9. This is the time when the antichrist is waging war against the saints; then when the two witnesses appear, the antichrist wages war against the saints. But nowhere does it say that Satan or the antichrist is waging war against the 144,000 chosen Jews. If they were given their resurrected bodies at the time they are sealed, then Satan could not touch them as they are no longer living in a mortal body. Here is another thought that reinforces this explanation. These sealed Jews have a daunting task. They have to go throughout the world during this time when the antichrist will have them marked as terrorists. It will not be easy for them to travel freely, let alone be able to make it through airport security with a mark on their foreheads, telling everyone that they are special emissaries sent from God.

If they have been given their resurrected bodies, they will be able to get their assignments supernaturally from God and will be able to travel supernaturally as Christ did when He came back to the earth with His resurrected body. This allowed Jesus to appear and disappear or walk through walls. So, if the 144,000 specially chosen Jews will be able to move freely and instantly to whatever destination God sends them to without any fear of harm from the antichrist or man, they will accomplish God's will to reach the Jews scattered throughout the world in record time.

Now think about this. If it makes sense that the 144,000 Jews are sealed and given resurrected bodies in Revelation 7, and they are the first-fruits of the Resurrection, then how can the Rapture of the church be Revelation 4:1? The saints and the 144,000 Jews cannot both be the first-fruits. **Also think about this: first-fruits denotes a small portion of the harvest, before the full harvest takes place. It makes more sense that the 144,000 are first-fruits (a portion of the harvest) than the harvest of the saints that cannot be numbered in Revelation 7:9. Also, realize**

the 144,000 cannot be the first-fruits if the Rapture happened in Revelation 4:1.

I said earlier I would cover some of the events contained in these chapters in Revelation that John the Revelator was instructed to prophesy again, concerning the peoples to be raptured. I believe the section that contains these events is from the beginning of Revelation 11 to the second description of the Rapture in Revelation 14:14. This section is out of chronological order. Some of these events covered here go back before the Rapture, and some events go forward to when Christ physically returns to the earth and stands on Mt. Zion. Some events occur between these two.

The first event I believe John was prophesying about, which would have a connection to the people who would be raptured, concerns the two witnesses. The two witnesses are on the earth for three and one-half years. If they are killed by the antichrist before the end of the seven years of the Great Tribulation, then this means that they appear at some point before the middle of the seven years. This makes it possible, if the Rapture happens at some point close to the middle of the seven years, for the saints to witness the appearing of the two witnesses before the Rapture. To me, this is very exciting, for this will be another supernatural event God will send to the earth to show those who are lost that Jesus is coming soon and wants to attract as many as possible to Himself before the Rapture. As I study Revelation 12 and 13, there is so much to grasp for each piece of the prophetic puzzle to fit together. I believe some of the prophecies here will not be fully understood until future events begin to unfold.

In conclusion to this section of my study, I would like to point out an event I believe we will witness before the Rapture. This portion of my study is found in Revelation 14 before it talks about the harvest of the earth mentioned in Revelation 14:14, which I believe is a second description of the Rapture. Revelation 14:6-11 covers the coming of three angels sent by God to bring a message to the world. If we reread Revelation 7:1-2, we will read about four angels on the earth. Then it says in Revelation 7:2, *Then I saw another angel coming up from the east, having the seal of the living God...* This angel goes on to call the other four angels to help him put the seal of the living God on the 144,000 Jews. Read Revelation 7:3: *Do not harm the land or the sea or the trees until WE put the seal on the foreheads of the servants of our God.*

If we read this portion carefully, we realize these angels who are asked to help seal the 144,000 Jews are the ones who will deliver the wrath of God, but they have been asked to hold off until some point after the sealing of the 144,000 Jews. **This is another key scripture pointing out that the wrath of God does not start until some point after the sealing of the 144,000.**

Another interesting observation is there will be many angels involved during this seven-year period. When we read Revelation 14:6, the same phrase is used: *Then I saw another angel flying in midair...* This angel has a mission to those living on the earth. Read Revelation 14:6-7, *Then I saw another angel flying in midair, and he had the eternal gospel to proclaim to those who live on the earth - to every nation, tribe, language, and people. He said in a loud voice. "Fear God and give him glory, because the hour of his judgment has come. Worship him who made the heavens, the earth, the sea and the springs of water."* It is so exciting that this angel is sent to proclaim the gospel to those who live on the earth.

Going into detail, the angel describes the people he is speaking to in the same terms as those who will be involved in the Rapture later in Revelation 14:6-7 as the people from every nation, tribe, language, and people. He is speaking again of the Gentiles who are eligible for the Rapture. As we read further, the angel proclaims what man is to do before the judgment of God begins, for it says, *Fear God and give him glory, because the hour of his judgment has come.* This verse is important to understand.

What I have been showing is these chapters are not in chronological order. As you see, it says the hour of His judgment has come. But when you read Revelation 8 and 9, the judgment or the wrath of God starts after what I see as the Rapture in chapter seven. This is illustrated with the warning from the first of three angels for the nations to repent before the wrath of God to come, as described in the second description of the Rapture in Revelation 14.

Therefore, the first angel is given the mission of helping the saints to bring in the last part of the harvest before the Rapture happens, and the wrath of God begins. **There are not two raptures but rather two accounts describing the same event with God's wrath following.**

Next, Revelation 14:8 goes on to talk about the second angel: *A second angel followed and said, "Fallen! Fallen is Babylon the Great, which made all nations drink the maddening wine of her adulteries."* I believe that Babylon the Great which will fall is America. I go into this in greater detail later in this study. I believe when it says Babylon the Great has fallen, it is referring to governmental, social, and economic collapse, not the full destruction of Babylon that is to come later as described in Revelation 18.

I believe this collapse could be triggered by several possible events. One possible choice would be that we would be destroyed by our enemies. Another could be the catastrophic event described in the sixth seal of Revelation. I go into this event in greater detail later in my chapter called "The Window of the Lord's Return." This event would bring America to a new low.

Next, Revelation 14:9 talks about the third angel following the first two, and the wording conveys that the three angels will appear in chronological order. The third angel is proclaiming the judgment of God and the eternal punishment about to come on those who fail to heed this message. At a time when the church will be under great persecution and will have moved underground to avoid the oppression of the antichrist, these angels will move about openly proclaiming the gospel. This will take away any excuse that man would have about knowing God's plan of redemption.

As you read these verses in Revelation 14:9-12, you will see that the mark of the beast is being forced on the world at this time. Christians and all who do not want to come under God's judgment must at all costs refuse this mark and the system of the antichrist. Remember, the wording of the three angels shows this is chronological; verse twelve is a message to the saints. It is telling the saints that this will be a trying time, but we must remain faithful to Jesus, as the rewards are great.

The next verse confirms there will be trying times, and we must be faithful at all costs. Hebrews 10:35-38 states, *So do not throw away your confidence; it will be richly rewarded. You need to persevere so that when you have done the will of God, you will receive what he has promised. For in just a little while, he who is coming will come and will not delay. But my righteous ones will live by faith. And if he shrinks back, I will not be pleased with him.*

Read Revelation 14:9-12. *A third angel followed them and said in a loud voice: "If anyone worships the beast and his image and receives his mark on the forehead or on the hand, he too, will drink of the wine of the wrath of God's fury, which has been poured full strength into the cup of his wrath. He will be tormented with burning sulfur in the presence of the holy angels and of the Lamb. And the smoke of their torment rises forever and ever.* **There is no rest day or night for those who worship the beast and his image, or for anyone who receives the mark of his name.** *" This calls for the patient endurance on the part of the saints who obey God's commandments and remain faithful to Jesus.*

As we approach the coming of the Lord, we will be facing challenging times. Many Christians are fearful they will have to go through any part of the Great Tribulation. Some Christians wonder how a loving God could allow His people to go through any of this tribulation.

I believe we must have the same resolve to serve God as the saints of the early church had. They were not just willing to live for God; they were willing to die for God. This was not as a way of obtaining grace and salvation. It was because they already had God's grace and salvation. Look at what happened to the disciples who were first imprisoned and then released by an angel. When they were brought before the religious leaders who wanted to kill them, listen to the attitude of these early believers who were experiencing trials and persecution. Acts 5:40-41 says, ... *They called the apostles in and had them flogged. Then they ordered them not to speak in the name of Jesus and let them go. The apostles left the Sanhedrin, rejoicing, because they had been counted worthy of suffering disgrace for the Name.*

Look at what happened in China when Mao took over; he had thousands of Christians killed. The 80,000 Christians in China had to go underground, but did they give up their faith? No! The church oppressed with tribulation and persecution in China grew from 80,000 to somewhere between 100 to 200 million Christians today. We are God's army, and we must recognize that as we get closer to the Lord's return, Satan will be ramping up his attack on the earth to keep people from getting saved.

It just does not make sense that God would take the saints out before the harvest is complete. Read 2 Peter 3:9, *The Lord is not slow in keeping his promise, as some understand slowness. He is patient with you, not wanting anyone to perish, but everyone to come to repentance.*

If God is so determined to bring the lost to Himself that He would send angels to help in the last days before His return, does it not make sense that God would leave His army here to lead the lost to Christ until the last minute and THEN rapture his saints off the earth just before He pours out His wrath and judgment on those who have rejected Him?

— CHAPTER FOUR —

HOW DOES THE UNITED STATES FIT INTO THE PROPHETIC PICTURE?

This is a question that has intrigued me forever. The Bible does not address the United States in plain-speak, so you have to wonder how do we fit into all of this? I guess an easy answer would be that we just become absorbed into and under the rule of the antichrist. Our Constitution is cancelled, and the USA becomes irrelevant as we know it. **I was told by one pastor that it might be that the United States will be left out of the events concerning the antichrist and the mark of the beast altogether. Do not hold your breath on that hope. That is truly wishful thinking. Do you really think that Satan, indwelling a world leader who has designs to rule the planet forever, would think of leaving America as a Christian nation to be free to do its own thing? To fully dispel this thought, read Revelation 13:7** *He was given power to make war against the saints and to conquer them. And he was given authority over EVERY tribe, people, language, and NATION.* **America is a nation.**

Over the years, my thoughts on this subject have led me to see that we have been the main protector of Israel, thus causing the United States to be standing in the way of many of the prophetic events that have to fall into place. As long as the United States is a strong superpower, we would not stand by and let Israel be attacked and destroyed, for we have always provided them with armaments and supplies. The early thoughts I had were as follows:

1) We would be defeated in a world war, and we would not be around to do any more protecting.

2) The United States would have an economic collapse which would make us so poor that we could no longer hold the position as Israel's protector and as the world cop. Also, our problems would be so severe at home that we would need all our military and police forces to keep things under control at home, resulting in a deficit of resources for dealing with world problems any more. This is difficult to envision and I do not want to see these kinds of hard times. I certainly do not want to experience an event like the Great Depression of the thirties that hit my father's generation, but I have always believed that for the end-time events to unfold, according to that which has been laid out in the Bible, then America and the world would have to experience a widespread economic collapse.

3) My next thought is a long one and the most thought provoking. I have questioned the scriptures I am about to share with you, wondering for years if they could be talking about the United States. If it were not for the fact that I have read other prophetic writers sharing my questions and possible conclusions, I would hesitate to share these thoughts

Where do we begin? If you read Revelation 18 about the destruction of "Mystery Babylon," you have to wonder if America could be a spiritual type of the actual, physical and geographically-located Babylon. Most Bible teachers believe these scriptures are talking about Iraq. But when you carefully read the passage, you will see many scripture verses that show the country of Iraq does not fit the description of the country to be destroyed in judgment

Here is an example: Revelation 18:10 says, *Woe! Woe! O great city, O Babylon, city of power! In one hour your doom has come!* **Iraq is not a city of power today;** they had their day, and so the question I have is whether these scriptures are talking about a country that has the spirit of Babylon rather than the geographic location of Iraq. If you read these scriptures with that thought in mind and apply the thought that the city of power being referred to is the United States, then see if it makes sense to you.

For example, read Revelation 17:1-2: *...Come, I will show you the punishment of the great prostitute, who sits on many waters. With her the kings of the earth committed adultery and the inhabitants of the earth were intoxicated with the wine of her adulteries.* Geographically, the United States sits on many waters and contains many peoples from many nationalities, and Iraq does not. Now read Revelation 17:15, *The* *waters you saw, where the prostitute sits are peoples, multitudes, nations and languages.* America is a land known as a land of many peoples and languages, and Iraq is not. Revelation 17:18 says, *The woman you saw is the great city that rules over the kings of the earth.* This sounds like the United States, not Iraq

Revelation 18:1-3 talks about the fall of this great city and Revelation 18:4 says, *Come out of her, my people.* I have been doing a bit of a study on this verse, focusing on the two words "my people;" at first, I thought it referred to Christians. Now I see the strong possibility it is addressing the Jews as God's chosen people. In 2 Chronicles 7:14 it says, *If my people who are called by my name will humble themselves and pray and seek my face and turn from their wicked ways, then will I hear from heaven and will forgive their sin and heal their land.* This verse is God speaking to His people, the Jews, in answer to their prayers when they were praying to God during the dedication of the temple. This phrase, "my people," is most often used to refer to God's chosen people, the Jews. If you look at Romans 9:25, you will see it can also mean the Gentiles who have been accepted as God's people because of Christ's sacrifice on the cross. Romans 9:25: *...I will call them 'my people' who are not my people; and I will call her 'my loved one' who is not my loved one.* When you study Revelation, you will see the Christians are spoken about collectively as the church or referred to as saints. It is my conclusion the reference to "my people" in Revelation 18:4 is speaking to the Jews after the Rapture has taken place. I will go into greater detail in the next chapter entitled, "God's No Man Left Behind."

Read Revelation 18:17-18. *In one hour, such great wealth has been brought to ruin! Every sea captain, and all who travel by ship, the sailors and all who earn their living from the sea, will stand far off, when they see the smoke of her burning, they will exclaim, "Was there ever a city like this great city?"* Does this sound like Iraq or the United States? Also, ask yourself, "What other country could this chapter be talking about?" Well, any Bible scholar would eliminate Russia and China. It would not be Europe, as this is the center of the antichrist's rule, and the revived Roman Empire is the country that is ready to destroy Mystery Babylon. Some say Mystery Babylon is Rome, ruled by the Pope. I do not see this as a land of commerce over which the merchants of the world would mourn. Could it be a Middle Eastern country like Iraq? I would have to say no for two reasons. First, the description of this country just does not fit any of the countries of the Middle East, and the Bible says the antichrist wants to ultimately destroy Israel. If the Middle Eastern countries want Israel destroyed, then this makes these countries friends of the antichrist. I am sorry; I just do not see any choice but to say this is describing the fall of the United States. This country is described as "Mystery Babylon." Think about this: the United States is the only superpower today that did not exist when the Bible was written. If the country that is being described did exist during the writing of Revelation, then would it be a mystery?

If you were to ask, "Does the Bible really tell us who God would use to destroy the country we are talking about?" The answer lies in Revelation 17:16. *The beast and the ten horns you saw will hate the prostitute. They will bring her to ruin, and leave her naked; they will eat her flesh and burn her with fire.*

Now after hearing about the fall of the dollar, the rise of the euro, and the choosing of a permanent European leader, it gets easier to see what this verse in Revelation is talking about. I believe "Mystery Babylon" is America, based on my discussion above about the fall of "Mystery Babylon" spoken about in Revelation 18. The leaders behind the new revived Roman Empire and the antichrist will not want to see the US dollar rise again and certainly will not want to see the United States rise to world power again.

An update now shows us that the United States, under the leadership of those who do not support Israel, will pull back our support and ultimately let Israel stand on its own without any outside help.

In concluding this chapter, let it be fully realized that Israel will never be left alone without protection. When it looks like Israel is without allies, the armies of God will be encamped around Israel, and Israel will never be destroyed.

— CHAPTER FIVE —

GOD'S "NO MAN LEFT BEHIND"

I f this study has given you some second thoughts, as it has me, that the Rapture does not happen until Revelation 7, then maybe you will also be convinced that we will not see the Rapture until after the sealing of the 144,000 Jews. This is explained in Revelation 7:3-8. Now read Revelation 7:9 (NIV): *After this, I looked and there before me was a great multitude that no one could count, from every nation, tribe, and people and language, standing before the throne and in front of the Lamb. They were wearing white robes and were holding palm branches in their hands.* I believe this is the rapture as seen from the throne in heaven. After we meet the Lord in the clouds, our Savior will lead us to His home and throne where we will worship God and our Lord and Savior Jesus Christ.

Revelation 8 prophesies of seven angels who hold the seven trumpets of God's wrath that is about to be poured out on the earth. You realize how God manifests His grace to His saints by rescuing them from the earth just before the out-pouring of His wrath.

Going back to the sealing of the 144,000 Jews, there is an important sequence in this event. These Jews are sealed in Revelation 7:1-8. Then at some point after the sealing, the Rapture of the saints takes place. Think about this--it is perfect timing. When Christ was on the earth and His people, the children of Israel, rejected Him as a nation. At that time, He promised to graft the Jews who rejected Him back into His family. We must realize that the Jews will be an important part of the bride of Christ.

In Revelation 7, we see the turning-point. God is getting ready to move his saints out of harm's way through the Rapture, and He turns His attention to bringing the nation of Israel back into His family. He has just commissioned the 144,000 Jewish evangelists to preach Christ to the Jews throughout the world. Now you might wonder how God could pour out His wrath on the earth while His chosen people Israel are still on the earth. After further study, I believe once God seals the 144,000, there will be only a short time before the Rapture. During that short time, the 144,000 Jewish evangelists will launch the greatest evangelistic blitz of all time to let the Jews around the world know Jesus is their coming Messiah, and He is coming imminently to take them to His heavenly Father and introduce them as an important part of His bride.

I believe that when the Rapture occurs, many Jews will go up at this time. God will still extend His hand of protection to those who are left behind. I want to show you how I believe God will protect His people, the Jews who are left behind. The Bible teaches that the plagues cannot hurt the 144,000 sealed Jews. Read Revelation 9:1-6. *The fifth angel sounded his trumpet, and I saw a star that had fallen from the sky to the earth. The star was given the key to the shaft of the Abyss. When he opened the Abyss, smoke rose from it like the smoke from a gigantic furnace. The sun and sky were darkened by the smoke from the Abyss. And out of the smoke locusts came down upon the earth and were given power like that of scorpions of the earth. They were told not to harm the grass of the earth or any plant or tree, but only those people who did not have the seal of God on their foreheads. They were not given power to kill them, but only to torture them for five months. And the agony they suffered was like that of the sting of a scorpion when it strikes a man. During those days men will seek death, but will not find it; they will long to die, but death will elude them.*

When the Rapture occurs, those Jews who have just accepted Christ in this massive evangelistic effort will go up in the Rapture along with all the Christian Gentiles, including the dead in Christ and those Christians who are alive at that time. Recently, I believe God gave me further insight on a verse that previously confused me in Matthew 24:30-31. *At that time the sign of the Son of Man will appear in the sky, and the nations of the earth will mourn. They will see the Son of Man coming on the clouds of the sky, with power and great glory. And he will send his angels with a loud trumpet call and they will gather his elect from the four winds, from one end of the heavens to the other.*

I used to be confused as to why the nations of the earth would mourn at the time of the Rapture. Those who are left behind will have rejected Christ and accepted the antichrist as their god and they will not be mourning, they will be cursing the true and living God. I believe once someone takes the mark of the beast, they will no longer have a heart capable of repenting." So who is the nations of the earth refering to?

The King James Version uses the term "tribes" instead of "nations.". I believe this verse is speaking of the tribes of Israel in all the nations of the world. I believe when the 144,000 Jewish evangelists reach out to every Jew on earth, many will recognize Jesus as their Messiah and Savior and will go up in the Rapture. Those Jews who still reject this message will be allowed to witness Christ's coming in the clouds at the time of the Rapture. Those Jews will realize that they have just rejected Christ Jesus as their Messiah for the second time. The first time was at Christ's Crucifixion and then again at His Second Coming for His bride. The Jews from all nations around the world will mourn when they realize what they have done.

In the book of Zechariah, we read that at the time of the Second Coming and the battle of Armageddon, the Jews have their eyes opened, and they cry in repentance for rejecting Christ as their Messiah. Zechariah 12:10-11: *And I will pour out on the house of David and the inhabitants of Jerusalem a spirit of grace and supplication. They will look on me, the one they have pierced, and they will mourn for him as one mourns for an only child, and grieve bitterly for him as one grieves for a firstborn son. On that day the weeping in Jerusalem will be great, like the weeping of Hadad Rimmon in the plain of Megiddo.*

Now, let us return again to the subject of God's provision for His 144,000 special servants after the Rapture. The Bible says the Antichrist cannot harm them. When we carefully read Revelation 9:4, we understand it specifically points out that only God's 144,000, sealed with His mark, will be spared from this tormenting plague. This brings up two very important questions. The first is, "If there were tribulation saints, as many prophetic scholars believe, where is the provision for their protection from these plagues?" I consider this further reason to believe there are no tribulation saints after the Rapture. The second question is, "What will happen to God's chosen people Israel during this time?" I will show you how I believe God has made provision to protect His chosen people during this time.

Let us go back to the 144,000 Jews who have been sealed and commissioned to take the gospel of Christ to the nation of Israel. I believe part of their commission is to warn the Jews that Jesus is their Messiah, and He is coming for those who accepted Him. After this, the plagues of God's wrath will fall on the earth. I believe I can show you from God's Word that the children of Israel who miss the Rapture will be told to leave all nations where they are living and head back to the Holy Land before the plagues start to fall.

Remember when Moses told his people in Egypt to get ready for the Passover by sacrificing a lamb to cover and protect their homes and families from the angel of death? The 144,000 sealed Jews have this same kind of protection from the plagues that are about to come upon the earth. Remember when God was sending plagues like the locusts that ate all the crops of the Egyptians? If you read carefully about this account in the Old Testament, you will notice in the land of Goshen, the children of Israel were protected. The plagues did not harm the land of God's people. I believe it is possible to show from Scripture that God is going to call His people home to Israel just before His plagues and wrath fall upon man and the earth.

This is a good time to read Revelation 18, which talks about the fall of "Mystery Babylon." I have already said that I believe that "Mystery Babylon" is the United States, which happens to be the home of millions of Jews. Before the destruction of "Mystery Babylon," the Jews will be warned to leave. Remember, God's wrath and plagues start to fall in Revelation 8 **following** the Rapture. The saints in the United States and around the world have already left in the Rapture. The Jews who have not accepted Christ as their Messiah will be left behind at the time of the Rapture, but God will still make provision for them to escape His soon coming wrath.

Read Revelation 18:4. *And I heard another voice from heaven say, "Come out of her, my people, that ye be not partakers of her sins, and that ye receive not of her plagues."* I used to think that this was either a rapture verse or a command for Christians to leave the United States before God's wrath fell. There are two problems with this thinking. If this were a verse about the Rapture, God would not have to ask us to leave. We would just go instantly. If it were to mean the Christians are to leave the United States physically, then where would millions of Christians go? Would Canada or Mexico open its borders for all of these Christians? I do not think so.

Another writer on the End Times wrote an interesting explanation in his book on the last days. He said he believes the text in Revelation that says, *"Come out of her, my people,"* is speaking to American Christians, telling them to leave the United States and take flight to Israel for protection. I see a real problem with this interpretation. Do you believe that Israel will open its doors for millions of American Christians to come to Israel to wait for the Lord's return? I do not think so.

The only thing that makes sense to me is that God will instruct the Jews who missed the Rapture, after their indecision to accept Christ. They will be warned by the 144,000 sealed Jewish evangelists to head for cover, to leave "Mystery Babylon" and the other nations of the earth, and to return to their homeland. Now think about this. If it were Gentile Christians trying to flee the United States, would Israel open its doors? Again, I do not think so. However, Israel has always had its doors open for the Jews to return to their own nation, Israel. I believe once these Jews flee to Israel, God will supernaturally protect them from harm just as he did the Jews in Egypt during the time of Moses.

A scripture verse that goes well with what I am sharing here is found in Ezekiel 39:27-28. *When I have brought them back from the nations and have gathered them from the countries of their enemies, I will show myself holy through them in the sight of many nations. Then they will know that I am the LORD, their God, for though I sent them into exile among the nations, I will gather them to their own land, not leaving any behind. I will no longer hide my face from them, for I will pour out my Spirit on the house of Israel, declares the Sovereign LORD.*

I covered more about the 144,000 in an earlier chapter where I showed how I believe these specially chosen Jews will be able to accomplish their mission for God with supernatural, resurrected bodies. The two witnesses will also have supernatural powers but will have mortal bodies, for the Bible clearly states that they will be killed and lay in the streets of Jerusalem for three and one-half days before being resurrected for the whole world to see (Revelation 11:7-13). These two witnesses will also be on the earth at the time when the Jews are being evacuated to Israel.

— CHAPTER SIX —

CAN GENTILES BE SAVED AFTER THE RAPTURE?

Over the years, I have heard a few scenarios concerning this question. Some may ask, "But who are the Gentiles?" They are anyone from any nation or people group who are not Jewish.

1. One scenario could involve tribulation saints who knew about God's plan of salvation but did not accept Christ or live for Him before the Rapture. They would turn to Christ during the Great Tribulation and not accept the mark of the beast. They would struggle through the Great Tribulation and become the tribulation saints. This explanation is necessary in order to have a pre-tribulation rapture theory. If the Rapture does not happen until Revelation 7, then the term "tribulation saints" would not be necessary, for all the saints would be raptured at the same time. Further evidence of this scenario is the fact there is no mention of saints on the earth during the outpouring of God's wrath. Also, God makes provision for His wrath not to hurt the 144,000 Jews but makes no provision for tribulation saints! The best example is the scorpion creatures that cannot harm the 144,000 sealed with God's mark. Why is there no provision for the saints to be protected from these creatures of God's wrath? The best explanation is all the saints are raptured before this time of God's wrath on the earth.

2. Here is another scenario. The Holy Spirit would be removed during the Great Tribulation. The basis of this statement comes from the teaching that the saints are raptured off the earth and have the Holy Spirit living in them. When this happens, the Holy Spirit's influence will be taken off the earth with them. The question this generates in my mind is: if the Holy Spirit is not working to draw sinners to Christ, how will people be saved during this time? Some might say if you cannot accept and serve God with the Holy Spirit's help, how can you do it without the Holy Spirit's help? Yet as I see it, the Holy Spirit is God, who is omnipresent, and you cannot remove God from the earth.

3. My father-in-law, the Reverend Edgar Rasmussen, has always maintained that to tell people they can be saved after the Rapture is a shaky position at best. It gives people a false hope of a second chance. Holding out a second chance does not draw the unsaved and the backsliders to Christ. It tells them they can stay in their unsaved condition and still have a way back to God after the Rapture.

There are many who believe the saints have to be raptured before the Great Tribulation because the Bible says, *He that restraineth, must be taken out of the way before the antichrist can be revealed.* I believe this view has too many contradictions in God's Word. Basically, this view says the Rapture has to come before the antichrist can be revealed; therefore, the Rapture is a pre-tribulation event. But this interpretation contradicts 2 Thessalonians 2:3. *Don't let anyone deceive you in any way, for that day will not come until the rebellion occurs and the man of lawlessness is revealed, the man doomed to destruction.* I do not believe the restrainer is the Holy Spirit, and I will offer a compelling argument for who the restrainer is later in chapter nine .

My position on this question has become clearer while doing this study on the End Times. If we take the position that there is a pre-tribulation Rapture, then we have to assume the saints mentioned during the opening of the seals in Revelation 6 are tribulation saints. This is traditional thinking. As I have pointed out, if the Rapture does not happen until after the opening of the sixth seal in Revelation 6, actually happening in Revelation 7:9-13, then a very interesting observation can be made. Before I make this observation, I should point out that we can see the rapture event along with other important events happening in two sections of Revelation. We will see the 144,000 Jews and the Rapture following in both Revelation 7 and 14. You need to read these chapters together to get the whole picture, just as you would read the first four books of the New Testament to see the whole story of the Gospel.

This brings me to that very interesting observation I mentioned above and possibly the answer to the question, "Can Gentiles be saved after the Rapture?" If you look at Revelation 7 and 14, which contain the same rapture event, and if you continue reading on to the coming of Christ at the end of the Great Tribulation, you will see no living saints mentioned after the Rapture. Think about this: if the church has to go through the first half of the Great Tribulation, many exciting things will happen. Those who have fallen away will come back to Christ. The church will wake up and get the message of salvation out like never before in history, and as the day of the Gentiles is coming to a close after the sealing of the 144,000 Jews, every wise Christian will realize that we are in the final countdown of days on this side of eternity. Our 401k's will not do us any good, and only what is done for Christ will last. I believe that during this time, super-evangelism will be taking place, and all who will come to Christ will come. These will certainly be exciting times. Any tribulation we go through will be worth it in the end.

During this time, the church will see a time of spiritual warfare unlike anything the world has ever seen. Everyone will have to make a decision to either accept what Christ has to offer: eternal life with tribulation for a little while or the comfort and benefits of what the antichrist has to offer, a full belly. Hmmmm, is this not what Esau took for his birthright? The point is there will be no need for any more decisions to accept Christ after the Rapture. The time will be over for making decisions. I realize there will be exceptions to this; I believe there will be some people living in remote areas of the earth who will be outside of the influence of the antichrist, and if they survive the last years of the Great Tribulation, they will be included among those who will repopulate the earth during the millennium.

In closing, consider this. If the Rapture is pre-Tribulation, the church will continue in its lukewarm condition, waiting around for the Rapture while millions of people get left behind. On the other hand, with a mid-tribulation rapture happening after the opening of the seals during the first half of the Great Tribulation, then what happens in this instance is exciting. The church will wake up to what is about to take place, and we will see the greatest revival in the history of the church. I believe we will also see a great falling away at the same time. It is possible that when the church realizes what they were told about a pre-tribulation rapture was in error, many Christians will become bitter towards God. They may feel God has abandoned them, and they may give in to the New World system.

Even though this scenario is scary, look at the positive things that would happen. The church ushers in the greatest revival the world has ever seen, and the saints are purified into the pure bride for whom, the Bible says, Christ is coming back. This makes so much sense to me. Going through the trials of the first half of the Great Tribulation will purify and grow the bride of Christ. The Bible says in 2 Peter 3:9b, *He is patient with you, not wanting anyone to perish, but everyone to come to repentance.*

If I had my choice, the pre-tribulation rapture would be a far more desirable option. Even though the mid-tribulation scenario is a scary option, it means that millions more of the lost will come to Christ. Remember, many of those millions who have not accepted Christ are your friends and relatives! They are the ones for whom Christ died.

— CHAPTER SEVEN —

OTHER BIBLE TEACHERS' PERSPECTIVES CONCERNING THE RAPTURE

After studying the Bible and putting many of my thoughts on paper, I began an extensive search to look at other points of view about the Rapture. As this study progresses, I would ask that you have an open heart and mind. Remember, we are in search of the truth as revealed in God's Word.

The viewpoint of the pre-tribulation rapture is held by several denominational ministers and scholars. In order to search this out effectively, I will present scriptures and the thoughts that are used by teachers who support the pre-tribulation rapture.

The first teacher whose position I will examine has had a great ministry that teaches the chronology of God's dispensations and prophetic plans using a huge time line chart set up on the platforms of churches and auditoriums.

While this perspective is popular, I want you to consider that the pre-tribulation teachings may be flawed. Could it be possible that teachers of this position are defending a teaching to the point of possible spiritual blindness, a teaching handed down from their fathers and other generations before them?

I am not Paul, but what he wrote in the book of Acts is a worthwhile challenge to all of us, specifically in Acts 17:11. *Now the Bereans were of more noble character then the Thessalonians, for they received the message with great eagerness and examined the Scriptures every day to see if what Paul said was true.*

When I recently studied the small roll-out version of this chart, I noticed about a dozen Bible verses under the topic of the Rapture. Based on the placement of these verses on his chart, it is obvious that the chart represents a belief in a pre-tribulation rapture. The verses are placed on the chart between the seven churches of Revelation, found in Revelation 2 and 3, but before the opening of the seals, found in Revelation 6.

It is widely accepted that close to the opening of the seals is the beginning of the seven-year Great Tribulation period. Those who hold to the pre-tribulation view believe that the Rapture will take place before the Great Tribulation gets started. I studied through the list of verses on this teacher's chart, looking for ones that would show the timing of the Rapture. What I found in these verses was interesting. Basically, they attest to the resurrection of the righteous. They also attest to the Rapture, but they do not really show scripturally that the Rapture is a pre-tribulation event. In fact, there is one verse used that leans toward the Rapture being a post-tribulation event. Interestingly, this verse on the chart is the only one I have found so far that shows the timing of the Rapture as different from my conclusion about a mid-tribulation event. I will go over this verse in detail when I work my way through the verses on his list.

As I stated in a previous chapter, interpretation of scripture on any doctrinal issue should be backed up with at least two other verses in the Bible to assure the correct interpretation of God's Word. If I get confused over one verse because it contradicts my conclusion, I will stick with the interpretation I can back-up with two or more scriptures. I also believe that, as I continue to study God's Word, at some point the truth will come to light, and the verse that seems to contradict will eventually line-up with the rest of the Word of God.

Let us start by looking at the many Bible verses on the chart I mentioned above. I will show each verse, one at a time, and I will do my best to explain why it is relevant to the Rapture. I invite you to search with me to see if these verses actually show that the Rapture will be a pre-tribulation event.

SCRIPTURES UTILIZED TO TEACH A
PRE-TRIBULATION RAPTURE

Luke 21:34-36, *Be careful, or your hearts will be weighed down with dissipation, drunkenness, and the anxieties of life, and that day will close on you unexpectedly like a trap. For it will come upon all those who live on the earth. Be always on the watch, and pray that you may be able to escape all that is about to happen, and that you may be able to stand before the Son of Man.*

When I read this over, I see it talks about a horrible time coming on the earth. I believe there are two periods to which it could be referring. The time of the Great Tribulation is the first that comes to mind, but the Bible teaches there will be a time of birth pains before the Great Tribulation starts that will be so bad that many will think the Great Tribulation has already started. I will cover this period of birth pains in more depth in the next chapter on the coming antichrist. These verses are a warning to Christians not to be so caught up in this world that we do not recognize the time in which we are living. We need to be sure that we are watching for the Lord's return so that we are not caught unawares. These verses infer that we can see this time coming, and it will not be a surprise to us. Luke 21:36, in particular, was probably used on this chart under the Rapture because it would be easy to assume that to escape what is to come means to escape the wrath of God. Luke 21:36, *Be always on the watch, and pray that you may be able to escape all that is about to happen.* The chart indicates by the scripture placement that we would escape by being raptured.

I want to remind you that if you are a Christian, you do not have to pray that you will go up in the Rapture. The Rapture will catch up every Christian and take us off this earth in the twinkling of an eye. I believe the Bible teaches us that Christians will go through some trying times and that our God is more than able to protect us in the midst of tribulation. As we see these times approaching, we need to pray that God will protect us and sustain us as we go through these times. His Word assures us we can count on His help. It is a given that we will escape God's wrath through the Rapture.

Look at Daniel's three friends who had to face the fiery furnace. God helped them escape that trial, and I believe if we make God our all-in-all by putting our total trust in Him, we will see Him miraculously preserve us in the worst of times. Yet, the Bible says there will be martyred saints during this time. Remember, we will never face any trial alone, for God's Word says, "*I will never leave you nor forsake you.* Also, when you look at the following verse in light of other scriptures, such as 2 Thessalonians 2:1-3, you see the Rapture may be getting close, but until certain events take place, it will not happen.

2 Thessalonians 2:1-3: *Concerning the coming of our Lord Jesus Christ and our being gathered to him, we ask you brothers, not to become easily unsettled or alarmed by some prophecy, report or letter supposed to have come from us, saying that the day of the Lord has already come. Don't let anyone deceive you in any way, for that day will not come, until the rebellion occurs and the man of lawlessness is revealed, the man doomed to destruction.*

I know the man doomed to destruction is the antichrist and he is yet to be revealed. For the longest time, I did not know what the rebellion was about, but now I realize it is a great falling away that will take place before the Lord returns. This verse is talking about the coming antichrist and the falling away in the same verse. I believe that is because the falling away will happen during the time of the antichrist. After continued study I now realize that the falling away will start before the antichrist arrives. It is sad, but the church today is weak, and I believe many Christians are convinced the Rapture will take us to heaven before times get tough. If the church suddenly sees the hard times of the Great Tribulation and is not prepared for it, when faced with the choice of whether to buy into the antichrist's system or be denied the ability to buy or sell and face possible starvation, many will make the wrong choice. I believe this will be the time of a great falling away. In chapter nine I will expand on this great falling away when I cover my time line chart to the Rapture. As I have warned previously, Esau sold his birthright for food, so according to God's Word, the time will not be right for the church to be gathered to Jesus in the Rapture until we see these two events come to pass. In chapter ten, I cover a total of six events that must take place before the Rapture can occur.

The next verse presented in the pre-tribulation chart is John 14:1-3. *Do not let your hearts be troubled. Trust in God; trust also in me. In my Father's house are many rooms, if it were not so, I would have told you. I am going to prepare a place for you. I will come back and take you to be with me, that you also may be where I am.*

This is a great verse full of the promises of God. It has much to say to the church, but

I will share three points that are relevant to my study:

This verse attests to the resurrection of God's people.

It says Christ is coming back to receive His elect or saints to Himself.

It attests to the fact there will be a rapture, but there is no indication of the timing of the Rapture in relation to the Great Tribulation.

The next verse is I Corinthians 15:23. *But each in his own turn: Christ, the first fruits; then, when he comes, those who belong to him.*

This verse is quite self-explanatory. Jesus is coming for His bride. There is a rapture on the horizon. It says when He comes, those who belong to him will be resurrected. The ones who belong to Him are the Christians and the Jews who have accepted Christ. The Bible says we will each go in his own time. Yet there is still no indication of the Rapture event's timing in this verse.

The next text is 1 Corinthians 15:51-58. *Listen, I tell you a mystery: We will not all sleep, but we will all be changed -- in a flash, in the twinkling of an eye, at the last trumpet, for the trumpet will sound, the dead will be raised imperishable, and we will be changed. For the perishable must clothe itself with the imperishable and the mortal with immortality. When the perishable has been clothed with the imperishable, and the mortal with immortality, then the saying that is written will come true: "Death has been swallowed up in victory." Where, O death is your victory? Where, O death is your sting? The sting of death is sin, and the power of sin is the law. But thanks be to God! he gives us victory through our Lord Jesus Christ. Therefore, my dear brothers, stand firm. Let nothing move you. Always give yourselves fully to the work of the Lord, because you know that your labor in the Lord is not in vain.*

This is a great portion of scripture; it not only talks about the Rapture but also goes into great detail on how we will be changed into eternal beings. In light of God's grace, it behooves us to give all of our life and strength to the work of the Lord in whatever capacity God calls us.

This next verse has confused me a bit about the timing of the Rapture. Remember, this popular end-times chart promotes the pre-tribulation rapture. I am leaning heavily toward a mid-tribulation rapture, even though I would prefer a pre-tribulation rapture. (I think we all would prefer the easy way!) This verse gives evidence of a post-tribulation rapture. Read 1 Corinthians 15:52. *...in a flash, in the twinkling of an eye, at the last trumpet, for the trumpet will sound, the dead will be raised imperishable, and we will be changed.*

The phrase, *...at the last trumpet...*, begs the question, which last trumpet? The only last trumpet I am aware of is the last trumpet of the seven trumpets of God's wrath. I do not believe we will go through the wrath of God under the category of the seven trumpets. I believe, with study, this inconsistency will be reconciled, for there are too many scriptures placing the Rapture in Revelation 7 **before** the wrath of God. I would rather stay with an interpretation with multiple verses to support it. Later, in chapter eleven, I will explain an alternative to the last trumpet, and the accompanying inconsistency will go away.

After four years of working on this study, I now lean toward a mid-tribulation rapture because of the amount of scriptural support to back up this position. We especially need to weigh the scriptures that are plain and easy to understand as we attempt to build a doctrinal position. If the scriptures we use are vague, we could be building our position like building a house of cards.

The next verse in the end times chart is 2 Corinthians 5:1-8. *Now we know that if the earthly tent we live in is destroyed, we have a building from God, an eternal house in heaven, not built by human hands. Meanwhile, we groan, longing to be clothed with our heavenly dwelling, because when we are clothed, we will not be found naked. For while we are in this tent, we groan and are burdened, because we do not wish to be unclothed but to be clothed with our heavenly dwelling, so that what is mortal may be swallowed up by life. Now it is God who has made us for this very purpose and has given us the Spirit as a deposit, guaranteeing what is to come. Therefore, we are always confident and know that as long as we are home in the body we are away from the Lord. We live by faith, not by sight. We are confident; I say and would prefer to be away from the body and at home with the Lord.*

These verses attest to the resurrection and the promise of a new eternal body. They give us an expectant hope in the future of exchanging our earthly body for an eternal one that will allow us to live with Christ forever. However, these verses give no indication about the timing of Christ's return or the placement of the Rapture even though they give us significant assurance God has better things for us ahead for all eternity.

The verse shown next on the pre-tribulation rapture chart is Ephesians 5:27, which states, *...and to present her to himself as a radiant church, without stain or wrinkle or any other blemish, but holy and blameless...* Again, this verse attests to the resurrection of the believer, but there is no mention of the Rapture or the timing of Christ's coming.

Next, read Philippians 3:11 *...and so, somehow, to attain to the resurrection from the dead...* and 3:20-21, *But our citizenship is in heaven. And we eagerly await a Savior from there, the Lord Jesus Christ, who by the power that enables him to bring everything under his control, will transform our lowly bodies so that they will be like his glorious body.*

These verses also speak about the resurrection and our mortal bodies being transformed to be like Christ's glorious body. I can see these verses touching on Christ's power to bring about the Rapture, but there is no indication about the timing of this event.

Next, read Colossians 3:4. *When Christ, who is your life, appears, then you also will appear with him in glory.* This verse surely refers to the Rapture. It clearly says when Christ appears, we will be in glory with Him, but it gives no indication of timing for the Rapture.

The following verses for study are from the book of 1 Thessalonians:

1 Thessalonians 2:19: *For what is our hope, our joy, or the crown in which we will glory in the presence of our Lord Jesus when he comes? Is it not you?* This verse attests to the resurrection and Christ's coming for us, but again there is no indication of timing.

1 Thessalonians 3:13: *May he strengthen your hearts so you will be blameless and holy in the presence of our God and Father when our Lord Jesus comes with all his holy ones.* This verse points to Christ's coming for His saints, but as with the other verses, it gives no timing for the Rapture.

1 Thessalonians 4:13-17: *Brothers, we do not want you to be ignorant about those who fall asleep, or to grieve like the rest of men, who have no hope. We believe that Jesus died and rose again and so we believe that God will bring with Jesus those who have fallen asleep in him. According to the Lord's own word, we tell you that we who are still alive at the coming of the Lord, will certainly not precede those who have fallen asleep. For the Lord himself will come down from heaven, with a loud command, with the voice of the*

archangel and with the trumpet call of God, and the dead in Christ will rise first. After that, we who are still alive and are left will be caught up with them in the clouds to meet the Lord in the air. And so we will be with the Lord forever. This is a tremendous passage of scripture that affirms the resurrection of both the dead in Christ and those who are alive at His coming. It is saying, when Christ comes, those who are alive will be taken by the Rapture and not by death.

The next verse to examine is 2 Thessalonians 5:9-23. I will not write out this whole section of scripture, but all of chapter five should be read in this study. This chapter begins by discussing times and dates and being caught unprepared for Christ's coming.

I will, however, quote the first six verses of 1 Thessalonians 5:1-6. *Now, brothers, about times and dates we do not need to write to you, for you know very well that the day of the Lord will come like a thief in the night. While people are saying "Peace and safety," destruction will come on them suddenly, as labor pains on a pregnant woman, and they will not escape. But you, brothers, are not in darkness so that this day should surprise you like a thief. You are all sons of the light and sons of the day. We do not belong to the night or to the darkness. So then, let us not be like others who are asleep, but let us be alert and self-controlled.*

The church should not be caught by surprise at the coming of the Lord; it is only the unsaved world around us who are crying, "Peace and safety," who will be surprised as if by a thief in the night. Looking at 2 Thessalonians 5 as a whole is so important in understanding the Lord's coming, yet there is no sign of the timing of the Rapture.

The next verse posted on the pre-tribulation rapture chart is 2 Thessalonians 2:1. *Concerning the coming of our Lord Jesus Christ and our being gathered to him...* This verse attests to Christ's coming and the Rapture, but like the other verses it fails to provide any indication of timing. It is important to note that if this chart would have included the next two verses after 2 Thessalonians 2:1, we would see that Paul is telling the church that the Rapture will not happen until certain events take place. The key event is the revealing of antichrist. Therefore, this verse in full context gives some support to a mid-tribulation rapture.

Next, 2 Thessalonians 2:7, 8: *For the secret power of lawlessness is already at work;*

but the one who now holds it back will continue to do so till he is taken out of the way.
And then the lawless one will be revealed, whom the Lord Jesus will overthrow with the
breath of his mouth and destroy by the splendor of his coming. These last two verses are
quite interesting. They are generally accepted as referring to the antichrist, and many
believe that these verses are about the collective power of spirit-filled Christians being
able to restrain the antichrist. Therefore, the Rapture is looked at as the way that
the restrainer would be taken out of the way, giving the antichrist free reign on the
earth. If you really think about this explanation and look closely at these scriptures,
you will see a problem with this explanation. Look at the portion which says, but
the one who now holds it back will *continue* to do so till he is taken out of the way.
This verse describes the restrainer as "the one," not a collective force, such as from
masses of Christians. I have always had a problem believing that Christians have to be
raptured before the antichrist could have free reign. If the collective force and power
of all praying saints could restrain the antichrist, then why did not the prayers and
collective power of all Christians restrain Hitler and other tyrants who have lived and
attacked Christians and Jews on the earth, including stopping all the Christians from
being martyred throughout the ages?

Most Christians who believe in a pre-tribulation rapture also believe there will be
tribulation saints after the Rapture. Some denominations believe that the tribulation
saints will be comprised of those who had drifted away from God before the time of
the Rapture but came back to God after missing that event. There are some churches
that believe a few, who may have thought they were Christians by their good works
or simply by being a part of a church, will be left behind, much to their surprise. As
I have come to my conclusion that the Rapture will be a mid-tribulation event, I do
not see that scriptures support the idea of tribulation saints after the Rapture. All who
will come back to God or get saved during the early years of the Great Tribulation
will have made up their minds to serve God or not, and when the Rapture occurs,
those who are not Christians will have fully rejected Christ. The reason I bring up
this idea is because those who believe there will be tribulation saints would have to
infer that tribulation saints would be helpless without the power of the Holy Spirit.
Think about this. Could it be that scriptures are actually referring to someone else
being taken out of the way? I will go into detail to answer this question in chapter
nine where I talk about the four strongest arguments for the pre-tribulation rapture.

I do not mean to come off like a know-it-all, but I believe I have a reasonable explanation for who "he" is that has to be taken out of the way, in order to give the antichrist full reign on the earth. Do you remember the story of when Daniel fasted and prayed for God's intervention? He was visited by the Lord and His top warring angel, Michael the Archangel.

Read Daniel 10. Here are a few good verses to consider: First, Daniel 10:12, 13 (KJV): *Then said he unto me, fear not, Daniel: for from the first day that thou didst set thine heart to understand and to chasten thyself before thy God, thy words were heard, and I am come for thy words. But the prince of the kingdom of Persia withstood me one and twenty days: but, lo, Michael, one of the chief princes, came to help me; and I remained there with the kings of Persia.*

Next read Daniel 10:20, 21 (KJV): *Then said he, Knowest thou wherefore I am come unto thee? And now will I return to fight with the prince of Persia: and when I am gone forth, lo, the prince of Grecia shall come. But I will shew thee that which is noted in the Scriptures of truth: and there is none that holdeth with me in these things, but Michael your prince.*

So my explanation for this verse is that one of God's most powerful angels, Michael, is the one who is holding the antichrist at bay until it is time for Satan to unleash his full fury of evil on the earth, and he, Michael, will have to be taken out of the way or be told to halt his restraining work, not the church. I would have to say that the only verse that shows the timing of the Rapture as pre-Tribulation is this one here. Yet, if you agree that the church through the ages has not really been a restraining force with the power to stop evil, then you may conclude as I have that this scripture does not provide scriptural proof that the Rapture will happen before the antichrist is revealed or before the Great Tribulation starts. I will be going into greater detail on Michael the Archangel in a later chapter, showing why I believe that he is the restrainer who must be removed or told to stand down.

I will now examine a second teacher who also supports the pre-tribulation position. I will be drawing my discussion from a popular book on the subject of the Rapture and the End Times. The first statement in that book which caught my attention is that the scriptures clearly support a pre-tribulation rapture of believers. Please understand my motives in examining the teachings of these scholars. I have come to a point where I just do not think the pre-tribulation viewpoint of the Rapture is clearly supported by scripture. Yet, I hear this teacher make the statement that the Bible clearly supports the pre-tribulation viewpoint.

I see the mid-tribulation view of the Rapture clearly supported in the Bible. Some people might ask, "Just what difference does it really make?" If it did not make any difference, I would not be writing this, but it will make a huge difference when the Great Tribulation starts and millions of believers realize the Rapture did not happen. They will be upset at their Bible teachers and pastors who misled them. Please do not take offense at this last statement. I would love for a Bible teacher or pastor to show me clear scriptural support for a pre-tribulation rapture, but because our views on the timing of the Rapture are so opposed, I have to examine their evidence to see which view really is clearly supported by the Word of God.

The book I am drawing this discussion from covers five reasons for believing that the Rapture is a pre-tribulation event. I will examine each of the author's five scriptural reasons for his position in this context. I will then look at the author's views as compared to my position, which has evolved into a mid-tribulation Rapture position. You can decide for yourself which position is clearly supported by the Word of God.

The first reason for supporting a pre-tribulation position uses the following scripture reference. Revelation 19:11, 14 (KJV): *And I saw heaven opened, and behold a white horse; and he that sat upon him was called Faithful and True, and in righteousness he doth judge and make war.* Also, *The armies which were in heaven followed him upon white horses, clothed in fine linen, white and clean.* If we look at the context of the text, we will notice it is the nineteenth chapter of Revelation. The wrath of God is finished and Christ is returning with His saints. I agree with the author's statement that the saints have to go to heaven before this event happens in order for the saints to come back to the earth with Jesus from heaven. This teacher does not address the fact that if the Rapture is a mid-tribulation event, as shown in the second half of Revelation 7 before the wrath of God starts in Revelation 8, the saints would be in heaven in more than enough time to return with Christ as indicated in Revelation 19.

The author of this book makes the comment that the post–tribulation position is not logical. I agree with the author on this point because the post–tribulation position teaches that the Rapture does not happen until the end of God's wrath. The main point

I would like to make is that his first scriptural support for a pre-tribulation rapture does not contradict the mid-tribulation position. Therefore, the Word of God is not clearly supporting a pre-tribulation rapture from this scripture verse.

The second argument for a pre-tribulation rapture from the author's book on the Rapture and the End Times is from Revelation 7. The author points out how the four angels who have power to harm the earth are told to hold back until the 144,000 Jews are sealed. He then goes on to say that if there is no sealing of Christians to protect them, then they must be already raptured; therefore, on that basis, he sees the Rapture as a pre-tribulation event. If you read Revelation 7, where the 144,000 are sealed, the Rapture from the mid-tribulation view occurs sometime after the sealing of the 144,000 in Revelation 7, but before the wrath of God is poured out in Revelation 8.

What is interesting is that the author states that the sealing of the 144,000 is before God's wrath. God never pours His wrath upon the righteous. Look closely and you will see that at the point of the sealing of the 144,000, the six seals of Revelation 6 have already been opened. In this case, the author says that the seals are not the wrath of God. At other times, he says the seals are the wrath of God. I will give further reasoning why the seals are not part of the wrath of God in chapter nine . The mid-tribulation view I share in this study goes on to say the saints, or the church, will go through the opening of the seals of Revelation 6. Then the 144,000 Jews will be sealed in Revelation 7, and after the sealing of the 144,000, the mid-tribulation Rapture will take place before the wrath of God begins in Revelation 8. Again, the author's second argument for a pre-tribulation Rapture does not conflict with the mid-tribulation view. Therefore, this scripture passage does not clearly support the pre-tribulation view of the Rapture.

This teacher's third argument for a pre-tribulation Rapture is that the restrainer must be taken out of the way. He uses 2 Thessalonians 2:6-8 *And now you know what is holding him back, so that he may be revealed at the proper time. For the secret power of lawlessness is already at work; but the one who now holds it back will continue to do so till he is taken out of the way. And then the lawless one will be revealed, whom the Lord Jesus will overthrow with the breath of his mouth and destroy by the splendor of his coming.* When we read this scripture carefully, we see the antichrist cannot be revealed until the restrainer is taken out of the way. So if the restrainer is the church or the saints on earth, then the antichrist cannot be revealed until after the Rapture of the church. When we read 2 Thessalonians 2:1-3, we really have a problem: *Concerning the coming of our Lord Jesus Christ and our being gathered to him, we ask you brothers not to become easily unsettled or alarmed by some prophecy, report or letter supposed to have come from us, saying that the day of the Lord has already come. Don't let anyone deceive you in any way, for that day will not come until the rebellion occurs and the man of lawlessness is revealed, the man doomed to destruction.* This scripture says that before the church can be gathered to Christ, the antichrist must first be revealed. His argument totally contradicts 2 Thessalonians 2:6-8. That text says that the restrainer must be removed first. Which is it? You cannot have it both ways. If the restrainer is not the church, the problem goes away. I cover this contradiction later in this study, pointing out it makes more sense that the restrainer is not the church but is Michael the Archangel, the chief warring angel who came to Daniel's aid when he prayed and fasted for twenty-one days. But the bottom line is that this third argument from the book on *The Rapture and the End Times* is not clearly supporting a pre-tribulation rapture.

The last two points in the book, supporting this author's view, are handled as one, so I will try to cover them as one. First, the author says, "The Lord commands the church to always be watchful for Christ's coming." Then he goes on to say, "...which could happen at any time...", quoting 1 Thessalonians 5:6 and Luke 12:40. *Therefore let us not sleep, as do others, but let us watch and be sober.* Then it says, *Be ye therefore ready also: for the Son of Man cometh at an hour when ye think not.* As I look at 1 Thessalonians 5:6 where it says "...but let us watch...", my question is this: If the Lord's coming and the Rapture are without warning, why do we have to watch? If we are told to watch, there has to be something for which to watch. Furthermore, if there is something for which we are to watch, then how can we say that the Rapture is an imminent event? For an event to be imminent, by definition, there cannot be anything that has to happen before that imminent event. If there is anything that has to happen, for which we have to watch and wait, then that event is not imminent.

The author's viewpoint is interesting because he teaches that the Rapture has been an imminent event for two thousand years. My question is, "If we had to wait for Israel to be reborn as a nation, which happened in 1948, then how could the Rapture have been imminent before 1948?" Also, the apostle Paul talks about the Lord's coming and our gathering to Him as not taking place until the man of lawlessness is revealed. Read 2 Thessalonians 2:1-3. *Concerning the coming of the Lord Jesus Christ and our being gathered to him, we ask you, brothers, not to become easily unsettled or alarmed by some prophecy, report or letter supposed to have come from us, saying that the day of the Lord has come. Don't let anyone deceive you in any way, for that day will not come until the rebellion occurs and the man of lawlessness is revealed, the man doomed to destruction.* So how can anyone say the Rapture is imminent if the man of lawlessness is not revealed? Does it not make sense that the Rapture will not be imminent until sometime after the antichrist is revealed? There are other events that must also take place before the Rapture. I will discuss these events in chapter ten.

Some people say no man knows the day or the hour of the Lord's return. I agree with this, as this is what the Bible says, and once the antichrist is revealed, we will still not know the day or the hour of Christ's return. It will be time for us to obey the words in Luke 21:25-28. *There will be signs in the sun, moon and stars, on the earth; nations will be in anguish and perplexity at the roaring of the sea. Men will faint from terror, apprehensive of what is coming on the world, for heavenly bodies will be shaken. At that time, they will see the Son of Man coming in a cloud with power and great glory. When these things begin to take place, stand up and lift up your heads, because your redemption is drawing near.* If we have to wait for these things to begin to come to pass, and if we have been commanded to watch for these things, then how can we say the Rapture is imminent?

In closing, the book on *The Rapture and the End Times* quotes from <u>Webster's Ninth New Collegiate Dictionary</u>, which defines "imminent" as ready to take place, especially hanging threateningly over one's head. The author explains that a fellow colleague noted in his book on the End Times, "Other things may happen before the imminent event, but nothing else MUST take place before it happens...If something else must take place before an event can happen, that event cannot be counted as imminent."

The author concludes that because the Rapture is pre-tribulation, it has to be imminent. But this statement is based on flawed, scriptural support. If the Rapture is a mid-tribulation event, then it cannot be imminent until the Great Tribulation is in motion, the 144,000 are sealed, the antichrist arrives, and other events take place. In closing, the author's last scriptural arguments do not clearly support a pre-tribulation rapture.

The third teacher I will be critiquing has written many books and taught many times on television, often covering topics concerning the Rapture and the End Times. The other night when I was watching television, I noticed he was teaching on the Rapture, and he said that there are some people teaching that the church is going through the Great Tribulation. He said, "Let me shoot that down right here." When he said that, I was all ears. At the time I started this study, I had a multitude of questions on the timing of the Rapture. I had always held to the pre-tribulation view of the Rapture. It was my hope when I started this study, I would find scriptural strength from the Word of God to prove to myself that the pre-tribulation view is the correct view. However, as this study progressed, the opposite has happened. I am now convinced that the mid-tribulation view of the Rapture is the most accurate interpretation, based on the weight of scripture from God's Word. When this teacher said, "Let me shoot the mid-tribulation rapture teaching down right here," he had my attention.

Thank God for a DVR on my television. I record my favorite evangelists every day so that I can listen to them on my schedule. I replayed this teachers program several times, about why the Rapture is a pre-tribulation event. I dug out several Bibles to check his Bible quotations, and this is what I found.

The teacher began by explaining that the first three chapters of Revelation talk about the seven churches of Asia, and after that, the church is not mentioned again until the end of the book of Revelation. "Why?" he asked. "Because the church goes up in the air."

He went on to say that in Revelation 4:1, John was snatched up into heaven where he saw the twenty-four elders who were seated, robed, and crowned. The teacher used the phrase "snatched up into heaven." But this is not what the Bible states. This phrase makes it sound as if this is a Rapture event while, in reality, the verse simply says, "...Come up here." When it is time for the Rapture, God will not be asking us to come up because, without notice in the twinkling of an eye, we will be "...caught up..." We will not be asked to come up.

The television evangelist continued his teaching, saying because the elders are wearing robes and crowns; this represents the church. I see a problem with this interpretation. First, I do not read of a multitude that would represent the saints or the church in heaven in white robes until Revelation 7:9. *After this I looked, and there before me was a great multitude that no one could count, from every tribe, people, and language standing before the throne and in front of the Lamb. They were wearing white robes and were holding palm branches in their hands.* If you read this carefully in the book of Revelation, you will notice it does not mention this multitude as having crowns. Why? A good explanation for this is the saints will not be given crowns until the Judgment Seat of Christ for believers takes place. It is reasonable to believe this judgment of believers will not happen until all of the saints are in heaven. Doesn't it make sense that the saints being martyred in Revelation 6 at the fifth seal would not receive their crowns and rewards until all the saints are united in heaven? The first pre-tribulation teacher who used the time line chart puts this judgment of believers during the period when God is pouring out His wrath on the earth (after the Rapture of all believers). Then the Marriage Supper of the Lamb happens after the Judgment Seat of Christ. This makes sense to me.

If the saints and the church have to wait to receive their rewards until all the saints are in heaven, then how can someone say the elders in Revelation 4:4 represent the church wearing their robes and crowns? Therefore, the reference to the elders wearing robes and crowns in Revelation 4:4 must point to the twenty-four elders. They would be in heaven before the Rapture and could have already received their crowns that represent the rewards for what they did with their lives on earth. I have read that many people believe the twenty-four elders are leaders from the twelve tribes of Israel and the twelve disciples. This makes sense to me, but other people say they would not be in heaven around the throne until the Rapture of the church. I can see two scriptural reasons why they can be in heaven before the Rapture of the church.

The first reason is found in Matthew 27:51-52, These verses are about what happened when Christ died on the cross and was later resurrected. The Bible says, *At that moment, the curtain of the temple was torn in two from top to bottom. The earth shook and the rocks split. The tombs broke open and the bodies of many holy people who had died were raised to life.* These holy people were resurrected after Christ was resurrected, and they were seen by many people. Also, if God chose to take Enoch and Elijah to heaven before they died, and if God resurrected these holy people at the time of

Christ's resurrection, then it is not a violation of scripture to imagine God could resurrect the twenty-four elders before the church is resurrected at the Rapture.

The second reason is found in Revelation 7:13-14. *Then one of the elders asked me, 'These in white robes -- who are they, and where did they come from?" I answered, "Sir, you know." And he said, "These are they who have come out of the Great Tribulation..."* Revelation 7:9 says a great multitude in white robes suddenly appeared in heaven. I see this plainly describing the Rapture. So how can the elders represent the church in Revelation 4:4 if the multitude in white robes does not appear in heaven until Revelation 7:9? They do not represent the church; they are just the twenty-four elders who are at the throne of God when the church arrives in Revelation 7.

The television preacher explained that the church is raptured in Revelation 4, and the antichrist shows up in Revelation 6. He went on to say that if four comes before six, then we are out of here. If you want to stay, that's your business. But consider the wording of 2 Thessalonians 2:1-4. *Concerning the coming of our Lord Jesus Christ and our being gathered to him, we ask you, brothers, not to become easily unsettled or alarmed by some prophecy, report or letter supposed to have come from us, saying that the day of the Lord has already come. Do not let anyone deceive you in any way, for that day will not come until the rebellion occurs and the man of lawlessness is revealed, the man doomed to destruction. He opposes and exalts himself over everything that is called God or is worshiped, and even sets himself up in God's temple, proclaiming himself to be God.*

Here we see clear wording. Paul is teaching that the Rapture, or as Paul says, "... the gathering to him....", will not take place until the antichrist is revealed. If the antichrist is not revealed until Revelation 6, then the Rapture cannot happen until sometime after the revealing of the antichrist occurs in Revelation 6. I hope it is clear that, based on the Word of God. With all due respect, I cannot agree with this television preacher.

— CHAPTER EIGHT —

THE COMING ANTICHRIST

W hen I first wrote the outline for this study, I included a chapter on the antichrist. Well, as this study was taking shape, it seemed that all I would be writing concerning the antichrist would be a rehash of what everyone else had said or written. I felt unless I had something fresh to write, I should just drop this topic from my study. A few weeks later, as I was reading the book of Revelation, two fresh truths jumped out at me. As I studied further to confirm if I was seeing the Word of God correctly, I had further insights jumping out at me. At that point, I realized I had to write this chapter.

To begin with, I must set the backdrop where I believe the antichrist first appears on the world's stage. If you will read the following verses, I will explain where I am going with this. Read Revelation 13:1-3. *And I saw a beast coming out of the sea. He had ten horns and seven heads, with ten crowns on his horns, and on each head a blasphemous name. The beast I saw resembled a leopard, but had feet like those of a bear and a mouth like that of a lion. The dragon gave the beast his power and his throne and great authority. One of the heads of the beast seemed to have had a fatal wound, but the fatal wound had been healed. The whole world was astonished and followed the beast.*

I do not pretend to understand all that is written in these verses, but what I do understand, I will explain. These verses begin with a beast coming out of the sea with ten horns, ten crowns, and seven heads, and it is a bit confusing, but what we can infer is the beast is a rising government which will grow to become one-world government. The passage describes one of the heads of the beast as seeming to have a fatal wound. From this verse, I conclude that the antichrist will come from one of the heads of the beast. What is interesting is before one of the heads of the beast is wounded, the whole being described here as the beast with ten horns (or ten leaders or heads of state) must be fully in place. Once the antichrist comes from one of the heads of the beast, <u>then</u> the antichrist is referred to as "the beast." If you read the following verses, it will help clarify the description of the beast that becomes a one-world government consisting of ten kings or leaders. Read Revelation 17:12 and 14. *The ten horns you saw are ten kings who have not yet received a kingdom, but who for one hour will receive authority as kings along with the beast. They will make war against the Lamb, but the Lamb will overcome them because he is Lord of lords and King of kings and with him will be his called, chosen and faithful followers.*

As a point of clarification there have been many world leaders who have had the spirit of antichrist, but just having the spirit of antichrist does not make them the antichrist. Hitler certainly had the spirit of antichrist, but he was not *the* antichrist. If you believe as I do that the man who will become the antichrist is alive on the earth today, you have to realize even though he is destined to become the antichrist, he will not be the antichrist until Satan literally possesses his body and brings him back from death.

Now, if we draw from the accepted teaching about the coming antichrist, we will see most prophetic teachers believe that the man who will become the antichrist will be the leader of this one-world government, and then this world leader will be mortally wounded. Many believe he will have a mortal head wound, and his miraculous recovery will usher in the antichrist. Let's read Revelation 13:3. *One of the heads of the beast seemed to have had a fatal wound, but the fatal wound had been healed.* **This verse does not say the leader of this one-world government will be wounded. NO!! It says one of the <u>heads</u> of this government will be wounded. This means to qualify as a candidate for the antichrist, you must be one of the ten heads.** Let me further explain. The European Union is getting ready to elect a permanent leader to lead the countries or regions that are aligned with this new one-world government. Tony Blair, the former leader of England, is one of the leaders who has tossed his hat into the ring to run for this position. I have already heard of Bible teachers who believe that Tony Blair is going to be the antichrist. But no, this is not what is being said in the Bible. **The Bible says one of the ten heads is fatally wounded, not the leader of the ten heads.**

An important point to understand is the event that leads to one of the ten heads of state being fatally wounded cannot occur until the one-world government is in place. This means that according to 2 Thessalonians 2:1-3, the gathering of believers or the Rapture cannot occur until the one-world government is in place and the antichrist is revealed.

Many Bible teachers are now saying the future one-world government will not be comprised of ten nations but ten <u>regions</u> of the world. The ten crowns and ten horns represent ten leadership positions. This verse says one of the heads is wounded with a fatal wound, which means the leader over the ten heads or the president of the European Union does not qualify to become the antichrist. He must be one of the heads of the beast to qualify. Now, if you think about this, any one of these ten horns or heads of state that comprise the new one-world government could end up being the antichrist. This means that we will not know for certain who the antichrist is until one of the ten heads of state is fatally wounded.

The powers behind the formation of this future one-world government have already laid out the division of this future global government. The future antichrist must come from one of the following regions. It is from this global division that we get the ten heads of the beast.

1. America, Canada and Mexico

2. South America

3. Australia and New Zealand

4. Western Europe

5. Eastern Europe

6. South Asia

7. Central Asia

8. North Africa

9. South Africa

10. The Middle East

If we refine this list a bit further, we realize that some of these ten regions don't qualify to produce the antichrist. We know the Russian region and the Asian region both have separate parts to play in end-times prophecy, and the leaders from these regions would not be the antichrist. We know that the Middle East region will accept a seven-year peace pact with the antichrist, and Israel would never go along if the antichrist came from the Middle East region. This brings the list of ten down to seven. If you look further at the leaders of the other regions, some of them are a lesser caliber then what would probably be accepted by the world as the new global leader, thus making it easier to see who of these leaders will rise as the antichrist.

This leads to another interesting thought. If any one of the heads that comprise the one-world government can be tapped to become the antichrist, then consider the following idea. I only know of one End Times teacher, Dr. Jack Van Impe, who has said our current president is being groomed to be "The Man." I have said all along I just do not see how he could be "The Man," but personally, I do not know of any leader who is more qualified. If you are following my reasoning here, you may come to the same conclusion as I. If the United States becomes the North American region of the new world government, and its leader is the president, then the president would become one of the heads of the beast. This would make the President of the United States a qualifying person who could become the antichrist. WOW! What a thought.

Another important thought to keep in mind as these events start to unfold is this: BEFORE the United States would be willing to sign up and join the one-world government and become part of the North American region of this global government, the United States has to fall apart economically, as well as suffering a complete breakdown of society as we know it. A period of time from between six months on the short side and up a year and a half on the long side could occur before we would be willing to give up our independence. We might see events like terrorist attacks on our cities, hyper-inflation, and the collapse of our dollar, food shortages, famine, and anarchy in our cities. This stretch of time will seem like the end-of-the-world to many. Many Christians will believe the Great Tribulation has started. This period of time is only part of the birth pains that will be coming on the world before the Great Tribulation begins, merely setting the stage for the antichrist to come to power. Personally, I believe this period, before the Great

Tribulation starts, will be on the short side of my predictions. Once things start falling together, world events will move rapidly to the prophetic destiny of the Lord's return.

Imagine how these coming events will affect our lives. This coming time of upheaval will be a window that will last from the time the world economies collapse until the ten-region, one-world government is formed. This window will be unlike any time in American history. Life as we know it will be over. This special window will last until the antichrist comes to power. We need to be ready to take advantage of the greatest evangelistic opportunity the world has ever seen. People's lives will be turned upside down. Churches will be filled with people looking for answers. If we know this time is coming, we can prepare to have a part in this great harvest of souls. Once the antichrist comes to power, this open window to share Christ's love will close.

Recently, as I was preparing this study for the printers, I was watching a well-known televangelist. He was talking about the soon-coming collapse of the dollar and America's economic collapse. He made the statement that he knows when this is going to happen. He then predicted that America's dollar and economy would collapse when the church is raptured out of here. This statement is giving a false sense of security to all his followers. If you recognize from this study that the one-world government has to be in place before the Great Tribulation starts, then you must also realize that the church will see a period of tribulation, even if the Rapture were a pre-tribulation event. I would not want to be in the shoes of this preacher when the US economy collapses, and his church fills up with all these people who are asking him, "Where is the Rapture that is supposed to get us out of here?" The store shelves will have been emptied by panic-buying. People will not be ready for what lies ahead. In fact, I believe most of the churches in America are not ready for what lies ahead.

If you have followed me this far, you will realize this one-world government will have a leader who does not become the antichrist. This global government will probably be faltering, and the stage will be set for a greater leader to rise from its ranks. Then, when one of the heads of the beast or one of the leaders of this ten-region, one-world government is fatally wounded and lies at death's door, he will be brought back to the land of the living. He will arise with the wisdom and the cunning of Satan. He will show the world he is the one they are to follow. Read Revelation 13:3. *One of the heads of the beast seemed to have had a fatal wound, but the fatal wound had been healed. The whole world was astonished and followed the beast.*

Another verse that helps to understand the nature and makeup of the beast is found in Daniel 7:20-21. *I also wanted to know about the ten horns on its head and about the other horn that came up, before which three of them fell - the horn that looked more imposing than the others and that had eyes and a mouth that spoke boastfully. As I watched, this horn was waging war against the saints and defeating them.* The portion of this verse that says *The horn that looked more imposing than the others* is a phrase that gives evidence that one of the ten horns will rise up from the others to become the antichrist. Once this horn or head of state has been fatally wounded, he will come back as Satan in the flesh, and then it will be evident who the antichrist is.

Another verse that gives many insights to the nature of the antichrist is found in Daniel 8:23-25. *In the latter part of their reign, when rebels have become completely wicked, a stern faced king, a master of intrigue will arise. He will become very strong, but not by his own power. He will cause astounding devastation and will succeed in whatever he does. He will destroy the mighty men and the holy people. He will cause deceit to prosper and he will consider himself superior. When they feel secure, he will destroy many and take his stand against the Prince of princes. Yet he will be destroyed but not by human hands.*

These verses give some incredible insights to this coming global leader. First, the scripture says he will be a master of intrigue. When you look up the word "intrigue" in the dictionary, what you learn is this leader is a master of deceit and lies. This global leader will make war against all that is good and against God's people. He will even stand up against the Prince of princes, yet he will be defeated but not by human hands. Can it be any clearer? Jesus will win, and we win. Come, Lord Jesus.

As we study the scriptures, we will come to realize there is one sure way to know who the antichrist is before his coming to power. The Bible says he who has wisdom may be able to figure it out. Revelation 13:18 (KJV) says, *Here is wisdom. Let him that hath understanding count the number of the beast: for it is the number of a man; and his number is Six hundred threescore and six.* Think about this. If the antichrist were to be the leader of the European Union, such as Tony Blair, it does not take any wisdom at all to figure out who the antichrist would be – the president of the European

Union. However, if you try to figure out which of these ten horns or leaders is to be the antichrist, you would need to see all of these leaders' birth certificates so that you could see the name with which they were born. The original birth certificate of one prominent world leader, who could some day be one of the ten leaders of this new world government, is cloaked in uncertainty and not available for close examination.

As we continue to study Daniel 7, we will see more hints as to what kind of leader the antichrist will be. These hints could help discern who of the ten world leaders will be the antichrist. The first hint is found in Daniel 7:20b, ...*the horn that looked more imposing then the others and that had eyes and a mouth that spoke boastfully.* This verse says this leader will be imposing in stature, boastful and arrogant. Unfortunately, many world leaders match this description. Then read Daniel 7:25a. *He will speak against the Most High and oppress his saints and try to change the set times and the laws.* This leader will be a leader who will bring in many changes to customs and established laws.

An important point to consider is a one-world government must be in place <u>before</u> one of the ten heads of state can be fatally wounded, and this has to happen before the antichrist can rise to power. This seriously puts the imminent return of the Lord on hold until a one-world government is in place.

Next, I want to point out that we have been misled concerning the kind of mortal wound this world leader would have. As I mentioned earlier, most Christians believe the world leader would recover from a fatal head wound. This is taken from Revelation 13:3a. *One of the heads of the beast seemed to have had a fatal wound, but the fatal wound had been healed.* **This verse does not say this leader will recover from a head wound. No, what it is saying is one of the ten heads of the beast is fatally wounded. What does "one of the heads" mean? What it means is the beast is comprised of a number of leaders or heads of state, and one of these ten heads of state is fatally wounded but not necessarily from a wound to the head.** Why is this important? I believe this event will reveal the antichrist and the beginning of the Great Tribulation will soon follow. If most Christians have been taught the antichrist would arise after a miraculous recovery from a fatal head wound, then when this leader does not recover from a head wound but maybe from a fatal wound to other vital organs, this will leave many confused. They will not know if this really is the antichrist. When the antichrist rises to deceive even the elect, if possible, he will have confused Christians who are open to deception.

Another point, that could lead to confusion concerning who the antichrist is, could originate with the type of wound that this world leader receives. I have heard teaching that this leader who is fatally wounded will be wounded from a sword. The Bible does say he is wounded with a sword. Revelation 13:14b (KJV): *...saying to them that dwell on the earth, that they should make an image to the beast, which had the wound by a sword and did live.* The point I would like to make is, when John the Revelator wrote this, the weapons we have today did not exist. When my wife and I traveled across the country doing Kids Crusades, we did a message on the whole armor of God. We substituted modern weapons for the weapons used by a Roman soldier in Bible days. For the Sword of the Spirit, we substituted a rifle. It is possible the future antichrist will be wounded with a sword, but I do not believe we should be adamant about what type of weapon will be used. John the Revelator had never seen a rifle.

ADDITIONAL CLUES TO IDENTIFY THE COMING ANTICHRIST

Since the first book, I have received a rush of new insights on the coming antichrist. What is interesting about these insights is that they are all pointing in the same direction. Out of respect for the office of our world leaders, I will limit the use of specific names so as to protect the innocent or the guilty. Now realize, I am not saying I know for sure who the antichrist is. I see clues pointing in a certain direction, and I see this one leader as the most qualified choice to date. I must also say, "So far I just don't see a more qualified candidate".

I continue to keep my ears open to hear about a better candidate for the antichrist. Many of the people throwing their best guesses out there don't understand that for a leader to qualify for this position, he must be one of the ten heads of the new global beast government. As I have mentioned earlier in my book, I explain where God showed me that to qualify for the antichrist you have to be one of the ten heads of state that will make up the new one world government. The world will be divided into ten regions with ten heads of state, and one of these ten leaders will be fatally wounded.

If there has been one strong suggestion as from where the antichrist will come, it has been said that he will arise from a country in the Middle East. I have had a hard time accepting this because that would mean that Israel would have to accept a seven year peace treaty from its enemies. This is not logical to me, also, I have been told that the King of Jordan is a good candidate because he has been a silent friend of Israel working behind the scenes. I don't believe that a person who has been seen as a good man will instantly turn into an evil man. I believe the man of sin will be recognized as having had an evil way about him before he becomes the antichrist.

Another choice that has been thrown out as a candidate for the antichrist has been the new leader of Greece. One problem I see with this candidate is he would have to end up being one of the ten regional leaders, however he would also have to be accepted by the major players of the world. In closing on this thought, personally, I believe if we want to look into the direction from where the antichrist will come, we need to follow the money.

In this section called "Additional clues to the Coming Antichrist", most of these clues will be covering new insights that were not covered in this chapter, with the exception of number one below. They are as follows:

1. Read Daniel 8:23 and 24: *"A stern faced king, a master of intrigue, will arise. He will cause deceit to prosper, and he will consider himself superior."* If you will study these verses you will see many clues to the coming antichrist. **"A master of intrigue,"** points to a leader that will have an air of mystery about him. This could mean that much of his background and history are unknown. **"He will cause deceit to prosper",** points to a leader who commonly deceives those he rules over. This is a nice way of saying that he will be a skilled liar.

2. Another clue comes from Daniel 11:37; this is another case where many have not seen what I believe is the true meaning of this text. "He will show no regard for the god of his fathers or for the one desired by women, nor will he regard any god but will exalt himself above them all". This scripture is talking about three different clues.

a. He will show no regard for the god of his fathers.

b. He will show no regard for the one desired by women.

c. He will not regard any god but will exalt himself above all gods.

The first clue above has been taken by some prophetic teachers to mean that the antichrist will have Jewish blood in his genealogy and will therefore have no regard for the God of Abraham, Isaac, and Jacob. I heard the current leader of our country has Jewish ancestry on his mother's side. I tried to research this and came up blank. I asked a friend who is very good at this type of research and he came back to me saying that much of his mother's and his history has been scrubbed clean. This does not surprise me, as the Bible says the antichrist will be a person of intrigue or mystery. If we can't even prove if he is an American citizen, it does not bother me that we can't prove his genealogy.

The focus of my second clue is in the second part of the scripture above. "He will show no regard for the one desired by women" In the King James version it says **"Neither shall he regard the desire of women"** It has bothered me that many have said this means he will have no desire for woman and will be a homosexual. This is not what this verse is saying. It says "He will show no regard for the one desired by women" So the question is, who is "the one desired by women". I was talking to a friend about this and as we chatted about who was the one, it dawned on us that God has given woman a desire from the beginning of creation, this desire has been recently perverted, but this God-given desire of women is to have babies and raise a family. When you realize that the one desired by woman is babies, then when you read this verse about the antichrist, it is saying "He will show no regard for babies desired by women". Now what world leader comes to mind that has no regard for babies? I am thinking of a leader who is making abortion on demand available for all teenagers, a leader who is forcing even Christian businesses to make abortion available to all employees. This leader has said he would not want his daughters to be cursed with pregnancy. I don't want to mention any names, but when I look at this clue and the others, I see a certain world leader is still in the running to be the man of sin.

3. I have developed a friendship from Uganda, a young pastor with a nice young family. He expressed to me that he and other Christians in Uganda are upset that the leader of our country is promoting homosexuality. He then went on to say that the leaders of his country will not stand up in opposition to this agenda that his people find so offensive because his country is getting food and financial aid from America. They cannot afford to rock the boat and lose this aid. It then dawned on me that this well known world leader is using financial and food assistance to blackmail countries into going along with his agenda. It further dawned on me that this leader is using the same tactics to get senators and congressmen to go along with his agenda by promising pork barrel projects to certain states that go along with him and threatening those states with financial cutbacks if they oppose his agenda. It finally dawned on me that this is the system of the antichrist. If you do not buy into his system you cannot buy or sell. You will not be able to buy food for your family.

4. Recently a prominent world leader visited Israel. It was his first visit to Israel and Jerusalem. It is interesting that this visit took place on the Jews most Holy day, Palm Sunday, the same holy day that Jesus arrived in Jerusalem riding on a donkey. His arrival was in fulfillment of Bible prophecy. What we need to realize is when the antichrist arrives, he also will point to instances where he fulfilled Bible prophecy. What was also interesting about this visit is how obvious it is that this world leader wants to be seen as the one who is pushing for a peace treaty between Israel and the Middle East. We already know who will succeed in delivering a seven year peace in the Middle East don't we? Yes, the antichrist. Mmmmm... do we have a match? Also, keep in mind this same unnamed world leader was given the Nobel Peace prize before he accomplished anything. Was this prophetic, that he would be the one that will establish peace in the Middle East?

5. Some are saying the antichrist has to come from Europe. Where is this in scripture? If he is to come from the Roman Empire, remember the Roman Empire was the super power of its day. What country today is the world super power? America.

6. It is interesting to note that the leader, who is from one of the 10 regions of the world that will make up the new one world government, must be hated and feared enough for someone to want to assassinate him, thus helping to fulfill prophecy that he would be fatally wounded but come back to life.

7. In closing, there has been a lot of talk about the last pope predicted in the 12th century and his part to play when the antichrist comes on the scene. I believe the last pope is in office today. If this is true, and my suspicions are correct, we could be watching the last elected president of the United States.

I originally wrote and posted these seven clues to the coming antichrist in 2013 and posted them on my site. In the last two years, mostly in the last few months, many prophetic voices are saying there will be no presidential election in 2016, and the president currently in office will stay in office and lead America into the Great Tribulation.

— CHAPTER NINE —

PRE-VS.-MID-TRIBULATION VIEW OF THE RAPTURE

For most of my thirty-eight years as a Christian, I have held to the pre-tribulation view of the Rapture and know this position quite well.

A challenge I would like to make to the readers of these next two chapters is to, first, have an open mind. Then, either prove my conclusions to be wrong with sound arguments from the Word of God, or shout my conclusions from the housetops. There can be no middle ground. To be wrong on this doctrine would leave the church ill-prepared for what we will face leading up to the Lord's return.

I want to look at the four strongest arguments for the pre-tribulation Rapture position and then look at the soundness of each of these teachings in light of the mid-tribulation position.

1. The restrainer must be removed.

I am going to start off with one of the most common scriptural verses that scholars who believe in the pre-tribulation rapture use to support this viewpoint. It is found in 2 Thessalonians 2:7-8a. *For the secret power of lawlessness is already at work; but the one who now holds it back will continue to do so till he is taken out of the way. And then the lawless one will be revealed.*

The pre-tribulation position states that the restrainer is the Holy Spirit or the Spirit-filled church that holds back the coming reign of the anti-christ. The reason this verse is so important to the pre-tribulation position is because those holding this position believe that as long as the church is on the earth with the indwelling Holy Spirit, the Holy Spirit's power in us will restrain the antichrist from fully rising to power. **I have mentioned earlier in this study that I see a weakness in this interpretation. I do not see either scriptural or actual evidence that the Spirit-filled believers have been able to restrain evil on the earth. We could not restrain Hitler or the evil of other tyrannical leaders of the past. When the saints were being tortured in Rome, Spirit-filled Christians could not stop the martyrdom of the saints, so why do we think we have the power to hold back the antichrist now?**

I would like to propose a question to help solve a second problem regarding the belief that God needs to remove the Holy Spirit (and thus the church) in order to keep us from preventing the antichrist's rise to power. "Does God answer all our prayers affirmatively?" No! God answers our prayers if they are in His will. If we pray for something outside of the will of God, He will not grant our petition. When you think about the greatest attacks in history against those whom God loved, you realize those attacks always led to great victories. Without the enslavement of the Israelites in Egypt, we would not have seen the exodus. Without the persecution of eighty thousand Christians by Chairman Mao in China, there would not be one to two hundred million Christians in China today. Without Hitler and the Holocaust, Israel would not have been reborn as a nation. Without the crucifixion of Christ, we would not have our salvation. Without the coming of the antichrist, we would not have the coming of the Lord. The question I would like to pose is, "Would it have been possible, through prayer, to have stopped these events from happening?" We know from God's Word that Jesus had to go to the cross; this event could not be stopped. I do not believe these other events were supposed to be stopped. I believe during extraordinary times of persecution, the church and believers are to pray for personal intervention and protection. During these times, believers need to pray for the salvation of people our lives touch. We need to look at these times of tribulation as opportunities to win the lost and accomplish God's will.

Before it is time for the Lord to come back, will it be God's will for the antichrist to come to power? The answer is "yes!" So, if it is God's will for the antichrist to come to power, why would God answer our prayers to prevent the antichrist from coming to power? Therefore, if God is not going to answer prayers that are contrary to His will concerning the antichrist, then why would God have to remove the church for this reason? Yet if removing the church is the correct interpretation of this verse, where is the weight of other scriptures to back it? To the best of my knowledge, they are totally absent.

The next question is, "If we have been misinterpreting this scripture, what would be an alternative interpretation, and does that view have the strong weight of scripture to back it?" I will now give a scripturally-backed alternative as to why I believe the first position I have discussed is wrong. The alternative position that keeps getting stronger as I study this is that the restrainer referred to here is Michael, God's chief warring angel. Jude 9 refers to Michael as the archangel. Webster's dictionary says an archangel is an angel of high rank.

After Daniel had fasted and prayed for twenty-one days, he had an encounter with the Lord, and an angel told him it took all of those days to break through spiritual battles. Daniel 10:13 describes this experience. *But the prince of the Persian kingdom resisted me twenty-one days. Then Michael, one of the chief princes, came to help me, because I was detained there with the king of Persia.*

This verse is saying Michael is one of God's top warring angels who can step in to help us when we call out to God for help. Plus, Michael has the power to restrain evil. To me, this is compelling, but is there weight from other scriptures to back up this idea? Read Daniel 12:1. *At that time, Michael, the great prince who protects your people, will arise. There will be a time of distress such as has not happened from the beginning of nations until then.*

This is a very compelling verse. First, it talks about Michael, the Great Prince who protects God's people. From whom is Michael protecting God's people? Spiritual forces of wickedness, undoubtedly. Then notice the context here is during the time of the end. **Now, if Michael, one of God's generals who commands the armies of God, can protect us from evil forces, then does it not make sense that if God wants to allow the forces of evil to rise up on the earth in the person of the antichrist, that God could tell Michael, one of his top Generals, to stand-down?**

During World War II, we had a few top generals who commanded the U.S. armed forces. One was General MacArthur in the Pacific theater of the war, and another was General Patton commanding the Third Army in Europe. When the war against the Germans and the Japanese was coming to a close, both of these generals wanted to press onward. General MacArthur wanted to roll into China and prevent it from being a future problem, and General Patton wanted to continue to roll into Russia and stop the threat of communism under Stalin. Well, when push came to shove, they had a Commander-in-Chief they had to obey. The President of the United States, Harry Truman told both of these generals to stand-down. So does it not make sense that God can tell His leading general, Michael, "the restrainer of evil," to stand-down?

There is another story to illustrate this point. I saw a Disney movie one time in which a bear cub was out on its own, and a great lion was stalking the little bear. When the bear cub saw the lion, he became bold and rose up to stand against this great beast. All of a sudden, you could see the look of fear on the lion and it ran away. Then they showed the huge mother bear standing tall behind the little bear cub. It was not the cub, after all, that made the lion flee. It was the mother that was backing the cub up that put fear into the lion. It is almost like the church thinks we are the ones who can hold the antichrist back, but no, it is the armies of God under Michael the Archangel's command who are holding back the powers of evil.

Again, do we have the weight of scripture to support this argument? There are so many stories in the Bible about angels executing God's judgment and being instruments of delivering God's children when they sought Him for help. The first verse I will show is found in the story of Sodom and Gomorrah, Genesis 19:12-13. *The two men said to Lot, "Do you have anyone else here, sons in law, sons or daughters, or anyone else in the city that belong to you? Get them out of here, because we are going to destroy this place. The outcry to the Lord against its people is so great he has sent us to destroy it."* These men were angels.

In another example, God sent an angel of judgment against Jerusalem and later told this angel to stand-down. Read 1 Chronicles 21:15. *And God sent an angel to destroy Jerusalem, but as the angel was doing so, the Lord saw it and was grieved because of the calamity and said to the angel who was destroying the people, "Enough! Withdraw your hand."* Another example is in 2 Chronicles when Hezekiah put his trust in the Lord to fight his battles. When God answered Hezekiah's prayer, the Lord sent angels to fight the forces of evil. The passage in 2 Chronicles 32:7-8 says, *Be strong and courageous. Do not be afraid or discouraged because of the king of Assyria and the vast army with him, for there is a greater power with us than with him. With him is only the arm of the flesh, but with us is the Lord our God to help us and to fight our battles.*

This next verse shows how God answered their prayers for help. In 2 Chronicles 32:20-21, the Word says, *King Hezekiah and the prophet, Isaiah, son of Amoz, cried out in prayer to heaven about this. And the Lord sent an angel who annihilated all the fighting men and the leaders and officers in the camp of the Assyrian king.* In 2 Kings, there are a few examples that show what kind of aid is available when we seek God's help and intervention. The first is found in 2 Kings 6:15-17. *When the servant of the man of God got up and went out early the next morning, an army with horses and chariots had surrounded the city. "Oh my Lord, what shall we do?" the servant asked. "Don't be afraid," the prophet answered. "Those who are with us are more than those who are with them." And Elisha prayed, "O Lord open his eyes so he may see." Then the Lord opened his eyes and he looked and saw the hills full of horses and chariots of fire all around Elisha.*

Next, read what happens to their enemies when God fights the battles for them in 2 Kings 19:35. *That night the angel of the Lord went out and put to death a hundred and eighty-five thousand men in the Assyrian camp. When the people got up the next morning, there were all dead bodies!* Also, let us not forget about the apostles who were thrown into prison for their witness for Jesus. When they were thrown into prison, angels came to their rescue as spoken of in Acts 5:18-19. *They arrested the apostles and put them in the public jail. But during the night an angel of the Lord opened the doors of the jail and brought them out.*

God's Word even says in the last days, at the time of the Lord's return, God will send angels to protect us from anyone who tries to harm us. What a promise in God's Word! It says in 2 Thessalonians 1:6-7, *God is just: he will pay back trouble to those who trouble you and give relief to you who are troubled, and to us as well. This will happen when the Lord Jesus is revealed from heaven in blazing fire with his powerful angels.*

There is much weight in the Word of God to prove that angels are the powers God uses to restrain. It is not the church that is the restrainer who is keeping the antichrist from coming to power, but it is the armies of God commanded by God's general, Michael the Archangel. The day is soon coming when the Commander-in-Chief will issue the order for the armies of God to stand-down. When that day comes, Michael may not want to go along with it, but he will stand down, and all hell will break loose on the earth.

I have to wonder if the following Bible verses that I have pondered for a long time could have something to do with what I have been describing here. Read Revelation 12:12b. *But woe to the earth and the sea, because the devil has gone down to you! He is filled with fury, because he knows that his time is short.* It gets even more convincing when you go back a few verses and read Revelation 12:7-9. *And there was war in heaven. Michael and his angels fought against the dragon, and the dragon and his angels fought back. But they were not strong enough, and they lost their place in heaven. The great dragon was hurled down, that ancient serpent, called the devil or satan, who leads the whole world astray. He was hurled to the earth, and his angels with him.* Now if you will skip a few verses ahead to Revelation 13:3, you will see what happens once chaos begins to break loose on the earth, for then the antichrist will truly be recognized after surviving a fatal wound. Revelation 13:3: *One of the heads of the beast seemed to have had a fatal wound, but the fatal wound had been healed. The whole world will be astonished and follow the beast.*

Review what I have been saying and showing you from the Word of God. It is not the church or the Holy Spirit; rather, it is Michael the Archangel, who is the restrainer of evil. If you will ponder these last verses I have just discussed in Revelation 12 and 13, it makes so much sense to me the restrainer of evil has just waged a great battle in the heavens, and Satan and his followers have just lost their place in heaven. The Bible says that Satan has had a place in heaven where he would go to God and bring accusations against the brethren or against God's people. Now he has just lost his place in heaven. Read Revelation 12:10, *Then I heard a loud voice in heaven say, "Now have come the salvation and the power and the kingdom of our God and the authority of his Christ. For the accuser of our brothers, who accuses them before our God day and night has been hurled down."*

Is there any doubt who has just restrained the power of wickedness here? It was Michael and the armies of God who have just cast Satan to the earth. I can imagine a bit here. Michael has just kicked Satan out of the heavens, and he has just won the war God commanded him to fight. Now if you will think about how General Patton and General MacArthur wanted to press on and finish off the enemies of the earth for all time, this is how I imagine Michael would similarly go to the Commander-in-Chief to seek permission to press on with the battle. I can hear Michael making his appeal to our heavenly Father, "This is our chance. Satan and his minions have been pushed back. We have them right where we want them. Just say the word, and I will command your armies to take satan out for all time." Then God replies, "No, Michael, your assignment is completed. I have a different plan for satan. It is now time for you and the armies you command to stand-down." Michael realizes God, in His infinite wisdom, has everything under control. This is where we need to read 2 Thessalonians 2:7-8a. *For the secret power of lawlessness is already at work, but the one who now holds it back will continue to do so till he is taken out of the way. And then the lawless one will be revealed.* If you will read this verse carefully, you will see it says the antichrist will not be revealed until the restrainer is taken out of the way.

When you think about this and about what we just covered in the book of Revelation, chapters 12 and 13, it is just a few verses after Satan is thrown down to the earth that a world leader is fatally wounded and then comes back from the dead as the antichrist! It makes sense to me that once Satan is thrown down to the earth, this will be the point when the restrainer has been removed.

You may have to be like the Bereans and read and study the Bible verses I have outlined, but what I have presented in this study is very compelling.

2. God has not appointed us to wrath.

There are two good verses in the Bible that support the teaching that God has not appointed us to suffer the wrath of God that will take place during the Great Tribulation.

The first is found in 1 Thessalonians 5:9. *For God did not appoint us to suffer wrath but to receive salvation through our Lord, Jesus Christ.*

The second is found in 1 Thessalonians 1:10. *And to wait for his Son from heaven, whom he raised from the dead - Jesus, Who rescues us from the coming wrath.*

From the pre-tribulation rapture viewpoint, these verses indicate the Rapture is a pre-tribulation event to spare the church from the coming wrath during the Great

Tribulation.

Consider that the Bible calls the time period leading up to His return, "the Great Tribulation", a seven-year time period that will become more and more intense as Christ's coming approaches. The Bible likens the increase of severe events to birth pains. I believe we are currently entering the time of the birth pains predicted. They could become so severe some Christians may believe the Great Tribulation has started, but if you look at the beginning of the Great Tribulation, with the opening of the seven seals, you will see events that are similar to what has happened for all of time: wars, earthquakes, famine, even the martyrdom of the saints, to which the fifth seal refers. Just as when a woman is getting closer to delivering a child and the intensity of her labor pain increases, that is how it will be when the seals are opened at the beginning of the Great Tribulation.

The intensity of war will increase, earthquakes will be more devastating, and famines will be widespread. Most Christians who hold to the pre-tribulation rapture believe we will miss out on the seals and all of the Great Tribulation.

Many quote 1 Thessalonians 1:10 to try to prove that point. If you look closely at this verse, it says, *...Jesus who rescues us from the coming wrath.* This means the wrath of God. This verse does not say we will be delivered from tribulation to come. In fact, **think about it; the Great Tribulation is not called the Great Wrath of God**. To me, it is obvious the seals are not the wrath of God, for God does not start wars, bring famine (and certainly he does not martyr His saints) as described in the fifth seal.

I believe the wrath of God does not start until Revelation 8 and 9, and then it picks up again in chapter fifteen. On the other hand, let us consider what the Bible teaches about tribulation. The Bible says that tribulation "worketh patience." It is interesting during the Great Tribulation, when the saints are battling with the antichrist. God's Word says in Revelation 13:10, *...if anyone is to go into captivity, into captivity he will go, if anyone is to be killed with the sword, he will be killed. This calls for patient endurance on the part of the saints.* I believe the Bible is teaching that the saints will be going through a period of tribulation that will bring about the purification of the body of Christ.

Does not the Bible teach us that Christ is coming back for a pure bride, worthy of being called the bride of Christ? To put this into further biblical context, read Revelation 13:7-10: *He was given power to make war against the saints and to conquer them. And he was given authority over every tribe, people, language, and nation. All inhabitants of the earth will worship the beast - all whose names have not been written in the book of life belonging to the Lamb that was slain from the creation of the world. He who has an ear, let him hear. If anyone is to go into captivity, into captivity he will go. If anyone is to be killed with the sword, with the sword he will be killed. This calls for patient endurance and faithfulness on the part of the saints.*

These verses are describing several different scenarios believers will be subjected to during the first part of the Great Tribulation. Basically, this is calling for our unswerving faithfulness and testimony to Christ. Some Christians will be thrown into jail and others will be killed, but we just have to stay true to Christ, knowing they can take our lives but not our eternal souls!

One question I have to ask is, "Does God's Word further support this teaching that the saints will go through a period of tribulation and persecution during this time at the end called the Great Tribulation?" I believe the Bible does give further weight to this thought in 2 Thessalonians 1:4-6: *Therefore among God's churches we boast about your perseverance and faith in all the persecutions and trials you are enduring. All this is evidence that God's judgment is right, and as a result you will be counted worthy of the kingdom of God, for which you are suffering. God is just; he will pay back trouble to those who trouble you.*

As you read further in this chapter, specifically verses 7-10a, you will notice the context for this chapter very much concerns the coming of the Lord. These verses are talking about a future time when Christ is revealed and returns to punish those who do not obey the gospel. The passage in 2 Thessalonians 1:7-10 says, *And give relief to you who are troubled and to us as well. This will happen when the Lord Jesus is revealed from heaven in blazing fire with his powerful angels. He will punish those who do not know God and do not obey the gospel of our Lord Jesus. They will be punished with everlasting destruction and shut out from the presence of the Lord and from the majesty of his power on the day he comes to be glorified in his holy people and to be marveled at among all those who have believed. This includes you, because, you believed our testimony to you.*

These verses are talking about a time of tribulation the saints will have to endure. These verses are also addressing the church. They clearly say the timeframe for this tribulation and the persecution of the saints will be during the time of the end, leading up to the Lord's return.

Earlier in my study, I mentioned I did not know what the rebellion was. Look at 2 Thessalonians 2:3 in the Kings James Version. You will notice the rebellion is referred to as a great falling away of believers. This is a key point for my position of a mid-tribulation rapture. I hear so many people say, "What difference will it make whether the rapture is pre-trib. or mid-trib. anyway? It will all pan out in the end."

I feel there is a huge difference. What would have happened if Noah had not built the ark or if Joseph had not prepared for the famine in Egypt? How will millions of Christians feel who have been taught Christ is coming to Rapture His church away before the Great Tribulation starts, when suddenly, the world is thrown into chaos? Imagine if Al Qaeda successfully pulls off their plan, which they have had in the works for many years, called the Hiroshima project. The project calls for Al Qaeda terrorists to set off seven or more nukes in seven or more major cities in the United States on the same day. World trade would come to a halt. All the food from store shelves would disappear in panic buying. Most major cities would be overrun with anarchy. All of a sudden, we would be thrown into great tribulation. This event could lead to the global collaspe of world economies, ultimately forcing the nations of the world to join a newly formed one world govenment.

From the collapse of the world economies to the forming of the one-world government could be six to eighteen months. This collapse will bring nations to their knees and make them willing to give up their independence and sovereignty as an individual nation to join the one-world government. Unfortunately, it is highly possible that those six to eighteen months will be a time of anarchy and famine and destitution on earth, but that does not mean the Great Tribulation has begun. The Great Tribulation cannot begin until the one-world government is in place. The Bible references ten heads of government forming the new one world government will be in place. Remember, the trigger event for the beginning of the tribulation is the seven-year peace pact with Israel, which cannot happen until the antichrist creates that peace pact.

My concern, and one of the greatest reasons why I am writing this book, is that millions of Christians at that time will question the teachings of their churches and wonder why the Rapture has not occurred. There is the potential for hundreds of thousands of Christians to feel that they were betrayed by their teachers and abandoned by God. When you consider this, you can see how the stage would be set for a great falling away that is talked about in the Bible.

And what about suffering? Some Christians today question that God would actually allow us to suffer through the Great Tribulation and emphatically believe that God would never abandon us to the torment of the antichrist. I do not want to be a pessimist or create fear, but it is important to know that while most Christians in the West have enjoyed great religious liberty, there have been more Christians martyred for their faith in the last century than in the previous centuries combined since the time of Christ. That is a documented fact. Persecution and martyrdom have stepped up significantly in the 20th and 21st centuries. In fact, if we were alive as adults during Hitler's era, most of us would have surmised that Hitler was the antichrist and that the Tribulation had begun with the annihilation of millions of Jews.

Suffering is not new to the Jew or the Christian. Have you ever read *Foxe's Book of Martyrs*? This book covers centuries of Christians who were killed for their unswerving faith in Christ, from the deaths of Christ's disciples and the persecution by the Roman Church in 1200 A.D. to the persecution and killing of Christians a few centries ago that caused them to leave their mother country and come to America for freedom of religion. I am not talking about water-boarding, which some in our society label as torture. NO! I am talking about Christ's disciple Peter being crucified upside down because he did not feel worthy to die the same death as Christ his Lord. I am talking about Christians being beheaded, torn apart by wild beasts, boiled to death, and burned at the stake.

One story that has always stuck in my memory is the story of a Christian who was to be burned at the stake, and he told a friend nearby that he believed God's grace would be sufficient for him to bear up to this death. The friend told the sentenced man that if God's grace is sufficient, raise one finger to let him know. When the flames were engulfing him, he raised up two fingers signifying God's grace was more than enough. When I hear pastors and Christians say God would never abandon

His church, I am reminded of Christ's death on the cross when Christ cried out in Matthew 27:46 (KJV): *And about the ninth hour Jesus cried with a loud voice, saying "Eli, Eli, Lama Sabachthani." That is to say, My God, my God, why hast thou forsaken me?* Did God forsake Jesus Christ His Son? Only in the sense He allowed His Son to die for our sins. If we as Christians have to suffer and die for our faith as martyrs did in ages past, does this mean God has forsaken us? No, because I am reminded of God's promise in Hebrews 13:5b-6: *...because God has said, "Never will I leave you; never will I forsake you." So we say with confidence, "The Lord is my helper, I will not be afraid. What can man do to me?*

I believe the first part of the Great Tribulation will be a time of great trials and tribulation that will wake up many in today's Laodicean-type church and call all believers to become the pure bride, without spot or wrinkle, for whom Christ is coming back. Most importantly, I believe the church will have a major part in the harvest of the lost souls who are not ready for the Rapture. To back up this thought, look at the rest of what Revelation has to say about the Laodicean church, namely Revelation 3:19-21: *Those whom I love I rebuke and discipline. So be earnest, and repent. Here I am! I stand at the door and knock. If anyone hears my voice and opens the door, I will come in and eat with him and he with me. To him who overcomes, I will give the right to sit with me on my throne, just as I overcame and sat down with my Father on his throne.* What a thought! Could Jesus be knocking on the door of our churches, calling the backslidden to come back to Him with all their hearts? Also notice that God is giving rewards to those who overcome. In order to be an overcomer, there must be trials and tribulation to overcome.

In conclusion, I agree with the pre-tribulation view that God has not accounted us to the wrath to come. However, I part company with the belief that the seals are the wrath of God. Up until now, I have believed the seals **are not part** of the wrath of God because the fifth seal is the martyrdom of the saints. God would not do this to His own.

Some time ago, I was talking to a pastor friend of mine about the timing of the Rapture. When I told him my viewpoint on the wrath of God, he said he believed the four horses or the first four seals are the wrath of God. Well, the first thing that entered my mind was the first horseman who is the revealing of antichrist. Therefore, how could this be the wrath of God? Then the thought hit me regarding the second seal; that shows peace would be taken from the earth. Again, this just does not sound like the wrath of God. Looking at the fourth seal, it says in Revelation 6:7-8: *When the Lamb opened the fourth seal, I heard the voice of the fourth living creature say, "Come!" I looked and there before me was a pale horse, its rider was named Death, and Hades was following close behind him.* This sounds more like the devil, and it sounds like it is coming out of hell and not from God.

I did not express all of these thoughts to my pre-tribulation, believing pastor friend. However, as I was driving home, I had a conversation out loud with God, and I kept asking how I might show or explain that the wrath of God does not happen until Revelation 8 with the seven trumpets of God's wrath. I kept asking what is the difference between the seals and the wrath of God. It was like this thought just popped into my head. (I believe the Holy Spirit answered my question right there on the spot). **The thought that came to me was, "The difference is in the delivery." Angels deliver all of the seven trumpets of God's wrath; angels also deliver the last seven bowls of God's wrath, BUT angels are nowhere involved with the opening of the seals in Revelation 6.** When I arrived home and studied my Bible, all these thoughts were confirmed from God's Word.

A couple of interesting points that go along with this conclusion are about the scroll. Revelation 5:2-3: says, *I saw a mighty angel proclaiming in a loud voice, "Who is worthy to break the seals and open the scroll?" But no one in heaven or on the earth or under the earth could open the scroll or even look inside it.* **What I notice here is the seals are not <u>in</u> the scroll, they are on the <u>outside</u> of the scroll, and the wrath of God is inside the scroll!**

Also, when we look at the many examples of God's judgment on the nations, we continually see angels involved in the delivery of judgment. There is the angel of death in Egypt and the angels again in Sodom and Gomorrah. Also, there is the angel of the Lord who slew 185,000 Assyrians in one night and the angel who killed thousands in Jerusalem when David took the census against God's wishes. I have to say the weight of scripture is compelling here; angels are involved in God's wrath and there are no angels involved with the seals.

I further believe the Rapture is clearly described in Revelation 7, before the wrath of

God begins in Revelation 8 and 9. What I will do in the next section of this chapter is show why I believe Revelation 4:1 does not describe the Rapture. I will also explain why I believe Revelation 7:9 <u>IS</u> describing the Rapture. I think I can show that scripture leans heavily on the Rapture occurring in the seventh chapter of Revelation.

In closing, I believe we will have to go through some unprecedented times. Yet, I am prepared in my heart, knowing in whom I have believed and am persuaded that He is able to protect me against that day. Man may hurt my mortal body, but man cannot hurt my eternal soul.

3. Revelation 4:1: The open door to heaven

Revelation 4:1: says, *After this I looked, and there before me was a door standing open in heaven. And the voice I had first heard speaking to me like a trumpet said, "Come up here, and I will show you what must take place after this."* Then Revelation 4:2: says, *At once I was in the Spirit, and there before me was a throne in heaven with someone sitting on it.*

These verses from Revelation 4:1-2 are interpreted to symbolically represent the Rapture of the church. I just do not see the Rapture of the church in these verses. I see John, the Revelator, being taken to heaven to the very throne of God where God told him, "I will show you what must take place after this." If you will go to Revelation 19:11, you will see heaven opened up again just like what happened in Revelation 4:1. Read Revelation 19:11: *I saw heaven standing open, and there before me was a white horse, whose rider is called Faithful and True. With justice he judges and makes war.* This is a revelation of Christ after the battles have been won and the marriage supper of the Lamb is about to take place. This door standing open does not mean a gateway is open for a rapture event because if you will go back to Revelation 19:6-8, you will discover the saints are already in heaven about to celebrate with Christ at the marriage supper of the Lamb. Read Revelation 19:6-8: *Then I heard what sounded like a great multitude, like the roar of rushing waters, and like loud peals of thunder, shouting: "Hallelujah, for our Lord God Almighty reigns. Let us rejoice and be glad and give him glory, for the wedding of the Lamb has come, and his bride has made herself ready. Fine linen, bright and clean, was given her to wear."*

I would like to know where to find a second or third scripture that shows the timing of the Rapture before the Great Tribulation starts. I was taught in Bible school that doctrine has to be backed with the witness of two or three other scriptures.

Now I will point out a third scripture verse that shows Paul, in this case, being caught up to heaven to see special revelations from God, just like John the Revelator. What Paul experienced does not represent a symbolic rapture of the church either. Read 2 Corinthian 12:3-4: *And I know that this man - whether in the body or apart from the body I do not know, but God knows - was caught up to Paradise. He heard inexpressible things, things that man is not permitted to tell.* Paul's experience is very similar to that which John the Revelator experienced. In fact, in Paul's case, he was "caught up" to Paradise, while John was asked to "Come up here." When the Rapture occurs, we will not be asked to come up; we will be caught up.

What I see happening here by those who want to interpret Revelation 4:1 as the Rapture of the church is they are strengthening their position on this doctrine based on the symbolic meaning of what they see in this passage. I believe all doctrine must be supported by the "plain speak" Word of God, and then let symbolism confirm it. We should not rely on symbolism alone. When you look at Revelation 4:1, it does not say the church is caught up to heaven. In fact, it does not even use the words, "caught up." No. Bible scholars have determined there is a symbolic meaning here, and our traditions have accepted it.

I firmly believe we should never interpret scripture symbolically to establish a doctrinal position. A doctrinal teaching must first be established as literal from the Bible. Symbolic use of scripture should only be used to supplement and support what the Bible teaches elsewhere literally, or you can make the Bible say anything you want. This type of interpretation is how cults are established.

I want to show you there are Bible verses that <u>plainly</u> speak of the Rapture. I will show you these verses, and then I will show you why Revelation 4:1 does not qualify as a verse that can be used to symbolically support the timing of the Rapture. This is very important to understand because, for someone who holds to the pre-tribulation view of the Rapture, Revelation 4:1 is really the only verse that alludes to the Rapture happening before the Great Tribulation begins. This means the timing of the Rapture as a pre-tribulation event is being established by the use of the symbolic meaning of Revelation 4:1, and that makes for shaky interpretation.

The first verse I will use to show the Rapture is 1 Thessalonians 4:16-17: *For the Lord himself will come down from heaven, with a loud command, with the voice of the archangel and the trumpet call of God, and the dead in Christ will rise first. After that we who are alive and are left will be caught up with them in the clouds to meet the Lord in the air. And so we will be with the Lord forever.*

Notice we who are alive are caught up in the clouds to meet the Lord in the air. Next, I will show you other verses that support the Lord's coming in the clouds to meet us at the time of the Rapture. Read Matthew 24:30-31: *At that time, the sign of the Son of Man will appear in the sky and all nations of the earth will mourn. They will see the Son of Man coming on the clouds of the sky, with power and great glory. And he will send his angels with a loud trumpet call, and they will gather his elect from the four winds, from one end of the heavens to the other.* Without writing them out, if you look up these other scripture verses, you will again see the Lord is meeting us in the clouds in Luke 21: 26-27 and Mark 13: 26-27.

Now as you study these verses, it is easy to see that the Lord will come in the clouds, and we are caught up in the clouds to meet the Lord in the air. When you go back and look at Revelation 4:1, John was not caught up in the clouds. In fact, he was not caught up at all. He was told to "Come up here."

Another point, John was not caught up at all. Revelation 4:1 says, *After this I looked, and there before me was a door standing open in heaven. And the voice I had first heard speaking to me like a trumpet said, "**Come up here**, and I will show you what must take place after this."*

When the Rapture happens, we are not asked to come up; we are <u>caught up</u>! God does not have to ask or tell us to come; we will be caught up instantly, in the twinkling of an eye. This verse is sometimes interpreted to mean the church is caught up. How can anyone get "church" from this verse? This verse does not line up with the literal verses that describe the Rapture; therefore, Revelation 4:1 cannot be used to symbolically represent the Rapture of the church.

To further support my viewpoint from the Word of God, I will show you that once we are caught up in the clouds, Christ the Son of Man, will lead us to the throne of God. We are not "caught up" to the throne. I think you will get my point if you read the vision of Daniel.

In Daniel 7:13 it says, *In my vision at night, I looked, and there before me was one like the son of man, coming with the clouds of heaven. He approached the Ancient of Days and was led into his presence.* As you study the rest of Daniel 7, you will see that the saints are released from the grasp of the antichrist and are given the Kingdom. This time when the saints are allowed to possess the Kingdom is the same time as the Rapture because it goes on to say that the amount of time the antichrist was making war on the saints was three and one-half years. This shows the Rapture taking place in the middle of the Great Tribulation. Read Daniel 7:21-22: ***As I watched, this horn was waging war against the saints and defeating them, until the Ancient of Days came and pronounced judgment in favor of the saints of the Most High, and the time came when they possessed the kingdom.*** Next, read Daniel 7:25. *He will speak against the Most High and oppress his saints and try to change the set times and the laws.* **The saints will be handed over to him for a time, times and half a time. (Or three and one-half years.)**

Now let us look at what is happening in Revelation 7 (what I call the Rapture of the saints). I believe it is a reasonable interpretation to consider the following as the Rapture instead of Revelation 4:1. Start reading Revelation 7:9-12: *After this, I looked, and there before me was a great multitude that no one could count, from every nation, tribe, people and language, standing before the throne and in front of the Lamb. They were wearing white robes and holding palm branches in their hands. And they cried out in a loud voice: "Salvation belongs to our God, Who sits on the throne and to the Lamb." All the angels were standing around the throne and around the elders and the four living creatures. They fell down on their faces before the throne and worshiped God saying, "Amen, praise and glory and wisdom and thanks and honor and power and strength be to our God forever and ever Amen!"*

Look at verse 9. It says, *A great multitude from every nation, tribe, language, and people were standing before the throne.* Now go down to verse 13 and hear what one of the elders standing there was saying about this: *Then one of the elders asked me. "These in white robes, who are they? And where did they come from?"*

Imagine this picture. One of the elders, who day and night is around the throne of God, suddenly notices millions, uncountable Christians standing around the throne worshiping God, and he did not know from where they came! See the answer in Revelation 7:14: *I answered, "Sir, you know." And he said, "These are they who have come out of the Great Tribulation. They have washed their robes, and made them white in the blood of the Lamb."*

We know these are Christians because their robes have been washed in the blood of the Lamb. My question is, "If these uncountable millions just showed up in heaven after the sixth seal but the Rapture happened in Revelation 4:1 before the Great Tribulation started, then who are these who just showed up? Is there a second rapture for the tribulation saints? I do not see that as scriptural. To me, what we are seeing here is the church going through part of the Great Tribulation until it gets to the part where the 144,000 Jews are sealed to be God's chosen messengers. They are commissioned to preach and reveal the love of Christ to the Jewish nation.

At one point, I believed this looked like the end of the day of the Gentiles and the start of God's plan to reach out to the children of Israel! I now believe there will be a period of overlap between the end of the day of the Gentiles and the time of reaching out to the Jews. I believe God is already working to lead the nation of Israel to Christ in time for the Rapture, as they are to become an important part of Christ's bride.

One argument I have heard against what I have said here is, "This is a second rapture, which is for the Jews." **Why would you have a separate rapture of the Jews when you just had the <u>sealing</u> of the 144,000 Jews to evangelize the Jewish nation?** I believe when the one and only Rapture occurs, millions of Christian Jews will go up in this Rapture; otherwise, they would not be part of the bride of Christ. Furthermore, the two witnesses, who play a part in this, are not even mentioned yet. They are to witness to the Jewish nation for three and one-half years. Also, if you will look at Revelation 7:9, it says these people who have just appeared in heaven came from every nation, tribe, people, and language. The same argument is used here: these are Jews who are living in every nation and speak in every language, but this verse speaks about every <u>people</u>, tribe, nation and language. This verse ties into another verse, which makes for a great deal of excitement. Look at Revelation 5:9. This is where only Jesus was qualified to open the seals, and it says, *You are worthy to take the scroll and to open its seals; because, you were slain and with your blood you purchased men for God from every tribe and language and people and nation.* THIS IS YOU AND ME!

THIS IS THE CHURCH THAT CHRIST REDEEMED WITH HIS BLOOD. Now look at Revelation 7:9, and you will see Christ gathering by the Rapture what He has already purchased with His blood! *After this, I looked and there before me was a great multitude no one could count, from every nation, tribe, people and language.*

Here is where I hope you will pay close attention to what I am going to suggest. I want to take you back to an event between Revelation 4:1 and Revelation 7:11-14. Remember, Revelation 4:1 is the accepted verse for the time of the pre-Tribulation Rapture. Now, look at Revelation 5:11-12: *And behold, and I heard the voice of many angels around the throne and the beasts and the elders: and the number of them was ten thousand times ten thousand and thousands of thousands, saying with a loud voice, "Worthy is the Lamb that was slain to receive power and riches and wisdom and strength, and honor and glory and blessing."* Notice the persons depicted around the throne-- angels, beasts, and elders. There is no mention of saints around the throne. If the church were raptured in Revelation 4:1, then the saints would be around the throne in white robes in Revelation 5. Also, when you read Revelation 7:11-14, notice the elder who is always around the throne, and he asks, *"Who are these in white robes...,"* who have suddenly shown up? The elder answers his own question and says they are the saints who have come out of the Great Tribulation. **If the Rapture had already happened pre-Tribulation in Revelation 4:1,** then the millions of pre-tribulation Christians would have been in white robes around the throne in both Revelation 5 and 7. **They would have blended in with the multitude about whom the elder was asking in Revelation 7:11-14.** Now do you still think there are two raptures? These verses plainly show the Rapture simply could not have happened in Revelation 4:1.

Next, go to 1 Thessalonians 4:15-18. This scripture shows why the Rapture could not have happened until after Revelation 5:11-12: *For this we say unto you by the word of the Lord, that we which are alive and remain unto the coming of the Lord shall not prevent them which are asleep. For the Lord himself shall descend from heaven with a shout, with the voice of the archangel, and with the trump of God: and the dead will rise first. Then we which are alive and remain shall be caught up together with them in the clouds, to meet the Lord in the air, and so shall we ever be with the Lord, wherefore comfort one another with these words.*

This scripture shows why the Rapture could not have happened until after Revelation

5:11-12. Read 1 Thessalonians 4:17. It says both the dead in Christ and those who are alive will both be raptured together to meet the Lord, and it says further, *...And so we will be with the Lord forever.* If from the time of the Rapture we will forever be with the Lord, think about it; we would be with the Lord in Revelation 5:11-12 around the throne. If there is no mention of saints in white robes around the throne in Revelation 5:11-12, then the Rapture has not yet happened. However, when the elder in Revelation 7: 9-14 asks, *"Who are these multitudes in white robes **which no man can number?"** he answers himself by saying, *"These are they who have come out of the Great Tribulation."* On the other hand, **those in Revelation 5:11-12 ARE numbered!** Can it be any clearer? The Rapture, the only Rapture, has just taken place in Revelation 7:11-14.

Another argument says that those who have suddenly appeared around the throne in Revelation 7:9 are the martyred saints. However, based on the reaction of the elder, what happened here happened suddenly! The fact that the elder asking the question is always at the throne proves it. It is as if he blinked, and all of a sudden, there are millions in white robes around the throne. This would mean if they were Great Tribulation martyred saints, they would have had to be killed at the same time. I do not think this is possible. Remember, it says the number of them could not be numbered! In Revelation 5:11, when angelic beings were worshiping around the throne, the numbers were in the millions, but when those in white robes appear, it says in Revelation 7:9: *After this I looked and there before me was a great multitude that no one could count.*

There is a second problem with the above interpretation. When the saints are being martyred, as described in the fifth seal in Revelation 6:9-10, it says the martyred saints are <u>under</u> the altar, not "...at the throne." And they are asking, *"How long until you avenge our blood?"* Then it says they were each given white robes. They are still <u>under</u> the altar, not at the throne. If these martyred saints were at the throne in Revelation 6:10 in the white robes given to them while <u>under</u> the altar, the elder in Revelation 7 would not have even noticed a second multitude showing up, for over the last two thousand years, millions of Christians have been martyred. At the Rapture, they would all have been at the throne. **Now think about this: if all the martyred saints of all time do not show up at the throne until Revelation 7, how can anyone say the Rapture happened in Revelation 4:1?**

When you look at what I have covered, concerning whether or not Revelation 4:1 discusses the Rapture, the lion's share of scripture shows this interpretation to be very weak.

4. The church is not mentioned after Revelation 4:1.

The fourth argument for the pre-tribulation position of the Rapture concerns the word "church". Because the word "church" is not mentioned after Revelation 4:1, it is taught that the church was raptured and is no longer on the earth.

My first response to this argument is that this is untrue. The scriptures say the saints would be martyred during the fifth seal of the Great Tribulation in Revelation 6. Then again, in Revelation 14:11-13, the Bible talks of those who are taking the mark of the beast and the needed patience of the saints during this time. It goes on to say many saints will be martyred at this time. Now I know there are some who teach those saints are tribulation saints. Tell me, where are the words, "tribulation saints," in the Bible? Plus, realize we are setting the time of the Rapture as pre-Tribulation not based on scripture verses but based on the omission of the word "church" after Revelation 4:1. Not only are we basing the timing of the Rapture on the omission of "church", but we are interpreting Revelation 4:1 with a symbolic meaning to make it mean whatever it has to mean to support a pre-tribulation rapture.

As I see it, the timing of the Rapture is too important to establish this doctrine without clearly stating scripture, chapter and verse to back it up. In addition, think about this, what is the church? It is the saints that make the church, so if the saints are mentioned after Revelation chapter 4:1, then the church is mentioned. Furthermore, if you study Daniel's vision found in Daniel 7, you will see he speaks about the Rapture of the saints taking place in his vision, and there is no mention of the church. It only talks about the saints. I will go into greater detail about the Rapture teaching found in Daniel in the following chapter.

Another point I would like to make concerning the argument that there is no mention of the church after Revelation 4:1 is that in order for this statement to be accurate, it would have to be true for the whole Bible and not just the book of Revelation. If the CHURCH is mentioned in any other book of the Bible in reference to the church going through the Great Tribulation, then this argument does not hold up. I believe 2 Thessalonians shows the church going through the Great Tribulation, and it is plainly worded without drawing a conclusion based on symbolism.

Read 2 Thessalonians 1:4-10. *Therefore, among God's CHURCHES, we boast about your perseverance and faith in all the persecutions and trials you are enduring. All this is evidence that God's judgment is right, and as a result you will be counted worthy of the kingdom of God, for which you are suffering. God is just: He will pay back trouble to those who trouble you and give relief to you who are troubled, and to us as well. This will happen when the Lord Jesus is revealed from heaven in blazing fire with his powerful angels. He will punish those who do not know God and do not obey the gospel of our Lord Jesus. They will be punished with everlasting destruction and shut out from the presence of the Lord and from the majesty of his power on the day he comes to be glorified in his holy people and to be marveled at among all those who have believed. This includes you because you believed our testimony to you.*

If you will continue reading 2 Thessalonians 2, you will see it is undeniable these chapters concern the time of the Great Tribulation leading up to the Lord's return, the time when Christ returns to put down all evil. Chapter 2 continues to make reference to the time of the antichrist, and 2 Thessalonians 2:1-3 specifically refers to the gathering to Christ, or the Rapture, as not occurring until some point after the antichrist arrives.

If this is where I were to stop and say that it is not a strong argument for a pre-tribulation rapture just because the church is not mentioned after Revelation 4:1, I would have been content. Many times during this study, I have felt the Holy Spirit prompting me to look deeper into His Word through what I would call spontaneous promptings of the Holy Spirit. What I have to share now comes from one of those promptings. I only say this because I know I could not have written this book without the help of the Holy Spirit, and I will not take credit that belongs to God.

I was prompted to study all references concerning the Rapture of the church, with the thought that the Bible does not teach that Christ is coming back for the church. My first thought was, "Could it be the Bible does not teach Christ is coming back for the church?" With that thought in mind, I opened my Strong's concordance and looked up every reference to church in the Bible. The church is mentioned eighty times. I looked up "saints," and "saints" is mentioned ninety-six times. What immediately jumped out at me was there is not one single mention of Christ coming back for the church.

There is no mention of the church in heaven, and, in fact, if you will read the following verses, you will see it is the saints for whom Christ is coming back. It is the saints who will rule with Christ in the ages to come.

Daniel 7:18: *But the saints of the Most High will receive the kingdom and will possess it forever – yes, forever and forever.*

Zechariah 14:5 (KJV): *....and the Lord my God shall come, and all the saints with thee.*

1 Corinthians 6:2: *Do you not know that the saints will judge the world....*

1 Thessalonians 3:13 (KJV): *....at the coming of our Lord Jesus Christ with all his saints.*

Jude 14 (KJV): *And Enoch also the seventh from Adam, prophesied of these, saying, Behold the Lord cometh with ten thousands of his saints.*

In order to get a good handle on what I discovered, I had to ask myself, "Who or what is the church?" It is a given the church is not a building. A building only provides the saints a place to come together to worship and serve God.

So who are these who come together to make up the church? I call them the collection of all those who identify themselves as Christians, as children of God or believers. **We must realize not everyone who calls himself a Christian is or will be saved.** The Bible says even Satan believes in God, and we know he will not have a home in heaven.

Read Revelation 2 and 3 about the seven churches of Revelation. Interestingly, none of the churches were perfect. Some were better than others, but without exception each description of the churches ended with the statement, *To him who overcomes would receive a reward.* **This leads me to say that Christ is not coming back for the church but for the overcomer. How does God's Word describe who the overcomers are? They are referred to as the saints or the elect. So, it is noted that the word "church" is not mentioned after Revelation 4:1, resulting in the assumption that the church was raptured. This is not the case! There is not a single mention in the Bible that Jesus Christ is coming back for the church.**

No, Christ is coming back for his elect, the saints. The fact that the church is not mentioned after Revelation 4:1 is irrelevant. I believe it makes more sense to say the church age is over after Revelation 4:1, for nowhere in God's Word does it describe the church going to heaven. No, only individual children of God will go to heaven, and those children are the saints.

In closing, the saints are mentioned after Revelation 4:1 because the Rapture has not yet happened. In fact, the Rapture is described in both Revelation 7 and 14, and the saints are mentioned in the context of this event. In the next chapter, I present a study in Daniel, and I will show how God's Word clearly describes the Rapture, showing this most important event happening in the middle of the Great Tribulation.

— CHAPTER TEN —

POST-TRIBULATION VIEW
OF THE RAPTURE

In my studies, I have read that five to ten percent of Christians believe the Rapture will not happen until the end of the Great Tribulation. I was not going to cover this viewpoint in my book because I have always believed this position is indefensible. If you keep the integrity of God's Word, I do not believe you can defend a doctrinal position that contradicts other portions of God's Word. God's Word will not contradict itself. When I decided to cover this position, I decided I would pick the two most commonly used scriptural arguments in favor of the post-tribulation view and show why this position is flawed.

One of the arguments for the post-tribulation position found in God's Word is in 1 Corinthians 15:52: *In a flash, in the twinkling of an eye, at the last trumpet, for the trumpet will sound, the dead will be raised imperishable, and we will be changed.* Some who hold to the post-tribulation view will say there is only one last trumpet found in the Bible, which is the last trumpet of the seven trumpets of God's wrath found in the book of Revelation. One problem I see with using this verse for the post-tribulation position is the last trumpet of the seven trumpets of God's wrath still leaves the seven bowls of God's wrath to come. This would mean the Rapture occurs in the middle of God's wrath, not at the end of God's wrath.

In addition, read the reference in Revelation that has the last trumpet contained in it. Revelation 11:15: *The seventh angel sounded his trumpet, and there were loud voices in heaven which said, "The kingdom of the world has become the Kingdom of our Lord and of his Christ. And he will reign forever and ever."* This verse gives no hint of the Rapture having just taken place. It sounds like the victory over evil has been won. This does not sound like a rapture verse. If you could say this verse sounds as if the Rapture has just taken place, then you would have a serious problem keeping the integrity of God's Word, for as I have said, God's Word will not contradict itself. Take a look at 1 Thessalonians 1:10, and you will find a major contradiction: *And to wait for his Son from heaven, whom he raised from the dead - Jesus who rescues us from the coming wrath.* Then read 1 Thessalonians 5:9: *For God did not appoint us to suffer wrath but to receive Salvation through our Lord Jesus Christ.*

The Word of God clearly shows we will not be on earth when the wrath of God is happening. If you read these chapters in the Bible which contain the verses I am using, they show we will not experience the wrath of God. You will see both of these chapters are talking about the coming of the Lord and the Rapture. I know some will say God can protect us in the midst of His wrath, but if you study the wrath of God, you will see vast areas of the earth are destroyed. When the fifth trumpet of God's wrath is delivered, the scorpion creatures are released. It only says they are not to touch the 144,000 sealed Jews who were from the twelve tribes of Israel. **Why is there no provision for the saints to be untouched by the scorpion creatures? It is simple. The saints are not on the earth; they have been raptured before the wrath of God starts.**

I do not believe there is a contradiction in the Word of God that cannot be explained if you study and look for an explanation. Follow along as I present an alternative explanation concerning the last trumpet. I believe you will see it makes a lot of sense.

When the book of 1 Corinthians was written, the book of Revelation did not exist. In fact, it could have been forty more years before the aged Apostle John wrote the book of Revelation. I know it could be possible for God to reference a book that is not yet written, but we are dealing with a contradiction that compels us to look for an alternative explanation from God's Word.

A STUDY OF THE LAST TRUMPET

Those, who believe in a post-tribulation rapture based on the last trumpet, say there is only one last trumpet found in the Bible, namely in the book of Revelation. They are not entirely correct. Ask yourself, what would someone reading 1 Corinthians 15:52, when it was first written, have thought this verse was talking about, when it said, *At the last trumpet, for the trumpet will sound, the dead will be raised imperishable and we will be changed?* I believe, from a Jewish mindset, they would have thought it referred to the trumpets of the annual Feast of Trumpets celebrated every year. I have done a study on the Feast of Trumpets, and what I found is very interesting.

A significant reference to the Feast of Trumpets is found in Leviticus 23:23-24: *The Lord said to Moses, say to the Israelites; on the first day of the seventh month you are to have a day of rest, a sacred assembly commemorated with trumpet blasts.* This feast occurs in the seventh month of the Jewish calendar. It falls on the new moon, so the exact day is not known, but it is around the last day of the month of September on our calendar. The shofar, or ram's horn, is blown at different times during this event for the purpose of calling the faithful to repentance and consecration. Interestingly, the Feast of Trumpets is one of three religious festivals that fall in the seventh month. There are a total of seven festivals celebrated throughout the year, and three fall in a one-month period. The first of these three is the Feast of Trumpets, followed by the Day of Atonement and culminating with the Feast of Tabernacles. These three feasts are the only feasts left to be fulfilled in the New Testament. The next feast to be fulfilled is the Feast of Trumpets. I believe it can be shown that this feast will be fulfilled at the Rapture.

These festivals are celebrated as a memorial to past events. The Feast of the Passover in the Old Testament was fulfilled in the New Testament when Jesus, the Lamb of God, died on the cross for our sins. The Feast of Trumpets is a remembrance of God's meeting with Moses on Mount Sinai, the account of which is found in Exodus 19. At that time, God gave Moses the Ten Commandments, establishing the covenant of the Old Testament. If you will follow along with me in the text I will share, you will see a special event happened on the third day. It appears this blast of the trumpet on the third day is the important blast which the Jews were awaiting, for this is the LAST TRUMPET of this celebration.

To prepare for this event on the third day, they were to wash their clothes. It was to be a time of repentance and consecration. On the third day, there were lightning and clouds on the mountain of God, and when the last blast of a series of trumpet blasts went off, Moses was to lead the people to meet with God. It appears this biggest of the blasts was the last and most significant blast of this event. Now read Exodus 19:13b-17: *Only when the ram's horn sounds a long blast, may they go up to the mountain. After Moses had gone down the mountain to the people, he consecrated them, and they washed their clothes. Then he said to the people, "Prepare yourselves for the third day, and abstain from sexual relations." On the morning of the third day, there was thunder and lightning, and a thick cloud formed over the mountain, and a very loud trumpet blast was heard. Everyone in the camp trembled, and then Moses led the people out of the camp to meet with God.*

Think about this: when Christ comes again, we will get new robes washed in the blood of the Lamb. It was on the third day that Christ rose from the dead, and it appears this is the third day of the Feast of Trumpets. Then when we hear the last trumpet, the dead in Christ will rise first, and we who are alive will be raptured. Instead of Moses leading his people to the mountain of God, Jesus will lead us to the presence of our heavenly Father. Note that it mentions that a thick cloud formed over the mountain, and when Jesus comes for His bride, He will be seen coming in the clouds.

When we read Hosea 6:2 (KJV), we see another Old Testament example to this line of thought. *After two days will he revive us: in the third day he will raise us up, and we shall live in his sight.* Then read 1 Corinthians 15:52, and it all fits together. *In a flash, in the twinkling of an eye, at the last trumpet, for the trumpet will sound, the dead will be raised imperishable, and we will be changed.*

I see another problem with tying the last trumpet of 1 Corinthians to the last trumpet of Revelation. How can we be protected from God's wrath and still go through it? A second thought is if we are going through the wrath of God, "Why have a Rapture at all?" I just do not see this verse supporting the post-tribulation view.

In closing my examination of the last trumpet, I did a study to try to determine if the trumpets of the seven trumpets of God's wrath could be different from the trumpet that will sound at the Rapture. First, I need to remind my readers that I have shown good reason to believe the Rapture happens at the opening of the seventh seal. It is after the opening of the seventh seal that the seven angels who stand before God are given the seven trumpets. Revelation 8:2: *And I saw the seven angels who stand before*

God, and to them were given seven trumpets.

As I have continued to study the trumpets associated with the trumpet blast at the time of the Rapture, I discovered an interesting fact. The trumpet blast that will sound at the Rapture will be the **trumpet of God,** not the trumpet of an angel. There are two references in the New Testament that show that the last trumpet to announce the Rapture is the **trumpet of God.** Please read the verses below and decide if my conclusion makes sense. 1 Thessalonians 4:16: *For the Lord himself will come down from heaven, with a loud command, with the voice of the archangel and with **the trumpet call of God,** and the dead in Christ will rise first.* Next, read Matthew 24:30, 31: *At that time the sign of the Son of Man will appear in the sky, and the nations of the earth will mourn They will see the Son of Man coming on the clouds of the sky, with power and great glory. **And He will send his angels with a loud trumpet call,** and they will gather his elect from the four winds...*

The second argument, used to support the post-tribulation view, is found in Matthew 24:29-31: *Immediately after the distress of those days, the sun will be darkened, and the moon will not give its light; the stars will fall from the sky, and the heavenly bodies will be shaken. At that time, the sign of the Son of Man will appear in the sky, and the nations of the earth will mourn. They will see the Son of Man coming on the clouds of the sky, with power and great glory. And he will send his angels with a loud trumpet call, and they will gather his elect from the four winds, from one end of heavens to the other.*

Those who believe in the post-tribulation view take the first statement in these verses, *immediately after the distress of those days,* to mean immediately after the end of the seven-year Great Tribulation, then Christ will come for His elect or saints. There are several problems with this interpretation. One is the seven-year Great Tribulation consists of two major parts. There is the pre-wrath portion to the Great Tribulation, and there is the wrath of God portion. I realize some people believe the wrath of God starts with the opening of the seals. I feel I have addressed this topic adequately earlier in this book in chapter nine under the subtitle, "God has not appointed us to wrath." That chapter presents a discussion showing why it is reasonable that the opening of the seals is not the wrath of God set to begin in Revelation 8.

In order to better understand why I do not believe the above argument about the post-tribulation view is correct, we need to figure out where these verses in Matthew

24 line-up with what is happening during the Great Tribulation. If we look at the sixth seal of Revelation, we have to agree there is a match. Read Revelation 6:12-13: *I watched as he opened the sixth seal. There was a great earthquake. The sun turned black like sackcloth made of goat hair, the whole moon turned blood red, and the stars in the sky fell to earth, as late figs drop from a fig tree when shaken by a strong wind.* Now compare this with what is said in Matthew 24:29: *... The sun will be darkened, and the moon will not give its light; the stars will fall from the sky, and the heavenly bodies will be shaken.* Consider this: these two different books of the Bible were written years apart by two different writers, yet they are very similar. When read in full context, they are, in fact, describing the same event. It just makes sense the Rapture will happen after the distress of those days as explained in Revelation 6 before the wrath of God starts in Revelation 8.

This brings up another problem. If we believe the Rapture is a pre-tribulation event, Matthew 24:31 looks to be describing the Rapture, but the timing is not correct for a pre-tribulation rapture. Those who hold to the pre-tribulation view need to come up with an explanation because this looks like a mid-tribulation rapture.

One well-known teacher on the Rapture and the End Times has come up with such an explanation. I will share his view on this topic and show why it fails to fit in with the rest of scripture. In order to explain how this pre-tribulation teacher handles this problem, read Matthew 24:31: *And he will send his angels with a loud trumpet call, and they will gather his elect from the four winds, from one end of the heavens to the other.*

This teacher explains that the elect who are being spoken about here are the Jews and not the Christian church. If we do a study on the elect, we will realize God has called many different people His elect, and in fact, a study will show you His angels are His elect, some individuals are His elect, Christians are His elect, and the Jews are His elect. So what you have to determine is which "elect" is being referred to in Matthew 24:31.

The pre-tribulation teacher I was watching on television explained that when the book of Matthew was written, the church was not formally started; therefore, this verse is addressing the Jewish audience. So, according to him, the elect that are being raptured here are the Jewish remnant survivors of the Great Tribulation. There are a couple of problems with this explanation. The biggest one is when the disciples accepted Christ as their Savior and Messiah, that was the start of the church, and they were all Jews during the formation of the early church. I realize some teachers will say the church was not started until Jesus died on the cross. I do not go along with this because when Jesus was calling His disciples together He was not forming a Jewish synagogue. He was teaching a New Covenant and those who were accepting His teaching were the nucleus of the church. The church was open before the cross; Jesus dying on the cross was the grand opening of the church.

When the Rapture occurs, both Jews and Gentiles who have accepted Christ will go up to be with our Lord. The Jews who will go through the remainder of the Great Tribulation will go through it because they did not accept Jesus as their Lord before the Rapture happened. Think about this: how can the elect, spoken about here, be the Jews who would be raptured off the earth at the end of the sixth seal? There would not be any Jews in Israel for Jesus to come back and save at the battle of Armageddon!

In conclusion, this account of the Rapture is not describing a post-tribulation event because it happens after the opening of the seals before the wrath of God starts. It is too soon to be the post-tribulation rapture.

This description of the Rapture is not a pre-Tribulation Rapture because it happens after the opening of the seals; the Great Tribulation is well under way.

It is not the Rapture of the Jews because they have to be in Israel until the battle of Armageddon, except for those who accept Christ as their Lord. These Jews go up in the same Rapture as the saints.

Now, we only have one other choice: these verses are describing the Rapture of the believers in the <u>middle</u> of the Great Tribulation.

THE DANGER IN TEACHING A POST-TRIB OR LAST TRUMPET RAPTURE

I have been watching some round table talks recently with speakers covering pre, mid, and the post-tribulation positions for the rapture. As I listen to these different speakers defending their different views, I have to admit that they all sound convincing. No matter how convincing they all are, I still know that only one view is correct. I know the timing of the rapture has no bearing on our salvation, but it is important that we get it right. What I am going to explain is why it will be harmful to the body of Christ for us to hold to a view on the timing of the rapture that is in error.

The thrust of this study is not toward the error of the pre-Trib view, as I cover this topic in my book, "The Window of the Lord's Return", quite thoroughly. I will remind you that I believe the warning Paul gave in 2Thess. 2:1-3 when he warned that before the gathering unto Him, (the rapture), there would be a great falling away. I believe this falling away will happen when the global economies collapse and the rapture does not occur as those Christians who hold to a pre-Tribulation view believe.

I show from Scripture, in chapter 8 of my book, that the antichrist cannot arrive until the ten head one world government arrives. When this truth sinks in, you realize that the United States will go through trying times after an economic collapse (maybe around six months) before we are willing to cancel our Constitution and join this one world government. **Picture an economic collapse where our dollars lose most or all value. Imagine all credit cards being switched off like a light switch. Imagine the collapse of our food distribution system and other infrastructures. This would lead to food riots, martial law, food rationing, and famine in this country and around the world.** This event has to happen before the Great Tribulation even starts, if you believe, as I do, that we will go through 3 ½ years once the Great Tribulation starts. **Realize that once the antichrist arrives on the scene his system will force everyone to take the mark of the beast or you will not be able to buy food.** Imagine 3 ½ years without being able to go to the store and buy food. The Bible says there will be great deception in the last days. Many Christians do not read their Bibles. It would be easy for many to think that God would not want their families to starve, therefore; many will buy into the system of the antichrist.

This brings me to the thrust of this topic. I want to show why the post-Trib. view or even the Last Trumpet teaching for the rapture will cause great harm to the body of Christ. If it were just a matter of letting those who want to believe that they will go through much of the wrath of God or even just half of the wrath of God during the End-Times, it would be fine. Those who believe this at least know they will have a rough road ahead. It is not this simple, though. Realize, 80% or more of Christians in America believe the rapture, is a pre-Tribulation event. As a teacher of a mid-Tribulation rapture it is my goal and my burden, to warn this high number of Believers that they will not be prepared to go through what lies ahead.

Even though we will go through three and a half years of the Great Tribulation, we will not go through any of the wrath of God. I will show why The Seals are not the wrath of God and we are raptured at the end of the Sixth Seal. I will show that God has a purpose for our being on earth during this time: so we can be used to win the lost and stop our friends, family and neighbors from taking the mark of the beast. I believe that once people have made their choice to either serve God or the antichrist, our job is done and we have no reason to stay on this earth any longer.

Here is where the danger lies in promoting either the post-Trib position or the last trumpet position. These two positions are one and the same for many. As I have heard admitted, post-Tribulation teachers say that the rapture would happen at the last trumpet of Revelation. This would mean that the body of Christ would be going through Six Trumpets of God's wrath.

How can you believe that God would allow his saints to go through any of His wrath after we have already gone through 3 ½ years of war on the saints by the antichrist? (Dan. 7:21-22, bears this out). "As I watched, this horn was waging war against the saints and defeating them, until the Ancient of Days came and pronounced judgement in favor of the saints of the Most High, and the time came when they possessed the kingdom."

Even those who say we will be on the earth until the last trumpet are not thinking this through. The first trumpet of God's wrath says 1/3 of the earth is burned up. The earth is 2/3 water and water does not burn. How can you imagine that the saints could escape this if we were still on the earth? The 5th trumpet has scorpion creatures stinging all except for the 144,000 specially marked Jews. **Notice there is no provision for the saints because they are already at the throne of God.**

Here is where I see the real danger in the post-Trib and last trumpet teachings. The pre-Tribulation believers understand strongly from their study that the saints are not accounted to wrath or the wrath to come. This is the stand that they will take **when presented with any view that shows them going through the wrath of God. They will not accept this teaching and will therefore just stay right where they are and**

remain unprepared. The post-Trib, position does not give them anywhere to go. As a result, this 80% or more of all Christians are heading for great danger and a great falling away.

In closing, I am going to share a few new insights that show why the last trumpet teaching is flawed. Please realize this is not a personal attack on any one individual who may take this position. I have a friend in the faith, a great teacher who I love and respect, whom holds this position, yet we have to agree to disagree. I cannot change someone's views; it takes the Holy Spirit to do that.

The last trumpet teaching comes from 1Corinthians 15:52: **"In a flash, in the twinkling of an eye, at the last trumpet, for the trumpet will sound and the dead will be raised imperishable and we will be changed."** This teaching takes the position that there is only one last trumpet in the Bible, and that is the 7th trumpet of God's wrath found in the book of Revelation. Without going into great detail, I share in my book that the book of Corinthians was written to be understood at the time it was written. The book of Revelation would not be written for almost another 40 years. What would have gone through the minds of the Corinthian church when Paul sent them this letter? I believe they would have thought of the annual feast of trumpets that they celebrated every year, and in my book I show this feast illustrates an Old Testament type of the future rapture of the church. When you read chapter 11 of my book, you will get the full details of this study.

Another point, similar to the one above, is when the different books and letters that make up our Bible were written, these different writings that would one day make up the Bible we have today were scattered throughout the church. It wasn't until three hundred years after all the books of the Bible were written that they were assembled and arranged into the order we have today. This would mean that the interpretation from the verse in Corinthians 15:52 could not have been made for 300 years. Do you really think that when Paul wrote the letter to the Corinthian church that they were not to understand this verse for 300 years of church history?

In doing further study, what I have uncovered is quite interesting and backs up my position that we are not to go through any of the wrath of God. The Seven Trumpets are given to seven angels who stand at the throne of God in Revelation 8:2. It is shown throughout the Bible that whenever judgment is being delivered, that judgment is delivered by angels. I show that in The Seven Seals there are no angels involved because this is not the wrath or judgment of God.

There is only one reference in the Bible that refers to the rapture happening at the last trumpet. It was at the **final** trumpet of the Feast of Trumpets, when the high priest would blow this trumpet. Moses led the people at that time to the mountain to meet with God. Notice that the top of the mountain was covered with clouds. It makes so much sense this last trumpet is referring to the **final** trumpet in the celebration of the Feast of Trumpets.

When I examined other New Testament verses that speak about the trumpet that will signal the rapture, I found two examples that paint an interesting picture. One verse says **"the trumpet call of God would sound"**, not the trumpet blast of an angel, and the second verse shows that the angels were waiting to hear the trumpet that Christ would sound that would send them off to gather the elect in the rapture. Matthew 24:30, 31: "They will see the Son of Man coming on the clouds of the sky, with power and great glory. **And he will send the angels with a loud trumpet call** and they will gather his elect from the four winds," This is just as it was in the Old Testament Feast of Trumpets where the high priest would blow the final trumpet. When the rapture is to occur, our high priest, Jesus, will blow the trumpet that will send the angels out to gather His elect.

In closing, I have a major point I need to make as it applies to The Last Trumpet teaching. This will require you to look closely at what I will share with you. This is a very important teaching and takes several paragraphs to lay out. Once the wrath of God starts with The Seven Trumpets of God's wrath, there will be no recess or break from God's wrath. John, who is relating what he sees in the scroll as he is writing the book of Revelation, is interrupted. If you read Revelation chapters eight through ten you will see that John is giving us a blow by blow of what is happening as angels are delivering The Seven Trumpets of God's wrath. Then John is told to stop writing about the wrath of God. John is told to stop writing about the wrath that is unfolding and go back and write about those who were being discussed leading up to the rapture in Rev 7:9.

As the angel instructs John to read a second scroll, this is a different scroll from the one he had been reading previously. This scroll is called a little scroll. I will write out part of Rev.8-11, however, I encourage you to read this chapter and section to see that

I am keeping things in context. Rev.10:8.-10: "Then the voice I heard from heaven spoke to me once more: "Go, take the scroll that lies open in the hand of the angel who is standing on the sea and on the land." "So I went to the angel and asked him to give me **the little scroll**. He said to me, Take it and eat it." ...I took the little scroll from the angel's hand and ate it. It tasted as sweet as honey in my mouth, but when I had eaten it, my stomach turned sour. Then I was told: **you must prophesy again about many peoples, nations, languages and kings.**" John had been giving a blow by blow account of the wrath of God, when all of a sudden he is interrupted and told to take a break from the wrath of God and go back and prophesy again about the same ones that were discussed before the rapture.

If you will study all that is written in this parenthetical section that goes from The Seventh Trumpet until The Seven Bowls of God wrath starts up, you will discover this section is not in chronological order. A good example of this is Rev. 14:1: "Then I looked, and there before me was the **Lamb, standing on Mount Zion, and with him 144,000** who had his name and his Father's name written on their foreheads." This was really confusing to me before the Lord showed me what was happening with this section. You see, Jesus is on Mount Zion with the 144,000. This can not happen until after the battle of Armageddon, when Jesus returns and steps on the Mount of Olives. **This is out of chronological order.** When you read in Rev. 14 about the angels preaching and warning people not to take the mark of the beast, this has already happened before The Rapture that happens in Rev.7:9. Rev.13:1 describing the beast coming out of the sea. This is the forming of the one world government. This also has already happened before the antichrist arrives.

Because teachers have taken these chapters to be in chronological order, it has led to many misinterpretations of the word of God. Another example of confusion coming from this is Rev.13:5 where it says that the antichrist will exercise his authority for forty-two months. This has led teachers to say that the antichrist will only rule for three and a half years. This is not the case. The antichrist brokers a seven year peace with Israel and breaks it in the middle. What this verse is referring to is The War on the Saints that will give the antichrist authority and power over the saints for forty-two months. Rev. 13:7: "He was given Power (this is authority) to make war against the saints and to conquer them."Read Daniel 7:25: "The saints will be handed over to him for a time, times, and half a time." This is 42 months. If you will read further in Rev. 11, you will see the account of the two witnesses, and it shows them dying and lying in the streets which does not happen until they have been on the earth for three and a half years, another example of this parenthetical section of Revelation.

You can see that these chapters in Rev. 11-14 are not in chronological order. Some of these events go back before the rapture, some events go forward to after Jesus returns to the earth, and some events are real time. What I will show you now is a real time event that is happening in heaven during the time that the wrath of God is happening on earth. I will take you to the opening of The Seventh Seal in Rev.11:15: "The seventh angel sounded his trumpet, and there were loud **voices in heaven**." This verse establishes that this event is happening in heaven. When you read further down, you will see what is going on in heaven. Rev.11:18: "The time has come for judging the dead and rewarding your servants the prophets and your saints and those who reverence your name."

I believe those who think the rapture is at The Last Trumpet, see this event as the rapture. It makes more sense that while the wrath of God is being poured out on the earth, the dead in Christ will be having what is called the judgment of the Believers, and then we will receive our rewards. I believe after this awards ceremony, we will move on to the marriage supper of the lamb, maybe after the marriage supper of the lamb we will have a honeymoon period in our new home before returning with Christ for the battle of Armageddon.

Is "The day of the Lord" the Rapture?

This additional study also sheds light on the timing of the Rapture. When I heard a TV preacher recently try to explain away 2Thess. 2:1-3, saying that the Day of the Lord is not the Rapture, but a 1,000 year period starting with the Great Tribulation, I knew I had to challenge this thinking. If you read 2Thess.2:1-3, it says the Christians in the church were concerned that the Day of the Lord had already occurred. How can this mean1,000 years? They were concerned they had missed the Rapture, a one-day event, not fearing they had missed a 1,000 year event.

This verse also says that the gathering or Rapture cannot happen until a falling way occurs, and the antichrist is revealed. When you tell a Pre-trib teacher events have to happen before the Rapture can occure, this compels Pre-trib teachers to disarm this verse. Read 1Thess.5:1-2: "Now brothers, about times and dates we do not need to write to you, for you know that the Day of the Lord will come like a thief in the night." This is not talking about a 1,000 year period; (How can 1,000 years sneak up on you?) This is talking about the Rapture, coming after the revealing of the antichrist, with the wrath of God to follow.

I have discovered in my study that the Day of the Lord is actually the Rapture followed by the wrath of God. Read Joel 2:31: "The Sun will be turned to darkness and the moon to blood before the coming of the great and dreadful day of the Lord." Notice that this verse goes along with the opening of the Sixth Seal where the sun goes dark. Also notice it is described as the great and dreadful day of the Lord. It is great day because the Rapture is about to take place and it is a dreadful day for the wrath of God is about to be poured out. Rev.8:1 is the opening of the Seventh Seal and when it is opened there is silence in heaven for 30 minutes. "When he opened the seventh the seal, there was silence in heaven for half an hour." I believe this silence will start the moment the saints are led to the throne of God by Jesus who just met us in the clouds. When we arrive at the throne we will be in such awe to be in the presence of Almighty God that we will be speechless. All the angels and heavenly beings will also be speechless as they witness the unfolding of God's redemption. This silence will go on until our heavenly father breaks the silence and welcomes the Bride of his Son to their new heavenly home.

If you read further in Rev.8:2, it says, "And I saw the seven angels who stand before God and to them were given the seven trumpets". These trumpets are the seven trumpets of God's wrath. When you read Joel 2:31, you will see what I mean. It is a great day for the saints who are raptured and it is a dreadful day for the unrepentant that are left behind to face the wrath of God.

Some are trying to say that The Seven Trumpets are not the wrath of God. I believe the Rapture happens after the Sixth Seal when the sun goes dark and the moon does not give off its light. If you read further down in chapter six, you will see it is talking about the wrath of God that is about to be released. Rev.6:16, 17 "They called to the mountains and the rocks, "Fall on us and hide us from the face of him who sits on the throne and from the wrath of the Lamb! For the great day of their wrath has come, and who can stand?" Notice this is the wrath of the one who sits on the throne and the wrath of the Lamb. Almighty God sits on the throne, and there is no mistaking that this is the wrath of God that is about to take place after the Sixth Seal.

— CHAPTER ELEVEN —

MID-TRIBULATION RAPTURE?
I MAKE MY CASE.

This chapter has three parts. First, I will cover seven Bible-backed events that must take place in the last generation before the Rapture can happen. Only one of these events has happened to date.

Second, I will do a study from the book of Daniel that clearly shows that the Rapture will be a mid-tribulation event.

Third, I will present the teaching from my timeline chart showing a mid-tribulation Rapture.

Along with the teaching of a pre-tribulation rapture has been the teaching of the imminent return of the Lord regarding the Rapture. As I show in chapter seven, "Other Bible Teachers' Perspectives Concerning the Rapture," many pre-tribulation rapture teachers have taught that the timing of the Rapture has been imminent for almost two thousand years! I was discussing this point with one pastor friend and told him, "How could the Rapture have been imminent for even one hundred years if Israel had not been reborn as a nation until 1948?" His response was, "Well, now it is imminent." Below I will show six events that can be shown from scripture that must take place before the Rapture.

PART ONE:
SIX EVENTS THAT MUST TAKE PLACE
BEFORE THE RAPTURE CAN OCCUR

When I started this study, there was one verse that convinced me that the Rapture was not an imminent event. After over three years of working on this study, I believe with the help of the Holy Spirit, I now see that from the time of the rebirth of Israel, (the event that triggers the beginning of the last generation before the return of the Lord Jesus), there are at least seven events that must happen before the Rapture of the believers. Only one of these scripturally supported events has been fulfilled. That is the rebirth of Israel in 1948. You may want to go back and review this study concerning the rebirth of Israel in 1948 from my book's introduction. Below, I will go over the remaining six events that must take place before the Rapture can occur.

1. The one-world government must be in place before the Rapture can occur.

To avoid redundancy, I must encourage you to review chapter eight, "The Coming Antichrist." This chapter clearly shows from God's Word that before the antichrist can be revealed, the ten leaders, or as I call them, "the ten heads of state," and the one-world government must be in place before the Rapture can occur. (The antichrist cannot arrive until the one-world government is in place.) When we connect this to the following events listed below which show a great falling away, we see the antichrist must be revealed before the Rapture can occur. We then begin to see a sequence of events that must come together before the Rapture.

2. There must be a falling away.

3. The antichrist must be revealed.

As you read the following events that must happen before the Rapture can occur, you realize this is not my opinion; this is the Word of God.

2 Thessalonians 2:1-3: *Concerning the coming of our Lord Jesus Christ and our being gathered to him, we ask you, brothers, not to become easily unsettled or alarmed by some prophecy, report or letter supposed to have come from us, saying that the day of the Lord has already come. Don't let anyone deceive you in any way, for that day will not come until the rebellion occurs and the man of lawlessness is revealed, the man doomed to destruction.*

These verses are talking about the man of lawlessness, the son of perdition or the antichrist, who must come before the day of the Lord or the Rapture can occur. These verses also talk about the rebellion; this is referred to in other translations as a great "falling away." When I discuss my timeline chart, I will go into more detail as to why we will be set up for a great falling away before the coming antichrist even arrives. I have shared in my study in a coming chapter that some sort of global crises is coming; this event must happen to convince the world that the solution to these global problems is a global currency and one-world government. When this crisis arrives, America will experience a total breakdown of society as we know it. Many Christians will believe the Great Tribulation has already started. Many Christians will realize that they were not taught correctly concerning the Rapture, and I believe this will lead large numbers of Christians to leave their faith, causing a great "falling away."

4. The temple must be rebuilt before the Rapture can occur.

5. The antichrist must desecrate the temple before the Rapture can occur.

The following scriptures will show that both the temple must be rebuilt and the antichrist must desecrate the temple before the prophecy of these verses can come to pass. The Bible covers both of these events together.

Mark 13:14, 26, 27: *When you see the abomination that causes desolation standing where it does not belong--let the reader understand--then let those who are in Judea flee to the mountains. At that time men will see the Son of Man coming in the clouds with great glory. And he will send his angels and gather his elect from the four winds, from the ends of the earth to the ends of the heavens.* This passage refers to the antichrist standing in the temple in verse 14; then verse 27 shows the Rapture following this event.

To give a second witness to God's own words, you should read Matthew 24:15, 30: *So when you see standing in the holy place 'the abomination that causes desolation,' spoken of through the Prophet Daniel—let the reader understand . . . At that time the sign of the Son of Man will appear in the sky, and all the nations of the earth will mourn. They will see the Son of Man coming on the clouds of the sky, with power and great glory.*

These verses show that the Rapture cannot happen until the temple is rebuilt because how can the antichrist stand in a temple and desecrate a temple that has

not yet been rebuilt? If you will look up Daniel 9:27, you will see the timing of this desecration of the temple. A more detailed explanation of this is found in chapter fifteen called "A Possible Scenario Story Leading Up to the Rapture." On page 197 with the subtitle of "2017."

6. Heavenly events must also take place before the Rapture occurs.

This is another instance where it is best to let God's Word speak for itself.

Matthew 24:29-31: *Immediately after the distress of those days the sun will be darkened, and the moon will not give its light; the stars will fall from the sky, and the heavenly bodies will be shaken.* **At that time** *the sign of the Son of Man will appear in the sky, and all the nations of the earth will mourn. They will see the Son of Man coming on the clouds of the sky, with power and great glory. And he will send his angels with a loud trumpet call, and they will gather his elect from the four winds, from one end of the heavens to the other.*

Next, read Revelation 6:12-13: *I watched as he opened the sixth seal. There was a great earthquake. The sun turned black like sackcloth made of goat hair, the whole moon turned blood red, and the stars in the sky fell to the earth, as late figs drop from a fig tree when it is shaken by a strong wind.*

As you read these verses, notice they both refer to the stars falling from the sky. These would be meteor showers. The reference in Revelation 6 places this event at the sixth seal, and the reference from Matthew 24 shows the Rapture happening after this event.

Notice all six of these last remaining events occur during a time period that is recognized as happening during the Great Tribulation. When these events that I have just outlined come to pass, it will be the time for us to stand up and look up as God has told us. Luke 21:28: *When these things begin to take place, stand up and lift up your heads, because your redemption is drawing near.* Truly, the last thing that will happen before the Lord returns will be the blowing of the trumpet, or the last trumpet as it is referred to in 1 Corinthians 15:52: *In a flash, in the twinkling of an eye, at the last trumpet. For the trumpet will sound, the dead will be raised imperishable, and we will be changed.*

In chapter 11, I present a study on the last trumpet that goes well with the verse above.

PART TWO: TIMING OF THE RAPTURE FROM THE BOOK OF DANIEL

In chapter eight, I presented information about the coming of the antichrist. Upon further study, I have found more evidence the Rapture does not happen until the middle of the Great Tribulation. In the first half of Daniel 7, we have the vision of Daniel described and then explained in the second half. I will show parallel links in the New Testament that show the same events. I will conclude by showing you that Daniel's vision not only contains information on the antichrist's war against the saints, but it also shows the deliverance of the saints in the Rapture. Then I will take you on a further study of Daniel that shows beyond all doubt that the Rapture will be a mid-tribulation event. Please maintain an open mind as you proceed in this study. Many people who are reading this cannot believe they have never seen what I am showing plainly written in God's Word.

First, let us read the end of Daniel's vision found in Daniel 7:13-14: *In my vision at night I looked, and there before me was one like a son of man, coming with the clouds of heaven. He approached the Ancient of Days and was led into his presence. He was given authority, glory, and sovereign power; all peoples, nations and men of every language worshiped him. His dominion is an everlasting dominion that will not pass away, and his kingdom is one that will never be destroyed.*

When we read this, we recognize that Jesus is the one who is coming in the clouds. Jesus is coming in the clouds to deliver the saints from the persecution of the antichrist and to take them to His Father's kingdom. Looking further at this verse, you will see it is addressing the Gentiles, not the Jews, as this event is the Rapture of the saints out of all nations of the world. Read Daniel 7:14a: *He was given authority, glory, and sovereign power; all peoples, nations and men of every language worshiped him.* My point will become even clearer as the meaning of Daniel's visions and dreams are explained in the second half of Daniel 7. Read Daniel 7:21-22: *As I watched, this horn was waging war against the saints and defeating them, until the Ancient of Days came and pronounced judgment in favor of the saints of the Most High, and the time came when they possessed the kingdom.* I believe "kingdom" is referring to the kingdom of heaven. For the saints to possess the kingdom of heaven, they have to go to heaven.

I want to show you the parallel of Jesus coming in the clouds for His saints from Matthew 24:29-31: *Immediately after the distress of those days, the sun will be darkened, and the moon will not give its light; the stars will fall from the sky, and the heavenly bodies will be shaken.* **At that time** *the sign of the Son of Man will appear in the sky, and all nations of the earth will mourn. They will see the Son of Man coming on the clouds of the sky, with power and great glory. And he will send his angels with a loud trumpet call, and they will gather his elect from the four winds and from one end of the heavens to the other.*

These verses from Matthew are almost verbatim as those in Mark 13:24-27 and Acts 2:20: *The sun will be turned to darkness and the moon to blood before the coming of the great and glorious day of the Lord.* These events are also seen in Revelation 6 with the opening of the seals. Notice the fifth seal is the martyrdom of the saints, parallel to what is happening in Daniel and described as war on the saints.

Please stay with me, for it is about to get very interesting. For now, I will further link these scriptures to the book of Revelation and Acts. Read Revelation 6:12-13: *I watched as he opened the sixth seal. There was a great earthquake. The sun turned black like sack cloth made of goat hair, the whole moon turned blood red, and the stars in the sky fell to the earth, as late figs drop from a fig tree when shaken by a strong wind.* What is spoken of in Revelation 6:12-13 is the fulfillment of that which Acts 2:20 says must happen before the day of the Lord comes. Acts 2:20: *The sun will be turned into darkness and the moon to blood before the coming of the great and glorious day of the Lord.* Some may ask, "Is the Rapture the day of the Lord?" 2 Peter 3:10 throws light on this, *But the day of the Lord will come like a thief.*

I will show you the arrival of the saints in heaven as described in Daniel 7:13 and Revelation 7:9. First, read Daniel 7:13, 14a: *In my vision at night, I looked, and there before me was one like a son of man, coming with the clouds of heaven. He approached the Ancient of Days and was led into his presence. He was given authority, glory and sovereign power; all peoples, nations and men of every language worshiped him.*

Read Revelation 7:9: *After this I looked and there before me was a great multitude that no one could count, from every nation, tribe, people, and language, standing before the throne and in front of the Lamb. They were wearing white robes and were holding palm branches in their hands.*

To bring these thoughts to their conclusion, I want to share the meaning of Daniel's vision that was given to him in the second half of Daniel 7. First, I want to show the verse in Daniel that describes the antichrist waging war against the saints until God steps in and delivers them. This deliverance is the Rapture that is described as the Son of Man coming in the clouds in Daniel 7:13. It is shown in greater detail in Matthew 24:29-31. Next, read Daniel 7:21: *As I watched, this horn was waging war against the saints and defeating them, until the Ancient of Days came and pronounced judgment in favor of the saints of the Most High, and the time came when they possessed the kingdom.* What is interesting is this oppression or war against the saints has an ending point described in the verse above. It says the horn is waging war against the saints and defeating them until the Ancient of Days steps in to deliver them.

In reading the next verse, you will see how long the saints must endure oppression from the antichrist. Read Daniel 7:25: *He will speak against the Most High and oppress his saints and try to change the set times and the laws. The saints will be handed over to him for a time, times, and half a time.* The margin of my Thompson Study Bible says this time is three and one-half years. Think about this. The antichrist appears on the scene at the opening of the first seal of Revelation 6. The antichrist is not on the earth as the actual antichrist until Satan possesses one of the horns or heads of the beast and brings this head of state back from the dead. Once Satan is this world leader in human form, you can be sure he will lash out against the saints almost immediately. Daniel teaches that the antichrist will broker a seven-year peace with Israel soon after he comes to power. The Bible supports that this is the beginning of the seven-year Great Tribulation. What is interesting is the antichrist will only be able to make war against the saints for three and one-half years, according to Daniel 7:25. Why will the antichrist no longer be able to make war on the saints? Daniel 7:21-22 shows the reason: **God intervenes!** What is the form of this intervention? **Jesus is coming in the clouds and raptures the saints!** Put these thoughts all together, and you have the Rapture occurring three and one-half years into the Great Tribulation.

This part of my study is very compelling, showing a period of three and a half years of war on the saints, followed by our heavenly Father's intervention. What I will show you now is a parallel verse from Revelation 13:5-6. It confirms this three and a half year period which will end at God's intervention with the Rapture of the saints. Revelation13:5-6: *The beast was given a mouth to utter proud words and blasphemies and to exercise his authority for forty-two months. He opened his mouth to blaspheme God, and to slander his name and his dwelling place and those who live in heaven. He was given power to make war against the saints and to conquer them. And he was given authority over every tribe, people and language and nation.*

Notice, this verse says he, the antichrist, was given authority for forty-two months. Some have taken this to mean that the antichrist would only appear on the scene for forty-two months. This does not make sense because the antichrist makes a seven-year peace with Israel and breaks it in the middle. This verse is saying the same thing as what Daniel chapter seven is saying. The antichrist has been given authority over the saints for forty-two months, and after that period, just as Daniel 7:21-22 says, God intervenes. *As I watched, this horn was waging war against the saints and defeating them, until the Ancient of Days came and pronounced judgment in favor of the saints of the Most High, and the time came when they possessed the kingdom.*

I believe I have shown a strong case for the Rapture as a mid-tribulation event from the book of Daniel. I will outline below further biblical support from the book of Daniel that shows the Rapture as a mid-tribulation event.

If you read Daniel 12:1-2, you will realize these verses are talking about the time of the Great Tribulation. These verses then describe a deliverance from this time of Great Tribulation. (Notice that Michael the Archangel is standing up and ready to play a part in this coming deliverance.) What is the form of this deliverance that is being referred to? If you will notice who are included in this event, you will realize it must be talking about the Rapture of the saints. Read Daniel 12:1-2: *At that time Michael the great prince who protects your people, will arise. There will be a time of distress such as has not happened from the beginning of nations until then. But at that time your people – everyone whose name is found written in the book – will be delivered. Multitudes who sleep in the dust of the earth will awake: some to everlasting life, others to shame and everlasting contempt.*

When you see the dead in Christ who have their names written in the Book of Life, awakening from the sleep of death, clearly the event described here is the Rapture. Read 1 Thessalonians 4:15-18: *According to the Lord's own word, we tell you that we who are still alive, who are left till the coming of the Lord, will certainly not precede those who have fallen asleep. For the Lord himself will come down from heaven,* *with a loud command, with the voice of the archangel and the trumpet call of God, and the dead in Christ will rise first. After that, we who are still alive and are left will be caught up with them in the clouds to meet the Lord in the air. And so we will be with the Lord forever. Therefore encourage each other with these words.*

This is a WOW moment for me. When you read above where it says, *For the Lord himself will come down from heaven, with a loud command, with the voice of the archangel...* Michael is the archangel, one of the top generals in command of the armies of God, and Daniel 12:1 shows Michael getting ready to play his part in the Rapture of all those whose names are written in the Book of Life, who are the elect of God, or the saints.

It is interesting that after these coming events were described in Daniel 12:1-2, it goes on to say in Daniel 12:4 that these words were to be sealed up until the time of the end. Daniel 12:4: *But you, Daniel, close up and seal the words of the scroll until the time of the end...* Reading further, it gets very interesting as verses 5-7 describe two men standing on both sides of the river talking to a man in linen that was above them. I believe the man in linen was Jesus and the other two may have been Michael the Archangel (and maybe another angel). One of the men or an angel asks the question, *"How long will it be before these astonishing things are fulfilled?"* What are the astonishing things referred to? The things referred to in Daniel 12:1-2 are the time of the Great Tribulation up until the time of the deliverance of God's people whose names are written in the Book of Life, both the living and those who are dead in the Lord. Then the man in linen – whom I believe is Jesus – answers the question and describes this time as *a time, times, and half a time,* (or three and one-half years). This places the Rapture three and one-half years into the Great Tribulation.

Now read Daniel 12:5-8 and see if what I am saying makes sense. Daniel 12:5-8: *Then I Daniel, looked, and there before me stood two others, one on this bank of the river and one on the opposite bank. One of them said to the man clothed in linen, who was above the waters of the river, "How long will it be before these astonishing things are fulfilled?" The man clothed in linen who was above the waters of the river, lifted his right hand and his left hand toward heaven, and I heard him swear by him who lives forever, saying, "It will be for a time, times, and half a time. When the power of the holy people has been finally broken, all these things will be completed."*

Again, notice the last part of the answer from the man in linen. It says that once the power of the holy people has been broken, all these things will be completed. Realize that during this time of the Great Tribulation, the antichrist has been waging war against the saints. About this time, the antichrist will enter the temple and declare that he is God.

Now get the picture of what is happening here. Daniel just had it explained to him how long it would be until these astonishing things would be fulfilled. However, Daniel still does not get the full picture. So again, he asks another question. The question is not about the fulfillment of the astonishing things but about the outcome of all of these things. Read Daniel 12:8-11: *I heard, but I did not understand. So I asked, "My Lord, what will the outcome of all this be?"* He replied, *"Go your way, Daniel, because the words are closed up and sealed until the time of the end. Many will be purified, made spotless and refined, but the wicked will continue to be wicked."* **None of the wicked will understand. From the time that the daily sacrifice is abolished and the abomination that causes desolation is set up, there will be 1290 days.**

This is another revelation moment for me. Daniel has had two questions answered in Daniel 12. The first question concerned the time when the astonishing things would be fulfilled. He was told it would be three and one-half years until the time that the saints would be delivered, coinciding with the antichrist desecrating the temple. Then Daniel asked what the outcome of all this would be. The Kings James Version says, *What shall be the end of these things?* He was told it will be three and one-half years from the time the daily sacrifice is abolished, the same time that the antichrist is desecrating the temple, until all these things will come to their end. The answers to these two questions have established two things: how long from the beginning of the Great Tribulation to the deliverance of the saints (three and one-half years) and how long from the desecrating of the temple until the end of these things, again (three and a half years). I believe God's Word in Daniel 12 supports my conclusion that the Rapture of the church occurs in the middle of the seven-year Great Tribulation period.

In closing, consider the question that some will ask, "Is it really that important when the Lord returns? Should not we just be ready?" This is a good question. If the church has been taught that the Rapture will come before the Great Tribulation starts, this gives the church a false sense of security. I have heard pastors say God would not allow His church to go through suffering. Previously in Revelation 14:11-13, I showed from God's Word that the saints will have to have patient endurance during the Great Tribulation. This will also be the time when the antichrist is pushing his system of the mark of the beast.

If the saints who have expected the pre-tribulation rapture, suddenly realize they are in the Great Tribulation with no warning to prepare for this turbulent time, I believe it will cause many Christians to turn away from God. Some will believe God has abandoned them and that their Christian leaders have misled them. They will then accept the system of the antichrist, rather than starve to death. I believe the events happening today with the world economies on the verge of collapse are setting the world stage to make it easy for the world populations to accept a savior in the form of the antichrist.

We, as believers, have to be the ones looking for the signs of Christ's coming. I am convinced we must prepare for hard times as Joseph did, so when the hard times come, we will be able to take care of the needs of our families and others. We need to be in a position for God to use us for the greatest revival the world has ever seen! If what I have written in this chapter makes sense, I urge you to shout it from the housetops and help spread the message of this book, for the time is short.

PART THREE:
TIMELINE OF EVENTS LEADING TO THE RAPTURE

This timeline of events has what I call three layers, like a three layer cake, that brings us to the same conclusion: the Rapture is a mid-tribulation event. Then I conclude with what I call the "icing on the cake."

The first layer covers the seven events that I discussed earlier in this chapter which the Bible shows must happen before the Rapture can occur. Only one of these events having happened to date and that being the rebirth of Israel in 1948.

The second layer covers the seven seals. I will initially cover only the first six seals as this will show how this layer intersects with the first layer of my teaching.

The third layer covers the parallels between Matthew 24 and other Gospel accounts with Revelation 6 and the seven seals of Revelation.

You will have to wait until the end to see what the "icing on the cake" covers.

The charts above start with our current situation: global economies are in trouble. The collapse could start in Europe and domino to America or it could start in America and domino to Europe. The truth is the economies of the world are now all tied together. The timing of this collapse is a question mark on my chart. Global economies are so fragile; things could literally fall apart tomorrow. I believe all that is keeping this from happening is the timing of God.

Once the economic collapse happens, within days, life as we know it in America will be over. We will see panic buying of food. Credit cards will no longer work, and what real money you have will have little to no value. We will see riots, anarchy and the institution of martial law. Many Christians will believe the Great Tribulation has begun. The truth is the Great Tribulation cannot start until the antichrist comes to power and that cannot happen until a global one-world government is fully in place. I show on my chart that it could take from six months to a year or more before America will give up its Constitution, Bill of Rights, freedom of speech, freedom of religion and the right to bear arms and join the one world government.

During this time, I believe it will be the greatest opportunity to witness to the lost the world has ever seen. But if we don't see these events coming and get prepared for this time, you won't be able to help your lost friends and family. How can you help minister to the lost if you are a basket case yourself? Remember, God warned Joseph in Egypt, and his preparation saved his family.

As you study my chart, you will see the first layer I present was covered earlier in this chapter under the seven things the Bible says must happen before the Rapture. You may also want to review my chapter on the "Coming Antichrist" as this shows that the one-world government must be in place before the antichrist can arrive.

The next layer of my chart is the seven seals of the book of Revelation 6. I have already given an overview of the first six seals in chapter one, but for the sake of this chart, just looking at the order of the seals will suffice. Notice that the sixth event in my first layer and the 6th seal of Revelation 6 are the same event. The heavenly events from the first layer come from the book of Matthew and the other Gospels and the heavenly events in the second layer of my chart come from the sixth seal of Revelation 6, thus showing the first two layers intersect at this point.

The third layer of my chart draws parallels between Matthew 24 and the other Gospels, and the opening of the seals in Revelation 6. If you will study Matthew 24 and Revelation 6, you will recognize that these two books are covering the same events. Notice Matthew 24 contains almost a complete outline for the seals covered in Revelation 6.

If you will read each of the three Gospel references I show on the third layer of my chart, you will see that each reference shows the sun goes black and the moon will not give its light and then it says, ***At that time*** *the sign of the Son of Man will appear in the sky.* Matthew 24:29-31: *Immediately after the distress of those days, the sun will be darkened, and the moon will not give its light; the stars will fall from the sky, and heavenly bodies will be shaken.* ***At that time*** *the sign of the Son of Man will appear in the sky and all the nations of the earth will mourn. They will see the Son of Man coming on the clouds of the sky with power and great glory. And he will send his angels with a loud trumpet call, and they will gather his elect from the four winds, from one end of the heavens to the other.*

Look at Mark 13:24-26 and Luke 21:25-27. Notice the same sequence of events. The sun goes black and the moon will not give its light. Next it says, ***At that time*** the sign of the Son of Man appears in the sky.

Now we need to read about the 6th seal in the book of Revelation and see how it progresses to the Rapture. Revelation 6:12-13: *I watched as he opened the sixth seal. There was a great earthquake. The sun turned black like sackcloth made of goat hair, the whole moon turned blood red, and the stars in the sky fell to earth, as late figs drop from a fig tree when shaken by a strong wind.*

If I am making a good case for the Rapture happening after the opening of the sixth seal, then what I want to propose is that the opening of the seventh seal is the Rapture. Revelation 8:1: *When he opened the seventh seal, there was silence in heaven for about half an hour.* I believe when we arrive in heaven at the time of the Rapture, we will be in awe and all the heavenly beings will be in awe to see the plan

TIME LINE OF EVENTS

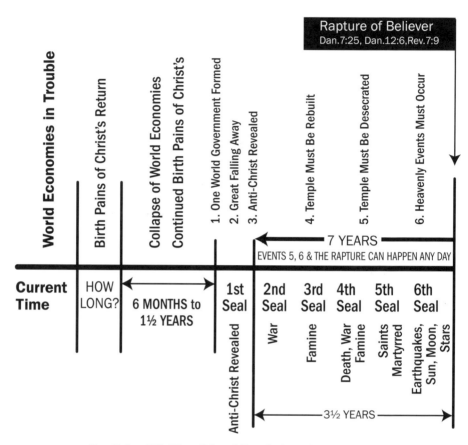

Parellels of Matthew24 and Revelations 6

of God's redemption unfolding at the throne of God. All will be silent (a holy hush, if you will) until our heavenly Father breaks the silence and welcomes us, the bride of His Son Jesus, to our new home.

In Revelation 7:9 we see the arrival of the saints at the seventh seal. Revelation 7:9, *After this I looked and there before me was a great multitude that no one could count, from every nation, tribe and language, standing before the throne and in front of the Lamb. They were wearing white robes and were holding palm branches in their hands.*

Then one of the elders who is always at the throne of God speaks. Revelation 7:13-14:

LEADING TO THE RAPTURE

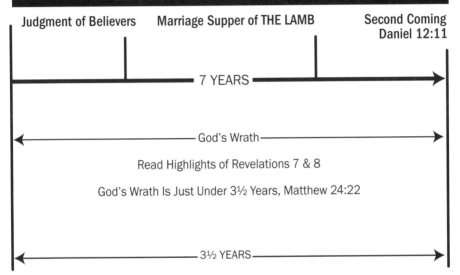

6 Things The Bible Says Must Happen Before the Rapture

1. Rev 13:1, One World Government Formed
2. II Thess. 2:1-3, Great Falling Away
3. II Thess. 2:1-3, Anti-Christ Revealed
4. Mark 13:14, Temple Rebuilt
5. Daniel 9:27, Temple Desecrated
6. Matt. 24:29-31, Heavenly Events Occur

7 Seals of Revelations "Intersect"

Parallels of Matthew 24 and Revelations 6

Judgment of Believers   Marriage Supper of THE LAMB   Second Coming Daniel 12:11

7 YEARS

God's Wrath

Read Highlights of Revelations 7 & 8

God's Wrath Is Just Under 3½ Years, Matthew 24:22

3½ YEARS

Look For "At That Time" After Heavenly Events
Matthew 24:29-30, Mark 13:24-26, Luke 21:25-27

*Then one of the elders asked me, "These in white robes, who are they and where did they come from?" I answered, "Sir, you know." And he answered, "**These are they who have come out of the great tribulation**; they have washed their robes and made them white in the blood of the Lamb."*

When we go back to the opening of the seventh seal, you will see after all the saints are safe at our heavenly Father's throne, the seven angels are given the seven trumpets and released to deliver the wrath of God to an unrepentant world. Revelation 8:1-2: *When he opened the seventh seal, there was silence in heaven for about half an hour. And*

I saw the seven angels who stand before God, and to them were given seven trumpets.

If you will take the time to look up the other Bible verses listed on my chart, I believe you will see the full picture of the Rapture unfold as I have described here.

Now for the "icing on the cake." A proper title would be, "**Darkness Comes Before Deliverance.**" As I already pointed out, there are three separate accounts in the Gospels showing that when the sun goes dark, *at that time the sign of the Son of Man will appear in the clouds.* When the sun goes dark, we can truly look up, for our redemption draweth near.

If we turn to the book of Exodus, we will see the account of Moses getting ready to lead God's people to freedom. The last plague before the plague of the firstborn was darkness. Exodus 10:21: *Then the Lord said to Moses, "Stretch out your hand toward the sky so that darkness will spread over Egypt, darkness that can be felt."* When Moses did as God instructed, it was dark for three days. This was the last plaque before deliverance. Following the darkness was the plaque of the first born. This event was deliverance for God's children who were under the blood. But it was judgment for those who were not under the blood.

If we go to the cross just before Jesus died, it was dark for three hours. Mark 15:33: *At the sixth hour darkness came over the whole land until the ninth hour.* Then we read a further account of the crucifixion found in John 19:30. *When he had received the drink. Jesus said, "It is finished." With that he bowed his head and gave up his spirit.* At the Crucifixion, it was dark for three hours before Jesus died, and we were delivered from sin.

Next are the events at the end of the sixth seal. Matthew 24:29-31, *Immediately after the distress of those days, the sun will be darkened and the moon will not give its light: the stars will fall from the sky, and the heavenly bodies will be shaken. **At that time** the sign of the son of man will appear in the sky, and all the nations of the earth will mourn. They will see the Son of Man coming on the clouds of the sky, with power and great glory. And he will send his angels with a loud trumpet call, and they will gather his elect from the four winds, from one end of the heavens to the other.* What does "**At that time**" mean? It's obvious to me. It means when the sun goes black and the moon does not give its light. "**At that time**" is the Rapture.

I will share one last verse from the Old Testament showing the Rapture after the darkness. Joel 2:30-31: *I will show wonders in the heavens and on the earth, blood and fire and billows of smoke. The sun will be turned into darkness and the moon to blood before the coming of the great and dreadful day of the Lord.* There are three key points to look at in these verses. Points one and two are from the verse that says *the great and dreadful day.* It will be great for God's people and dreadful for the unrepentant. Go back to the sixth seal of Revelation 6 where it says *The sun turned black like sackcloth made of goat hair.* This is the part of the sixth seal that causes us, the redeemed, to rejoice. When you go down a bit further, you will see where it is a dreadful day for the unrepentant. Revelations 6:14-17, *The sky receded like a scroll rolling up, and every mountain and island was removed from its place. Then the kings of the earth, the princes, the generals, the rich, the mighty, and every slave and every free man hid in caves and among the rocks of the mountains. "Fall on us and hide us from the face of him who sits on the throne and from the wrath of the Lamb! For the great day of their wrath has come, and who can stand."* This excites me. We have just been delivered from harm's way, the war on the saints is over, and we are about to be welcomed by our heavenly Father as Jesus leads His bride to the throne to meet Him.

The last point of interest in this verse in Joel 2:30-31 is the phrase, "Day of the Lord." This phrase, "Day of the Lord," is often referenced in the Bible as the time of the Rapture.

I have made my case. Now I ask you, the reader, to examine the scriptures to see if what I am presenting is sound.

MATTHEW 24 STUDY, THE SIGNS OF CHRIST'S COMING

I have just finished making my case for a Mid-tribulation Rapture. I believe I have made a very strong case. What I will present here is a further revelation God gave me since writing this chapter that I feel is too important not add to this chapter.

How this study came about was when I felt prompted to do a study on the signs of the times. Both the Old Testament and the New Testament speak of many signs that would indicate that we are at the time of the Lord's return. The thought hit me that

Jesus has told his believers that we are to watch for the signs of His coming. The Bible says that we would not be caught unaware if we are watching and waiting for Christ's return. **It will be those who are not watching** that will be caught unaware.

If we are, in fact, watching for these signs, and if we are now seeing these signs in the sun/ and the moon/ and stars, the events in Israel, wars and famine, droughts, and many calamities all hitting at the same time, if we are seeing these signs now, would Jesus have told us to watch for these events, if once they arrived they would have no meaning? If the converging of these signs do have meaning, then does this mean that we are at the time of Christ's return?

As we study Matthew 24, we see the parallel between Matthew 24 and Revelation 6, with the opening of the Seven Seals. What really nails this study is when you see Jesus explaining how "the sun will be darkened and the moon will not give its light". Then when you go to the opening of the Sixth Seal you see this same event. When you then look at what Joel says, "The sun, moon and the stars will go dark on the day of the Lord," you realize that what Jesus is explaining and what you read in Revelation 6 and Joel's prediction are all describing the same event.

Matthew 24:3 says, three of Jesus disciples came to him on the Mount of Olives, and asked Him, "Tell us, they said, when will this happen and what will be the sign of your coming and the end of the age?"

When Jesus' disciples asked this question, what they were asking Him was , "What will we see and what will we have to go through before your return?" What I realized when I was doing this study, was the answer Jesus gave his disciples was the outline of the future Seven Seals that would later be revealed to John when he wrote the book of Revelation. Jesus outlined what his disciples would see and what we would experience at the opening of the Seven Seals, as the signs of Christ's coming.

Jesus did not tell his disciples that everything would be going well, and that all of a sudden we would be raptured out of here. He said, we would see the coming antichrist, we would see war, famine and pestilence, and the saints would be killed for their testimony of Jesus. We would see the antichrist desecrate the

temple, which means we would see the temple rebuilt. Then we would see an event that would cause the sun and the moon and the stars to go dark, and at that time we would see the coming of the Lord to meet us in the clouds. Read all of Matthew 24, I am not making this up, all that I am saying is in this chapter.

Matthew 24 covers all of The Seals of Revelation 6, except the fourth seal,(Sword, famine and plagues.) The same account of the disciples meeting with Jesus on the Mount of Olives, found in Luke 21:11 covers the fourth seal plus more detail.

Luke 21:11 , *"Earthquakes, famine and pestilences in various places and fearful events and great signs from heaven."*

Matthew 24, also covers all six events that must happen before the Rapture, except for one, this being the formation of a global government. Revelation 12, shows this event must happen before the antichrist appears.

Jesus makes two important references to the Book of Daniel in Matthew 24.

1.   Matthew 24:15 makes reference to Daniel 9:27, concerning the antichrist in the temple

2.   Matthew 24:21 makes reference to Daniel 12:1, almost word for word. This reference talks about a coming time of great distress unequaled from the beginning of the world.

A time of distress worse than the 1929 Great Depression, because this time of distress did not lead to the coming of the Lord.

A time of distress worse than WW2 and the Holocaust, because these events did not lead the coming of the Lord.

Interesting Observation

The signs that Jesus describes to his disciples happening, leading up to His Coming at the Rapture, conclude at the Sixth Seal when the sun goes dark.

Jesus did not describe any of the events of God's Wrath happening before the event of His coming in the Rapture. **Why? " We are not accounted to Wrath"**

ANSWERING REBUTTALS TO MATTHEW 24 TEACHING

Some teachers are saying that in Matthew 24, Jesus was teaching his disciples, who are Jews, and this teaching only applies to the Jews as a separate Rapture for the Jews only. My response that shows why this line of reasoning makes no sense is very simple. Jesus did not come to make a new covenant for the Jews and a second new covenant for the Gentiles. No, all the promises in the New Covenant were given to the Jews first and the Gentiles were grafted into this covenant. There is not two Raptures; there are not two Brides of Christ or Two Marriage Suppers of the Lamb. We are now all one in Christ.

Some are asking. "Could what is being described in Matthew 24 be describing the Second Coming at the time of the Battle of Armageddon?" By sharing from the same account found in the Gospel of Mark, I am able to show why this would not be the case.

Mark 13: 26-27, *"At that time men will see the Son of Man coming in clouds with great power and glory. And he will send his angels and gather his elect from the four winds, from the ends of the earth to the ends of the heavens."* This is clearly describing the Rapture, and when you see the connection of these events tied to Revelation, chapter six, at the opening of the Sixth Seal, it cannot be at the time of the battle of Armageddon because the entire wrath of God is yet to happen from the time of the Sixth Seal to the time of the battle of Armageddon. Christ's coming at the battle of Armageddon does not happen until God's Wrath is poured out on the unrepentant.

CLOSING WITH READING OF MARK 13: 35,36

"Therefore keep watch because you do not know when the owner of the house will come back—whether in the evening or at midnight, or when the rooster crows, or at dawn. If he comes suddenly, do not let him find you sleeping. What I say to you, I say to everyone: 'Watch!'"

Realize, if we are told to watch, there must be something for which we are to watch. Matthew 24 outlines the things Jesus told his disciples for which to watch.

— CHAPTER TWELVE —

A WARNING TO THOSE WHO ADD OR SUBTRACT FROM GOD'S WORD

The Bible gives a warning to anyone who adds to or subtracts from the Word of God and, more specifically, adds to or subtracts from the prophecy of the book of Revelation. Revelation 22:18-19 says, *I warn everyone who hears the words of the prophecy of this book; if anyone adds anything to them, God will add to him the plagues described in this book. And if anyone takes words away from this book of prophecy, God will take away from him his share in the tree of life and in the holy city, which are described in this book.* I think it is interesting God puts this warning in the book of Revelation. It is as if God knew man would struggle to get its interpretation right.

There are rules for proper Bible interpretation, and some are so basic they should never be violated. One of these basic rules is to always take the Word of God in its proper context. What this means is when you are taking a scripture from a book in the Bible, you must look at what is being said before and after the scripture you are using as your text from which to teach or preach. This helps put it in its proper context.

I will give you an example of how a teacher of the Word of God can be guilty of taking away from the Word of God. Read 1 Thessalonians 5:2-3: *For you know very well that the day of the Lord will come like a thief in the night. While people are saying, 'Peace and safety,' destruction will come on them suddenly, as labor pains on a pregnant woman, and they will not escape.* Now this verse is often used to teach that the Rapture will come without warning, and we will not know when the Lord is coming. Also, it is often used to help teach the pre-tribulation position of the Rapture and the imminent return of the Lord. The problem with using this verse in this way is key words are omitted to make a point that is not true. If you look at the next two verses, you will see this scripture is teaching something different. Read 1 Thessalonians 5:4-5: *But you are not in darkness so this day should surprise you like a thief. You are all sons of light and sons of the day. We do not belong to the night or to the darkness.* **By putting these verses in proper context, we learn that those who are living in darkness will be caught like a thief in the night when the Lord returns, but those who are living in the light will not be surprised when the Lord comes back. Those who are in the light should not be caught off-guard. We should be looking for His coming, and when the signs of Christ's coming are happening, it will be time to look up, for the scripture says in Luke 21:28,** *Then look up, and lift up your heads; for your redemption is drawing near !*

That was an example of taking away from the Word of God. Now I will show a few examples of adding to God's Word. I will not mention the name of the preacher, but a well-known international preacher and teacher wrote a book on Revelation. In his book, he misquotes Matthew 24:36: *No one knows about that day or hour, not even the angels in heaven, nor the Son, but only the Father.* When he quotes this verse in his book, he says, "No man knows the day, the hour or the year." What he has done is add the word "year," and this changes everything. With the Word of God as God wrote it, when the signs of Christ's coming are happening, we will be able to look up and realize the Lord is coming at any time. We can truly expect His soon appearance. But when we add just this one word, "year," the pre-tribulation view of the Rapture is supported by changing the Word of God. This teaching says we will be raptured imminently, without warning.

Under the teaching of a mid-tribulation view, the Rapture will take place after the six seals of the book of Revelation 6. When these events are happening, the saints will realize it is time for Jesus to return. Even though we will not know the day or the hour, we will be able to know Christ is coming any day now.

Read Luke 21:25-28: *There will be signs in the sun, moon and stars. On the earth, nations will be in anguish and perplexity at the roaring and tossing of the sea. Men will faint from terror, apprehensive of what is coming on the world, for heavenly bodies will* *be shaken. **At that time** they will see the Son of Man coming in a cloud with power and great glory. When these things begin to take place, stand up and lift up your heads, because your redemption is drawing near.* When the word "year" is added, it gives weight to the pre-tribulation view because we are not to know the year. If the Rapture happens after the sixth seal, this would be a very good indication that the Lord is about to appear.

A second example of adding to God's Word involves what we are taught about the saints. Some people may be taught that saints who are being martyred and going through the time of war on the saints are "**tribulation saints.**" The title "tribulation saints" is not in the Bible. In order to teach the pre-tribulation position, we must explain who these saints are that are going through part of the Great Tribulation Adding "tribulation" to "saints" in our teaching infers that these saints were not ready for the Rapture and were left behind to go through the Great Tribulation. Again, when you have to add words to God's Word to strengthen your doctrinal position, you are violating God's command and building your doctrines on a house of cards.

In the book of Daniel, Daniel was told to seal up what he saw until the time of the end. When John the Revelator was writing the book of Revelation, he heard and saw things he was told not to write down. I do not know what he was told not to write, but it is clear from Daniel that some things were not meant to be revealed until the time of the end. Most people say the pre-tribulation Rapture doctrine originated less than two hundred years ago. Some teachers say this teaching goes back to about two hundred years after Christ's death. The truth is the pre-tribulation doctrine did not receive acceptance until around 1830 when John Darby introduced it.

I believe the doctrine of the pre-tribulation Rapture, in spite of how entrenched it is in our doctrines of faith, emerged because of the impatience of people who did not want to wait until the time of the end. With little weight of scripture to back up this teaching, we have insisted we can take a round peg and force it into a square hole. I believe the confusion that will arise from the discovery that the church will not be raptured before the seals of Revelation 6 will lead to mass confusion in the church. Many believers will fall away and follow after the lies of the antichrist; many will be convinced that he is the true God. Read 2 Thessalonians 2:3-4 (KJV): *Let no man deceive you by any means, for that day shall not come except there come a falling away first, and that man of sin be revealed, the son of perdition; who opposed and exalted himself above all that is called God, or that is worshiped; so that he as God sitteth in the Temple of God, showing himself that he is God.*

When this great confusion comes, who will be to blame? I believe the answer can be found in 2 Peter 3. This whole chapter is relevant to what we are studying about concerning the last days and the coming of the Lord for His believers. There are three sections very relevant to what I am saying here. The first is found in 2 Peter 3:3-4: *Knowing this first, that there shall come in the last days scoffers, walking after their own lusts, and saying, where is the promise of his coming? For since the fathers fell asleep, all things continue as they were from the beginning of creation.* **Think about what this verse is saying. Scoffers are taunting believers by saying, "Where is the promise of His coming?" Why would scoffers be saying this? It makes sense to me that when the Great Tribulation starts, the seals are being opened, and the Rapture has not happened, then scoffers and unbelievers will taunt the saints and say, "I thought all you saints were going to disappear and leave us behind, but it appears as if you have been left behind!"**

At this time, Christians will be looking for answers as to why the Rapture has not taken place. As you read further in this chapter, the Lord gives us the answer as to why we are to wait and why He has not yet come back for us. Read 2 Peter 3:9 (KJV): *The Lord is not slack concerning his promise as some men count slackness; but is long-suffering to us-ward, not willing that any should perish, but that all should come to repentance.* Think about what this verse is saying: *The Lord is not slack concerning his promise...* If you read this chapter and the verses on both sides of this verse, you will see he is talking about the promise of His return. **Why would men say the Lord is slack concerning His promise? I believe it is because when the Rapture does not happen according to OUR interpretation of God's Word, we will be complaining to God and asking Him why He has not come to take us out of here.** Then the Lord gives us the answer in this same verse. He goes on to say, *The Lord is long-suffering to us-ward, not willing that any should perish, but that all should come to repentance.* **Can it be said any more plainly? The Lord wants to hold off His coming for His bride, the church, or saints until as many as will accept Him do and are saved.**

If we are in God's army and we have been given the Great Commission to preach the

Gospel to the world, why would God want to take His army home when the greatest opportunity to win the lost will be during this time? I believe the doctrine of the pre-tribulation Rapture that says, "If you are not ready, one of these days you will be left behind" is a doctrine born by the nature of man. This doctrine would say, "If you do not accept Christ and live right, you will regret it and be left behind." I believe the nature of God, who so loved the world that He gave His only Son so that we could be saved, is a God of grace and love. He is not willing that any should perish. His desire is that all who will, would come to the knowledge of the truth.

If we read further in 2 Peter 3, we see a warning that we need to interpret the Scriptures carefully, or we might make some serious mistakes in establishing our belief system. Read 2 Peter 3:16 (KJV): *As also in all his epistles, speaking in them of things; in which are some things hard to be understood, which they that are unlearned and unstable wrest, as they do also the other Scriptures, unto their own destruction.* This verse tells us that all the epistles or books of the Bible have things which are difficult to understand. In this chapter, Peter has been talking of the Lord's return; so its immediate meaning is that it is hard to understand the meaning of the Word of God concerning the coming of the Lord.

2 Peter 3:16 goes on to say there are those who wrest or interpret the scriptures unto their own destruction. I believe when the saints realize the Rapture is not happening before the tribulation period, confusion will reign, and it will be a destructive event to the church. Many will believe God has abandoned them, and many will fall away from God as warned in 2 Thessalonians 2:1-3 (KJV): *Now we beseech you, brethren, by the coming of our Lord Jesus Christ, and our gathering together unto him, that ye be not soon troubled, neither by spirit, nor by word, nor by letter as from us, as that the day of the Lord is at hand. Let no man deceive you by any means; for that day shall not come, except there come a falling away first, and that man of sin be revealed, the son of perdition.* Can it be said any clearer? The gathering together unto Him is talking about the Rapture. It plainly says this event will not happen until a falling away happens, an event where many saints turn away from God. These verses state that the man of sin, or the antichrist, must first be revealed. This means the Rapture cannot happen until the antichrist is revealed. Yet, I hear it being taught by ministers of the pre-tribulation persuasion, "If you see the antichrist show up, then you have been left behind."

After recently studying the book of Zechariah, much of which concerns the Second Coming of the Lord, I noticed a reference to the prophets who were ashamed of what they had taught. They had been speaking and teaching as if their words were God's Words. Zechariah 13:4-5a: *On that day every prophet will be ashamed of his prophetic vision. He will say, "I am not a prophet."*

To be a teacher of God's Word places a great responsibility on the teacher. I write with fear and trembling, praying for God's guidance in preparing this study on the End Times. I fear many teachers have been careless, inferring what they write is, "Thus saith the Lord." I believe when the truth of the End Times is fully revealed, many teachers and prophets will react similarly to these prophets spoken about in Zechariah 13.

In closing, I believe what the Word of God plainly says, and I will not put my trust in any teaching or in a teacher of the Word of God who cannot back up his teaching with the "plain speak" Word of God.

— CHAPTER THIRTEEN —

CAN WE KNOW WHEN THE LORD IS ACTUALLY COMING?

I do not believe we can know when Christ will return at this time, but I believe once a series of events begins to happen, we can start to figure things out. In Matthew 24:36 it says, *No one knows about that day or hour...* This is the verse that is often quoted to reinforce that **no man knows when the Lord will return. The Bible says,** *No man knows about that day or hour...* **of His return, but it** does not say that we would not know the year.

Look at 1 Thessalonians 5:1-6: *Now brothers about times and dates, we do not need to write you, for you know very well that the day of the Lord will come like a thief in the night. While people are saying, "Peace and safety," destruction will come on them suddenly, as labor pains on a pregnant woman, and they will not escape.* **(Don't stop reading here like many who quote this verse, but read on.)** *But you brothers are not in darkness so that this day should surprise you like a thief. You are all sons of the light and sons of the day. We do not belong to the night or to the darkness, so then let us not be like others who are asleep, but let us be alert and self-controlled.* If I am reading this correctly, the lost and those who are spiritually asleep will not recognize it is getting close to the time for the coming of the Lord. Christians who are awake and watching will see it coming, not the day or the hour, but I believe we will know that this is the time, once it is about to happen!

Let me show you why I believe this. We have all heard the story of Noah. He was told to build an ark and get ready for God's judgment. He worked on the ark for about one hundred years. I imagine he took a lot of ridicule. Imagine hearing something like, "You are as slow as the Second Coming," except they were waiting for the flood. Well, Noah did not know exactly when the flood was coming; he just knew he had to get ready. When he finished the ark, he still did not know the day or the hour of God's judgment, but he was ready. Then something happened that tipped Noah off that the Day of Judgment was at hand. When the animals all started showing up and started filling the ark, this began a chain of events that let Noah know this was the year of the judgment of God. Once the ark was fully loaded with the animals, it was time for the rain.

The Bible says in Matthew 24:36-39: *No one knows about that day or hour, not even the angels in heaven, nor the Son, but only the Father. As it was in the days of Noah, so will it be at the coming of the Son of Man. For in the days before the flood, people were eating and drinking, marrying and giving in marriage, up to the day Noah entered the ark.* This verse is not talking about Noah and his family. This verse is talking about those living in Noah's time that had rejected the Word of God through Noah's preaching. The unrepentant knew nothing about what would happen until the flood came and took them all away. That is how it will be at the coming of the Son of Man. If we go back and read Matthew 24:39-42, it is saying both the sinner and God's people will be going about their day. Then, the Word of God warns the Christian in verse 42 to keep watch, so when the Lord returns, they will not be caught off-guard. Likewise, the owner of a home, if he knew a burglar was coming, would be waiting for him and not be caught off-guard.

Take a close look at this. It says no one knows the day or the hour, but it does not say one will not know the year. As I mentioned before, Noah knew something was up; he was not getting caught unprepared. He knew it was the time of God's judgment because God sent the animals to be loaded into the ark. Yet, when you read one book written by an international preacher who has written many books on the End Times, he quotes this scripture as saying, "...no man knows the day or the hour or the year..." This is not what the Bible says. It is sad that many Christians have been confused by teachers who are promoting a belief by distorting the real meaning of God's Word.

If we study the opening of the seals in Revelation 6, we see that the first seal concerns the coming of the antichrist. When we see the events described in chapter six, it is as if we are starting a time-clock to the seven years of the Great Tribulation. The Bible teaches that once the antichrist comes to power, he will soon after this make a seven-year peace pact with the nation of Israel. The beginning of this seven years of peace is probably a more accurate time for the start of the Great Tribulation.

The Great Tribulation is described in the book of Daniel in the Old Testament as Daniel's seventieth week. Historically, Daniel's seventy weeks were seventy weeks of years. These years were described in great detail, and history shows all were fulfilled except the last week of years, or the seven year period that is referred to as the Great Tribulation. This seven-year period is laid out in the Bible with great detail. Some events are being described as happening within days from the start of this last seven year period, leading up to the coming of the Lord.

The following point needs to be explained to some who may be confused about the coming of the Lord. The actual coming of the Lord will happen when Jesus Christ returns upon the earth. He literally comes down to the Mount of Olives at the end of the Great Tribulation. There are references to the day of the Lord as being the day of the Rapture. This is illustrated in 1 Thessalonians 5:2-3: *The day of the Lord will come like a thief in the night.* The Bible bears out the event of Christ's coming in the Rapture. The Rapture will not catch us, who are waiting and watching, by surprise like a thief, **but only those who are not watching and ready will be surprised. They will be caught unprepared, and Christ's coming will be like a thief in the night for them.**

STUDY POINT: Read Revelation 3:2-3 (KJV): *Be watchful and strengthen the things which remain, that are ready to die. For I have not found thy works perfect before God. Remember therefore how thou received and heard, and hold fast and repent. If therefore thou shalt not watch, I will come on thee as a thief, and thou shalt not know what hour I will come upon you.* **This verse is referring to those __not__ ready for Christ's return.** To them, Christ's return is coming as a thief in the night.

STUDY POINT: Read 1 Thessalonians 5:1-6: *Now brothers, about times and dates, we do not need to write to you. For you know very well that the day of the Lord will come like a thief in the night. While people are saying, "Peace and safety," destruction will come on them suddenly, as labor pains on a pregnant woman, and they will not escape.* ***But you, brothers, are not in darkness so that day should surprise you like*** *a thief. You are all sons of the light and sons of the day. We do not belong to the night or the darkness. So then, let us not be like others, who are asleep, but let us be alert and self-controlled.*

The key point to these scripture verses is verse four above, ***But you brothers, are not in darkness so that this day should surprise you like a thief.*** Verse six really nails it: *Let us not be like others, who are asleep, but let us be alert.* The Bible clearly tells us to be alert, watching and waiting for those last day events to unfold. Matthew 24:33 says, *Even so, when you see all these things, you know that it is near, right at the door.* Think about this verse. If we have to wait for these things to happen, it is not imminent, but once they have happened, then it will be imminent. So you ask, what are these things for which we are to wait? Earlier, I explained how the antichrist has to appear first; therefore, this verse above is talking about other things that must happen. What are those things?

Go back up a few verses to Matthew 24:29-31: ***Immediately after the distress of those days***, *the sun will be darkened, the moon will not give its light; the stars will fall from the sky, and the heavenly bodies will be shaken.* These verses give a list of things that will happen after the distress of those days. What is the distress of those days that happens before these other things can happen? If you remember, in chapter seven on the coming antichrist, I showed that before the antichrist can come to power, the ten-region one-world government must be in place. And before all the governments of the world will give up their independence, including the United States, we will experience some sort of event that will cause a global economic meltdown. This event will set the stage for the nations of the world to do whatever it requires to bring back order to our world. When the economies of the world collapse, this will certainly be some of the distress of those days.

The Bible also talks about birth pains coming before the return of the Lord. Signs of these birth pains include the increase of many natural disasters around the world, particularly some of the severest earthquakes of modern times in addition to other natural disasters will certainly add to the distress of those days.

As I was reviewing my chapter called, "A Possible Scenario Story Leading Up to the Rapture," a truth about the coming antichrist and his desecration of the temple jumped out at me. I saw that before the Rapture can take place, the temple has to be

Chapter Thirteen: Can We Know When the Lord is Actually Coming?

rebuilt. I could not believe what I saw in God's Word, but it is there. The rebuilding of the temple is just another sign of Christ's return.

In closing this point, I believe we need to be watching and waiting for these events and preparing for what will happen before this time. I believe these events will shake up our world, and before the Rapture, we will see the greatest revival the world has ever seen! These will be trying days, and we need to be ready to share the gospel with the lost who will be coming back to God and turning to Christians, looking for answers to what is happening in our world. If we realize the Lord's coming is soon, we can prepare to reach out to the lost and even to the Christians who are confused and offer them hope and assistance during these troubling times.

Concerning our knowledge of the year of the Lord's return, I would like to share a thought I have had for some time. I wonder if maybe we can look forward to a window of a few years that would make sense for the time-clock of the Tribulation to start ticking. I mentioned at the beginning of this section that I do not believe we can know the year of Christ's return at this time, but if we study the sixth chapter of Revelation regarding the opening of the seals, we will realize these seals mark the beginning of the Great Tribulation. Once the antichrist brokers a seven-year peace with Israel and the Middle East, a seven-year timetable begins, and from thereon in, until the return of Christ to rule and reign on the earth, every event will happen in an orderly, timed, and predictable manner.

For more than one hundred years, people have tried to predict the return of the Lord and have been wrong. I recently heard a pastor say everything has happened, and the Rapture should be upon us any time now. This statement has been worn out, and when the church hears this, they do not even blink. Think about this. If the Rapture was going to happen on a certain month in two years, and you knew that month, it would change your life because suddenly your retirement would not be as important anymore. In fact, a lot of the things we look at as important would suddenly not matter. The most important thing would be telling your friends and family about the coming of the Lord! However, because Christ's return is a big generational question mark, we do not even give this event much thought.

Back in the late eighties, a Christian sect posted billboards and wrote tracts entitled "88 Reasons Why Christ Will Return in '88." They spread them everywhere. They were so convinced it would happen that they sold everything they had and prepared for the coming of the Lord; some sold their homes and used the money to get the word out. Some had their pets put to sleep so that they would not starve when the Rapture occurred. When the Lord did not return as they expected, they were quite embarrassed and scattered to many different churches, starting their Christian lives over again. I am sharing this because I want to talk about one of the points this group and others have used in error to predict the year of the Lord's coming.

Matthew 24:32 talks about the fig tree and the unfolding of end-time events. Many believe this is referring to the rebirth of the nation of Israel. This verse goes on to say, *When you see these things; you know the Lord's coming is near, right at the door.* Matthew 24:34 further states, *I tell you the truth, this generation will certainly not pass away until all these things have happened.* This sect of Christians and many other prophetic teachers over the years have believed the length of a generation, which would not pass away until all these things happened, was the forty-year generation spoken of in the Old Testament. That generation died in the desert after forty years. When you consider that Israel was reborn as a nation in 1948 and add the forty year wilderness generation, this would add up to 1988. There is a real problem with using the forty-year generation in the wilderness because this was a generation under the judgment of God. This story in the Old Testament says those who were under twenty years old were not held accountable for the sins and decisions of their parents. They were not under judgment. But if you were twenty-one years old, in forty years you would die. Think about this: all those who were twenty-one years old in the wilderness would only live to be sixty-one years old. They would die young because their generation was under judgment.

The Bible says it has been accounted to man to live seventy years or more if he is strong. You see, the Bible tells us a generation is not forty but seventy years. If you take the forty years in the wilderness and add in the twenty years for the young who did not have to die, then add in the ten years for those who were sixty and died young, you are now back to the seventy-year generation or lifespan that God said we would live. If you now take the seventy years and add this to 1948, you have 2018. If this Christian sect that believed Christ was coming in 1988 had redone their calculations, it would have been 2018, based on a 70-year generation, but they were thirty years off.

I realize even if these calculations have merit, God does not have to hold to seventy years. The generation could be based on the fact that some live beyond seventy years. This would put things off to a future date. I really hope we have more time to get ready for the beginning of the Great Tribulation. Yet, if during the seven years of the Great Tribulation God is doing everything in a predictable and timely manner, it would make sense to me that He could use the seventy-year generation for the time frame leading to the return of Christ. In the next chapter, I will show many coming events that fit into this coming window of time, illustrating how close we really could be to our Lord's return.

— CHAPTER FOURTEEN —

THE WINDOW OF
THE LORD'S RETURN

In this chapter, the thought I would like to explore concerns the prediction of the Lord's return or the start of the Great Tribulation coming during an eight-year window of time from 2012-2020. As we approach the Lord's return, it may be possible to narrow the time down as we see the Great Tribulation actually getting started.

The Bible has predicted the rebirth of Israel along with other events, and one Bible prophecy says that when we see Israel reborn, that generation would not pass away until the return of Christ. I did a study on the rebirth of Israel, showing why 1948 was the fulfillment of the rebirth of Israel, an event predicted in both the Old and New Testaments. In 1948, a window of the Lord's return was opened that was seventy to eighty years wide, the time of a generation. Sixty-four years of that window have been used. The Bible says, *No man knows about that day or the hour of the Lord's return.* However, the Bible also says in Luke 21:25-28, *There will be signs in the sun, moon and stars, on the earth, nations will be in anguish and perplexity at the roaring and tossing of the sea, men will faint from terror, apprehensive of what is coming on the world, for heavenly bodies will be shaken.* **At that time** *they will see the Son of Man coming on a cloud with power and great glory. When these things begin to take place, stand up and lift up your heads, because your redemption is drawing near.*

What is interesting is the number of events of a prophetic nature I have listed in the following pages that are falling into this window of time, 2012 - 2020. Below, I will cover this list of coming events that either are happening or could happen during this window of time.

1. You have heard about the "2012" event that has been in the news about the Mayan calendar. The news media has said the Mayan calendar is predicting the end of the world. After some research, it turns out the calendar is just coming to its end and will reset to start again. Some are trying to say it is tied to solar events that coincide with the ending date of this calendar, but most who have studied this say the Mayans could not have known about these events.

We know as Christians, the world could not come to an end in 2012, for the Bible says there will be one thousand years of peace on the earth after the return of the Lord. If you have watched the movie that was released recently, called, *2012*, it could really put the fear of God in people. Is it not strange that people will believe something like this, but they will not believe the Bible? I believe, as we get closer to this date, many people will be living in great fear. I believe people will take similar steps to what happened as the calendar approached the year 2000, causing the Y2K scare.

If these same people would read the Bible, they would realize it is the coming of the Lord for which they need to be ready. If you read about the last plague that God will pour out on the earth, the last of the bowl judgments, you will see what God has in store as His wrath in judgment for man's wickedness is far worse than what is depicted in the movie *2012*.

Read Revelation 16:17-21: *The seventh angel poured out his bowl into the air, and out of the temple came a loud voice from the throne, saying, 'It is done.' Then there were flashes of lightning, rumblings, peals of thunder and a severe earthquake. No earthquake like it has ever occurred since man has been on the earth, so tremendous was the quake. The great city split into three parts, and the cities of the nations collapsed. God remembered Babylon the Great and gave her the cup filled with the wine of the fury of his wrath. Every island fled away and the mountains could not be found. From the sky huge hailstones of about a hundred pounds each, fell upon men. And they cursed God.*

If you look at what is described in these verses, you will see it describes the worst earthquake of all time, a quake literally being felt around the world! One great city, that some believe is Babylon, will be split into three parts. The cities of the nations will collapse. Imagine the skyscrapers of every city falling at the same time. Look at what happened to the city of Port de Prince in Haiti. Imagine this happening to cities around the world at the same time. Everyone would be on their own; the death toll would be in the millions. These verses go on to say that every island fled away. If you think about it, most of the islands are volcanic in origin and occur where there are weaknesses in the earth's crust, often where the tectonic plates of the earth come together. This earthquake, which God will use as part of His wrath on the earth, will be so severe that it will be as if every continental plate on the earth is moved out of place at the same time. It goes on to say the islands and the mountains will disappear. Islands are just underwater mountains anyway. This seems impossible; but the truth is if a quake is severe enough and the shaking lasts long enough, it causes the earth to turn into almost a liquid state. Buildings can actually sink into the ground. What is described here does not even mention what will happen with the tidal waves which will be generated by these quakes happening around the world. These tidal waves may have a part in causing the islands of the earth to disappear, almost like being washed off the map.

After this happens, the Bible says the hail will come. The King James Version of the Bible says these hailstones will weigh a talent apiece or about 125 pounds. These will be like bombs falling from heaven. Buildings not destroyed in the quake will be destroyed if hit with these hailstones. Yet the Bible says man will curse God. How can you curse a God you do not believe exists? Well, the truth is, man knows there is a God; they just do not want to obey Him. When God is done, man will have been given every opportunity to repent and will be without excuse when he stands before God on the Judgment Day.

2. A friend sent me a link to a site on the internet that talks about the return of the Lord happening in 2017 based on the year of Jubilee. The year of Jubilee is being calculated to have occurred in 1917, the year England made a decree that the Jews would regain their homeland. Fifty years later in 1967, after winning the Six Day War, Israel regained the city of Jerusalem and other lands that were part of Israel during the time of the Old Testament. The next year of Jubilee will be 2017. By the calculations of some scholars, this is the one hundred and twentieth Year of Jubilee or six thousand years since the creation of man. This would then lead into the one thousand years of peace that will happen after the Lord's Return during the

Millennium. Again, this prediction falls into the 2012-2020 window.

3. Solar Flares: There are scientists predicting the next solar maximum will occur in 2012 and 2013. I did extensive research on this, and one article I read said scientists have recently had growing concerns since the National Research Council gave a report, funded by NASA and issued by the National Academy of Sciences, entitled, "Severe Space Weather Events." Scientists were concerned there could be a repeat of the eight-day event that hit America in 1859 called the "Carrington Effect." This was a large solar flare accompanied by a coronal mass ejection, or CME, that threw billions of tons of solar plasma onto the earth's magnetic field, disrupting the early electronics of its day. It basically burned out our telegraph system, even setting some telegraph offices on fire. In more recent years, on March 13, 1989, six million people lost power in Quebec, Canada, after a huge solar flare caused a surge from ground induced currents that turned the lights out for a day. Again, in 2003, it was said we missed the big one, but the solar storm caused satellites to fail, blackouts to occur, and some planes to be re-routed.

These solar storms occur about every eleven years. The next cycle should peak in late 2012 and early 2013. Scientists say a perfectly aligned solar flare could so affect our modern electronics it could take out our way of life for months. A top official from the European Space Agency, space weather-head Mike Hapgood, said, "I don't think the National Academy of Sciences report is scare mongering." He went on to say, "Scientists are conservative by nature, and this group is really thoughtful." He also said, "The NASA report is a fair and balanced report."

On the flip-side of the coin, we have another voice saying the earth is actually very well-protected even if some satellites may not be. One report said when the earth is hit with a solar flare, the alignment of our magnetic field in relation to the sun is affected. Given the right conditions, solar flares could slide past the earth. Even if we do get hit with the big one, solar flares do not create an extinction event.

4. I was recently watching Perry Stone preach a message called, "Cosmic Prophecies in the Sun, Moon, and Stars." He was saying cosmic activity coming on the earth would be announcing the Lord's return. Giving these verses to back up this thought (Revelation 6:12-13, Matthew 24:29, and Joel 3:15), Perry Stone went on to say a certain kind of lunar eclipse will give a blood-red moon effect. He continued by saying these lunar events have coincided with Jewish festivals and with many events that have happened to the nation of Israel in its past history. In closing, he went on to say the eighth time one of these blood-red moon solar events will occur is 2014-2015. Without actually saying it, he was giving the impression that the predicted events of the book of Revelation could be tied to the events on these dates. Again, another prediction of end-time events is happening in the window of 2012-2020.

5. Are we headed for a world economic collapse? While economic leaders are trying to convince the public we have hit bottom and things will be improving shortly, many are not buying this. When the Great Depression hit America and the world in 1929, no one knew it would become so severe until it did. When it looked like things would improve, the next shoe would drop. It basically took four years for the Great Depression to hit bottom in 1933, and it remained there until the Second World War. If we are following the same track, we may not hit bottom until 2012 or 2013. It could even take longer for this depression to hit bottom because we currently have programs in place which take away the sting of a depression for the unemployed. These programs were not in place in the 1930's: welfare, food stamps, and unemployment compensation, to name a few.

We are currently printing and spending money like there is no tomorrow. Many states have run out of the money that is used to pay the unemployed. The longer we postpone hitting the bottom in this economic downturn, the harder we will hit, and the longer it will take to recover. I believe a world economic collapse is irreversible, and I believe the timing of this horrible event will fall in this window of time, 2012-2020. I believe this event will lead to a one-world government.

I was reading a book by David Wilkerson called *The Vision*, written in 1974. So much of what was shared in this book has come to pass, and in light of current events, there was a page in his book that really caught my attention. From page 99, "...the United States of the World is just a world depression away. A collapse of the world monetary system could lead to a world government headed by a global dictator." The premier of Belgium recently said, "The method of international committees has failed. What we need is a person of the highest order of experience, of great authority, of wide influence, of great energy, either a civilian or a military man, no matter what his nationality, who will cut all the red tape, shove all the committees out of the way, wake up all the people, and galvanize all governments into action. Let it come quickly…World anarchy and confusion can ripen this world for an antichrist dictator who will come in the name of peace to end the desperation and lawlessness that will abound."

More than ever, I see the stage is set for a world economic collapse. I believe the economies of the world are so fragile today that it will take very little to trigger a panic that will ripple into an economic collapse around the world. Again, I believe this event could very well happen in the 2012 – 2020 window of time.

6. Another coming event that can play an important role in the prophetic calendar will be the next presidential election in 2012. I am well aware that the printing of this edition will occur after the election of 2012. I have chosen to include these statements and insights in future print runs because I believe these insights may be helpful in our understanding the unfolding of events leading up to the coming of Christ.

It is generally accepted the current administration is trying its hardest to bring the United States into socialism, and this is only one step away from making a move to join the one-world government. The current presidential administration's success with this agenda is very important. The polls are saying this president's agenda is not getting the support it needs to complete his plan, so the question arises whether the president can win re-election in 2012. If he were to lose this next election, the plan to bring America into the fold of socialism and to join a one-world government could be set back for many years.

I have a gut feeling we are approaching the time of the Lord's return, and if everything is coming together, then the question I have is whether this current administration can be taken out of office in 2012. You probably know that a few years ago executive orders were signed into law, by a previous administration, which gives the sitting president certain rights during a time of national emergency. If this is true and if America were thrown into a national emergency situation, the president, without congressional approval, could declare martial law, suspend the rights guaranteed under the Constitution, and delay a national election until things return to normal. I believe if we really are approaching the time-table for the setting up of the one-world government and the system of the antichrist, there will be no stopping these events from happening. I believe a terrorist or an event of nature could happen to allow the current administration to stay in power under these executive orders.

As we are approaching the presidential election, I see three different choices on how this election could play out. I believe that if the president has a prophetic destiny and has to stay in office, somehow he will. So my first imagined scenario involves a terrorist attack on America just before the election which causes the election to be canceled by executive order, thus allowing our current president to stay in office.

Now that we are actually approaching the election, I see the **second** option being the reelection of our president, as a real possibility. Our current president has so many entitlement programs that most who are the recipients of these programs will try to reelect our current president to keep a free lunch on the table.

The third option is that our current president loses the election, but with the current state of the Union, we could be in such a bind that it would not matter who wins the election. The damage to our economy is already done and we are still facing the strong possibility of an economic collapse.

How would each of these three scenarios affect the Lord's coming in my projected window? The first option, a terrorist attack, would be the worst possible scenario. If this scenario happened just before the election, life as we know it will come crashing down in just a matter of weeks. It would cause widespread panic and would not leave the church any time to prepare for what is coming.

The second option involves the reelection of our current president. This could have the positive effect of alerting the church, that in spite of all our prayers and efforts, we could not stop this from happening. It is my prayer that this scenario would wake up the church, and we would have time, before the coming economic collapse to get prepared for these last days and for the harvest of souls. Realize that for us to have a part in this coming harvest, we must be prepared.

The third option would involve our current president losing the election. This option would really surprise me. A new president may be able to slow things down, but I don't believe the coming economic collapse can be stopped. Pat Robertson recently said, he believes we will see a change in presidents, but it will be like changing pilots when the jet is in a nose dive. The real downside to this third option would be that Christians and conservatives would think that we have dodged the bullet, and this could lull the church into thinking that the good old days are coming back. The church would be lulled into a sleep mode that would cause it to be unprepared for what is ahead. Again this coming election is falling into the window of 2012 - 2020.

I am not a prophet, but God has given me insights from His Word. About three weeks before the presidential election of 2012, I was talking to a close friend from Montana about the election, and we were discussing how the polls and current momentum was pointing to Romney winning the election. I had heard a conservative talk show host say that the Gallup Poll numbers had reversed, giving Romney the lead of 51 % to Obama's 45%. He went on to say that no candidate for President in recent years has ever lost with this strong a poll number at this stage of the race. He went on to suggest that for Obama to win, it would almost take stealing the election.

As I was talking to my friend that night, Chuck asked me, "If Romney wins this election can the time line of your book still be right?" I told Chuck that no matter the outcome of this election, we are still facing two imminent events that will thrust the US and the world into the seven last years before Christ's Return. They are as follows:

1. The economies of the world are hanging over a cliff, and Romney will not be able to stop this from happening. In fact, he could help speed up the coming collapse. It is already being said that banks will start lending more money if Romney wins. If a recovery starts and the velocity of money increases, it will force interest rates to go up. This increase in borrowing costs will hurt everyone and increase the payments on our national debt to a level that cannot be serviced.

2. The hot bed in Israel is not going to go away. I have been saying that an all-out war cannot breakout until after the antichrist arrives, and he will arrive in time to stop it by establishing a seven year peace treaty between Israel and the Middle East. Now, it is being said that Israel will not attack Iran until Romney gets elected, and Iran is said to have made gestures of talks to stall for time. Iran needs to have a nuclear capability before they take on Israel.

This being said, I told my friend Chuck there are four reasons why I don't believe Romney can win this election:

1. If Romney wins, he will be the President when events in Israel explode. When the last days wars that the Bible has predicted take place, Israel has to be standing alone.

Only Obama fits the bill as a President that will pull back his support for Israel. If Romney wins this election and he were to intervene, this could start World War III, as Russia has warned us that America better not attack Iran.

2. If Romney wins this election, he will be president when the economies of the world collapse, and he is too patriotic to sell the United States out to a One World Government. We know that Obama will sell America out in a heartbeat. I believe the evidence is there that Obama is in favor of a One World Government.

3. If Romney wins this election, a coming economic collapse will lead to food shortages and food rationing. Since Romney is a Mormon he would never allow the enforcing of laws that would make it a crime to have stored food. We know that Obama would not have a problem with this at all, as he believes in taking from the haves and giving to the have not's.

4. If Romney wins this election, the church will breathe a sigh of relief, believing that happier days are on the way, and the church will stay in its slumber. Then when things collapse without warning, there will not be time left for the church to get ready.

It is interesting that the figures for campaign contributions for September came out saying that Obama had 180 plus million dollars given to his campaign compared to Romney's 70 plus million dollars. If an election could ever be set up for being bought, this could be the one.

As we approached the election, I wondered about its outcome. I was considering putting my analysis on why Romney could not win this election in my book. I was talking to my Publisher about adding these thoughts to my book and he said "you can do what you want but let's talk about it this afternoon, because I don't want you to put things in your book that will date it and cause it to become irrelevant".

As I was waiting for the publisher to call me back, I was questioning God, asking if my book would become irrelevant. I thought I should spend some time in prayer and reading the Bible. After some time in prayer, I was getting ready to read my Bible and I said, "Lord, I sure wish I knew what was going on. I know you called me to write this book. Will my book become irrelevant?". Then I said to the Lord, "It would sure be nice if you would speak to me with a special word. It would be nice if I could just open my Bible, and you would show me a special verse that would tell me what is going on.", however I then said, "Lord I know that it is not right for me to ask for that kind of favor, so I won't ask". But when I opened my Bible it opened to Ezekiel 30. I read the first 3 verses and it seemed the Lord had a Word for me anyway. Below are the first three verses I read from Ezekiel 30: 1-3. *"The Word of the Lord came to me: Son of man, prophesy and say; this is what the Sovereign Lord says; Wail and say, "Alas for that day! for the day is near, the day of the Lord is near-- A day of clouds, a time of doom for the nations."* When I read this, it was as if God appeared in my office and answered my prayer, telling me that the day of the Lord is near, and my book would not become irrelevant. This was three days before the election, and I knew that no matter the outcome of the election, God's outcome and the timing of his coming will not be changed.

7. I have given much thought as to whether or not I should include this next event in my book. I initially had a hard time getting good info on this topic until I recently watched a study on television. It was entitled "The Prophecies of the Popes." The program was taught by a highly respected Bible teacher. I have since decided to include this topic in my book, and time will tell if I made a wise choice.

In the twelfth century a Catholic bishop named Saint Malachy, who lived in Ireland, was summoned to Rome. While staying in Rome, it was reported that he had a vision of the future popes. The teacher who presented this study emphasized that these prophecies are certainly not equal to the prophecies of the Bible. Bishop Malachy made predictions concerning all the popes in the future, leading up to the time of Christ's return. This document was lost for three centuries in the Vatican archives, but since its discovery in the fifteenth century, those predictions have been seen to be quite accurate. Saint Malachy predicted that there would be two hundred and sixty-eight popes. The current pope, Pope Benedict, is the two hundred and sixty-seventh. He is in his eighties, and he could easily pass away during the 2012-2020 window of time. Most interesting are the predictions concerning the two hundred and sixty-eighth pope, the last pope before the return of Christ. It was predicted that he would be known as "Peter the Roman," and this last pope would work with the antichrist. I do not really know what part the pope is to play concerning the antichrist. I know there is one called the false prophet who will work with the antichrist. Could this be the pope? Time will tell.

8. Another event I touched on earlier in this paper that I believe is worthy of being included in the list of events that can fall into the window of 2012 – 2020 is the next big hit on America by Muslim terrorists. I already mentioned the Hiroshima project in which terrorists are planning to set off nuclear bombs in several cities in America at the same time. I hope this never happens, but it is a real threat. Our leaders have warned us it is not a question of *if* but a matter of *when* the next big hit will strike America. In 1993, terrorists attempted to bomb the World Trade Center. They did not succeed, but did they give up? NO! Eight years later they succeeded. It has been nine years since the 911 attack, and they are past due to strike us again. Terrorist groups are constantly feeding us false chatter to keep us spending money on security. Another big hit could easily happen in the next few years, and if that terrorist hit comes while our economy is fragile, it could have a devastating effect on our country and the economies of the world.

9. This next event is one that keeps coming to mind, and I realize I should share my thoughts. It is 2012, and war between the Middle East and Israel has never been more pending in decades. The leader of Iran, Mahmoud Ahmadinejad, is pressing to gain nuclear weapons. He recently addressed the General Assembly of the United Nations and stated that Israel has no roots in the Middle East, and Israel will be eliminated. Another leader in Iran has stated that Israel will be destroyed by the end of 2013. Many believe that Iran will have nuclear bomb capabilities by 2013.

I have been hearing many prophetic teachers saying that the war of Gog and Magog is imminent. I do not agree.

The War of Gog and Magog would mean an all-out assault on Israel with the massive Russian Army assisting the countries of the Middle East. I do not believe the war of Gog and Magog can happen until the middle of the Great Tribulation. I will explain my reasoning, and you can decide if it makes sense or not.

We need to remember that the Bible has predicted that Israel will be granted a seven-year peace pact that is set up by the antichrist. This event cannot happen until after the one-world government is put into place. I show this from God's Word in my chapter on the "Coming Antichrist" when I state, "The antichrist cannot come to power until the one-world government is in place." Our current president (in 2012) has already said that the United States will not get involved if Israel goes to war with

Iran. Russia, an affirmed ally of Iran, has said that if the United States attacks Iran, they will look on it as an attack on Russia. This would start World War 3.

The countries of the Middle East are well armed with artillery, missiles, and weapons they have not had in past wars with Israel. This convinces me that if a war breaks out now with the United States saying that we will not interfere or help Israel, then this war would be stacked against Israel. With this little nation left alone and cut off from help, it would literally take the intervention of God to stop Israel from being wiped off the map. The Bible says that when the war of Gog and Magog happens God will not only defeat the enemies of Israel, but he will reveal his greatness to the nations of the world.

Read Ezekiel 38:21-22: *I will summon a sword against Gog on all my mountains, declares the Lord. Every man's sword will be against his brother. I will execute judgment upon him with plague and bloodshed; I will pour down torrents of rain, hailstones, and burning sulfur on him and on his troops and on many nations with him. And so I will show my greatness and my holiness, and I will make myself known in the sight of many nations. Then they will know that I am the Lord.*

Now I will explain why this battle cannot happen until around the middle of the Great Tribulation, after the antichrist has made a seven-year peace with Israel. This will cause Israel to put their guard down and rebuild their temple. If this battle happens now before the antichrist shows up, God will have to intervene and the outcome of the battle will open the eyes of Israel and the nations of the world to the fact that God is real, and he will not let harm come to Israel. God's intervention will be proof positive that he will watch the back of Israel. Once God shows himself to Israel in this manner, they will not need to accept a peace covenant with the antichrist because it will be shown that God would not allow Israel to be defeated.

This being said, I believe, if an armed conflict happens, it will be minor and contained. Somehow it will not escalate into a full-blown war. It might take Israel using a nuclear bomb on a single target in the Middle East to convince the rest of the Middle East that a war at this time would be too costly. The bottom line is that the hot bed of the Middle East cannot be put off much longer. The antichrist must show up in the next few years in order to stop this war from happening outside of the timing of God's prophetic Word. Again, what I have outlined here places this event in my "Window of the Lord's Return 2012-2020."

10. I will include an event that does not have a time prediction with it, but it is believed it could fall into the 2012 -2020 window. What is even more interesting about this event is that it could be part of the preparation for God's plan in the Great Tribulation. This event is the Yellowstone Park "Super Volcano." This event was highlighted recently in the movie, *2012*. Anyone can go online and read more about this possible coming event. After studying this, there seems to be a consensus that Yellowstone is not ready to go any time soon; yet, in January of 2010 the activity level had been increasing dramatically. The Yellowstone volcano's rim is about forty miles across with a magma pool the size of Lake Michigan beneath it.

Scientists have been measuring rises in ground surfaces, and bulges are forming in more than one location. The biggest bulge is forming under Yellowstone Lake. Measurements have shown that it has grown one hundred feet in the last few years. Scientists have estimated that this volcano has erupted every six hundred thousand years, and it is 20,000 years past due. Projections suggest an eruption would be catastrophic to the United States. It would cover most of the country with up to three feet of ash. By comparison, the Mount Saint Helen's crater is about two square miles, but the Yellowstone volcano would create a crater of several hundred square miles!

The last eruption of the Yellowstone volcano is estimated to have spewed over eight thousand times the amount of ash as Mount Saint Helen did in 1980. An eruption would ruin the crops across the farm belt of America. A BBC feature on such volcanoes said that after an eruption, "The sky will darken, black rain will fall, and the earth would be plunged into the equivalent of a nuclear winter." The Cascade Volcano Observatory calls the Yellowstone Caldera "...one of the largest and most active volcanoes in the world today."

The recent eruption of a volcano in Iceland caused extensive disruptions in air travel and caused billions of dollars in damages, threatening to put airline companies out of business. The size of the Icelandic volcano is so small compared to Yellowstone that it would be like comparing a marble to a basketball. If you read the following Bible verse, you will see why I believe this event may be what is being described in the Bible. Read Revelation 6:12: *I watched as he opened the sixth seal. There was a great earthquake. The sun turned black like sackcloth made of goat's hair, the whole moon turned blood red.*

One last thought on the Yellowstone volcano from a quote in *Time* magazine by the geologist Paul Doss, who said, "An eruption could very well happen now, for the simple fact that nobody was around the last time it blew. So nobody knows what the warning signs are. There may be sporadic earthquakes, strange geyser patterns or a lifting of the surface, but nobody really knows."

In addition to these coming events that could be pointing to the return of Christ, there are many other events lining up with the prophecies in the Bible that are signs God has given us to let us know it is time to "look up, for our redemption is drawing near."

In conclusion, in the last few years we have seen the coming together of the European Union, often referred to as the Revived Roman Empire, along with a lot of activity toward establishing a one-world government. As a sidebar to the coming one world-government, much has been happening to bring the United States into this alliance of nations. Laws are being signed that are referred to as international laws, and we, as a free country, are now being told we are bound by these laws. These new international laws will take away the rights we are guaranteed under the Constitution of this country. For some reason, our judges and government leaders are not doing a good job of defending our Constitution which they all swore to defend when they took the oath to serve our nation.

I have mentioned laws and executive orders in this book about which I have given very little backup support. I do not want to be accused of promoting fear and conspiracy theories, but I feel I should name two of these laws that are now on the books and share a few features of each. Research for yourself, to see if what I say is true. Laws are being put in place to allow our government to control the masses. The question is, "Why?" I believe the Bible teaches a global one-world government is inevitable. This leads me to believe that these laws are being put in place to reduce resistance from the people when our government decides to join the coming one-world government. If you research the Patriot Act, you will see that our president can declare a national emergency at his discretion, and during this time of national emergency, it would be a felony to possess more than one week's supply of food. If you control the food supply, you control the people. Also the John Warner Defense Authorization Act (already signed into law) allows the president to declare a national emergency at his sole discretion which would tie the hands of Congress for six months before Congress can challenge this declaration. This law allows the president to take control of the National Guard in each state, without the authorization of the governor of each state, and deploy them as he wills. Do not take my word for it. Look it up.

It has been said a one-world government cannot work without the United States being a part of it. One of the leaders behind the coming one-world government has said if the United States dollar and economy collapses, they are prepared to bail us out under the condition that we will suspend our Constitution and come under the unified laws of the new one-world government.

If I were one who believed in conspiracy theories, it would be easy to believe that steps are being taken to cause the American dollar and our economy to collapse. The truth is, our dollar and our economy are sliding in the wrong direction. We are praying for a turn-around, but many believe the fundamentals of our economy are in such trouble, it is only a matter of time before we will see an economic collapse. The question is how long will it take? Some believe it could take a long time. Our economy is so fragile all it would take is another 911 event or a large natural catastrophe to cause enough panic and economic disruption for a speedy collapse of our economy and the way of life that we have known in America. I believe it will be this type of a scenario that will weaken the resolve of Americans to keep our independence, thus making us willing to give in to the pressure of the new world system that will extend a helping hand to us.

A question I have to ask is, "Are two to eight years enough time to get everything in place for the antichrist to show up and for the Great Tribulation to start and for us to see the Rapture of the saints?" My answer is an absolute "yes!" You see, for the last several years, things have been happening in Europe that had to occur to pave the way for the antichrist. I think the biggest event to happen has been the coming together of the European Common Market and the making of a common currency, the euro. This makes all trade in these countries possible in one common currency. This common currency has been growing in importance over the last several years. In fact, since 2002 to the present time, the value of the euro has grown from being worth only eighty-eight cents to being worth as much as one dollar and fifty-seven cents in U.S. dollars. Recently, the euro has been rising and falling. The key point to realize is the world now has a second trade currency waiting in the wings. Up to the present time, the US dollar has been the currency of choice for world trade. In fact, most oil trade and a lot of international trade are done in US dollars. Some countries do not even have their own currency but trade in US dollars.

In the last few years, the United States has been spending money that we do not have. We have also been buying more goods from other countries than what we are selling to them. This creates a huge world trade imbalance with ramifications many Americans do not understand. The bottom line is that this out-of-control spending, huge trade imbalances, and lowering of the interest rates have made the dollar less appealing as a world trading currency! Currently, most of our trading partners are losing money by holding onto US dollars. If any bad economic event were to happen, like a global recession or another 911 event, our trading partners would be pressured into switching to a new global reserve currency.

With the euro falling at this time, some wonder if the European Union will even survive. I believe there are powers working behind the scenes that will do whatever it takes to insure the survival of the EU and a new one-world currency system. Even if the euro is not the future world currency, I believe, in the end, those who are working behind the scenes will look at America as expendable.

This brings up another huge recent event. Up until now, the countries of the Common Market have been using a common currency, but they have been self-governed. I read an article on the internet in 2008 giving reasons why many countries are not switching to the euro as their trading currency. One reason is because the euro is a currency without a country to back it. If the EU countries were to do what the original thirteen US colonies did in 1776 when they drew up a Constitution and became the United States of America, the world would have a new confidence in this new super power to back up their currency. The United States of Europe under the leadership of one leader would give a huge boost to the up-and-coming strength of the euro as a currency and to this new country as a super power.

In 2008, the countries coming together under the umbrella of the Common Market voted on establishing a single leader to rule over the combined European countries. This vote took place, but it needed a unanimous vote to pass. One nation, Ireland, did delay it for awhile, but a year later everyone signed-on. At first, this new power-block nation was voting on a new leader every six months. Now, even this has changed to a permanent leadership position. Currently, they have one country and one leader, leading a new country of over 500 million people. The euro currency is positioning itself to be the new world currency. This new country is already talking about creating a system that will make their currency system a digital currency system. This would require all of its citizens to have a computer chip implanted in their bodies. The technology is already in place, and they are saying that all the citizens of this newly formed country will have this implant sometime between 2012 and 2017. This is another event falling into the window of 2012-2020!

What we are seeing here is no longer the subject of end-time books and predictions we have heard preached so much for the last fifty years. These events are now coming to pass before our very eyes! We are now headed for the completion of the Revived Roman Empire that the Bible predicted would take place before the Lord returns to rule and reign on the earth. Chapter eight, on "The Coming Antichrist," shows why I believe the new one-world government will be in place before the Great Tribulation starts.

After reading about all these things and the signs of the Lord's return just around the corner, **one can see a perfect storm brewing that can rapidly propel the world into the time called the Great Tribulation. Another way to put this is, we are on a collision course to the return of the Lord, and just like the Titanic was unable to steer clear of the icebergs, we will not be able to avoid the forming of a one-world government, the coming of the antichrist, and the coming of the Lord. These are not events that can be stopped through prayer, but they are events for which we need to be prepared! Now is the time to wake up and do all we can to win our lost friends and family! Jesus is coming soon.**

WHAT COULD TRIGGER THE BEGINNING OF THE GREAT TRIBULATION?

I show in Chapter 11 of my book, "The Window of the Lord's Return" that a global economic collapse will probably be the event that will cause the nations of the world to give up their independence and join a one world government. The trigger event that sets the global economic collapse in motion could come in many different forms.

It could be a natural disaster of the greatest magnitude. Imagine an earthquake hitting the west coast equal to what hit Japan in 2011; it could bankrupt several states and cause a panic on Wall Street that could drag our whole country down.

When America was hit by terrorists on 9/11, it was a time when our economy was strong and we recovered; if we were to get hit today with another 9/11 event or larger, I don't believe with the condition of our economy today that we would recover. If a smaller country in Europe has an economic collapse, this event could trigger panic that could take down all of Europe and ripple to America.

One possible trigger event that came to me recently, is the effect of a national or regional electrical grid collapse. We just experienced an electrical power outage that took out the power to several towns in the area I live in Arizona. It only lasted a few hours, but it happened during critical hours of the day. I was going to the grocery store and it was closed. I was allowed in for other business purposes and I noticed that everyone was scrambling to protect the produce and everything in the coolers. Realize if this outage would have lasted for 24 hours, most of the fresh produce, meats and all the frozen foods would have been ruined.

I was also on my way to the bank and it was closed. I needed to go to the Post Office and it was closed. If a large region of the United States was to see its electrical grid collapse, it would not take long for the effects to ripple across the land. The stores would be closed immediately and if the power was not restored they would not be reopened. What food they had on their shelves would go to the owners and other employees. Banks would be closed and even cash machines would not work to allow you to take out needed cash. Stores and most other businesses cannot do business transactions without power, and massive layoffs would happen in short order.

America has enemies today that are working hard to create the capability to strike America with an EMP bomb, (Electrical Magnetic Pulse) this type of bomb would be nuclear in nature that would be set off high over America. It would not kill many people unless you're flying and it hits the electronics of your airplane. This type of weapon could shut down the electrical grid to a very large region in America. The damage would not only be to the electric grid but it could fry the electronics of automobiles and any appliances and electrical equipment that runs the businesses of this country. Scientists are saying we could see the same result from a solar storm. We are currently at the peak of the 12 year cycles that could cause this type of event.

In 1965 a critical electrical substation on the East Coast blew up and this one substation going down took down the electrical grid of the whole East Coast. What most people do not realize is that our whole electrical grid is made up of hundreds of substations that control the flow of electricity across our country. Each of these substations has large electrical transformers that work to distribute power. These large transformers are custom built to the specific load of that substation and the electrical companies do not have inventories to replace these transformers in the event that this was to happen. My brother in law is one of the top electrical engineers for General Electric. He works in the area of electrical power production. I asked him recently how long it would take to replace a large number of these substation transformers if this event were to happen. He admitted that they do not have replacement stock available and it could take a year or longer to rebuild these critical components. This single event would not happen slowly with a warning to get ready, it would happen without warning and we would be thrown into the dark immediately.

These are just some of the options that could trigger a global economic collapse. **There are other events lining up right now that could trigger this collapse in less than 30 days.** Please do not label me as a fear monger. I believe God wants his saints to be aware of Christ's imminent return and God has given me a trumpet to blow to wake up the church to what is soon coming. **The timing of a global collapse that will propel the world into the Great Tribulation is in the timing of God and not the timing of man.**

Right now there are three countries with their finger on the trigger of a nuclear bomb. The leader of North Korea is crazy enough to pull this trigger; Iran is racing as fast as they can to have this ability to hit Israel with a nuclear bomb. Israel when backed up against a wall will use a nuke to show their enemies that they will protect themselves with nukes if necessary. The Bible says that Damascus will be burned by fire, never to be lived in again. Right now it is Syria that is trying to push Israel up against a wall. Imagine what will happen when any one of these three countries pulls the trigger on a nuclear bomb. Most people will fear that World War Three was about to break out. With these thoughts going through people's minds, what will happen to food and other resources? It will be like a warning that a great snow storm is about to hit, where you see the masses buying up everything in sight to hold them over for 3 or 4 days. Imagine the masses wanting to buy enough food and resources for their families for an indefinite period of time. It will be impossible at that time to get ready for what lies ahead.

— CHAPTER FIFTEEN —

THE NIGHT OF THE BLOOD
MOON, A REVELATION REVEALED

Before I get into the core of this chapter, some may ask, "What is a blood moon? A blood moon is a lunar eclipse, where the earth passes between the sun and the moon. In the process of blocking the light of the sun from hitting the moon, this process causes the moon to take on a reddish tint, thus being called a blood moon. What makes a Tetrad most significant to Bible scholars is the fact that in each of these past tetrads, the four blood moons have all occurred on Jewish holy days.

In just over the last five hundred years there have been three occasions in history where four consecutive lunar eclipses called Tetrads have occurred on these significant dates - 1492, 1949-50 and 1967-68. A fourth Tetrad is currently unfolding in 2014-15. What makes this more significant is the fact that the next Tetrad of four blood moons will be over 400 years from now. What I notice that these events have in common is very interesting.

1. In 1492 when Columbus discovered America, this gave the Jews a place to escape the destruction and persecution from Spain, a future safe haven for the future in America.

2. In 1949-50, the dates following the rebirth of Israel, the people of Israel were given a place where they could go to escape the destruction and death following World War II.

3. Then in 1967-1968, Israel regained land at a time when it appeared they would be destroyed but again, escaped destruction and death at a time of war.

4. 2014-2015, I am seeing a number of possible events that would qualify as the type of events that would follow a Tetrad of four blood moons. These events would follow the last Blood Moon or September 28, 2015, happening in 2016 or 2017

a. I believe current events are set for war in the Middle East, possibly this year or in 2016. This war will be known as the Psalms 83 War. I discuss this in detail in my chapter called the (Five End-Times Wars). This war will look as though Israel will have no chance of victory. I see Israel being backed into a corner and having to use its nuclear bombs to turn the tide of this war, forcing their enemies to cry for peace.

b. A second event, that follows the pattern of events that brings safety to the Jews following a Tetrad of Blood Moons, will be the time when the antichrist has arrived on the scene, and it will be the signing of the 7 Years Peace Treaty in Israel. The timing for Israel to escape the destruction of a pending nuclear war.

c. A third possibility would be the Jews leaving America during a time that our country is seeing the collapse of its economy. They will be leaving to fulfill the prophecy of Revelation 18:4. This verse is leading up to the destruction of Mystery Babylon. I believe the Jews will see the hand-writing on the wall and recognize that leaving America to go to Israel will be their best option. Revelation 18:4 (NIV) *"Then I heard another voice from heaven say: "Come out of her my people, so that you will not share in her sins, so that you will not receive any of her plagues; for her sins are piled up to heaven."*

After further thought, I see how the prophecy from David Wilkerson ties into the coming Blood Moon events. The Blood Moon events from the past have always been one of two types of events, either an event where Israel is spared from annihilation in war like the example of The Six Day War in 1967, that followed a Blood Moon event, or an Exodus from harm as was The Blood Moon events of 1492 and 1949. Both of these Blood Moon events were followed by the Jews going to a place of safety from impending harm. I see much evidence that makes me believe that the event that will follow the second year of Blood Moons in 2015 will be the Jews leaving America after a financial collapse and going to Israel as a place of safety for the coming years.

David Wilkerson is predicting a coming economic collapse that will be followed by the destruction and invasion of America by our enemies. I believe Revelation 18:4 is a prophecy about the Jews, God's People, being warned to leave America before the destruction and a coming invasion that will make America an unsafe place for them to stay. These verses are talking about the destruction of Mystery Babylon, which I believe is America.

When the antichrist arrives and negotiates a peace treaty after a period of war has broken out in the Middle East. I believe the pre, Gog and Magog war (The Psalms 83 war) will have already taken place. Realize, after the Psalms 83 war, the Middle East will be at its highest alert for war. If the year 2016 is the year for the signing of a seven year peace treaty and the beginning of the seven year Great Tribulation, then I believe the Psalms 83 war will be taking place in late 2015 or early 2016, a war that will also be concluded with the children of Israel escaping destruction--a blood moon qualifying event.

In conclusion, if 2016 is the beginning of the Great Tribulation and the rapture happens in the fall of 2019 after three and a half years of the Great Tribulation, then the war of Gog and Magog would fall into a window of 2017 to 2019. This lines up with the end of the fifty year Jubilee cycle from the Six Day War in 1967 to 2017. As more light of prophecy is revealed, I see a strong case for the rapture happening in 2019. This is a significant year, as this year is seventy years after the budding of the fig tree. I discussed this prophecy in the introduction. This event is tied to the signing of a peace agreement in 1949 that allowed Israel to grow as a nation. A generation from 1949, seventy years from 1949, is 2019, the year I see as a possible date for the rapture.

THE NIGHT OF THE BLOOD MOON

On April 15, 2014, the night of the first Blood Moon, the first of four that happened in 2014 and 2015, I was on the phone talking with my friend Russell from the Adirondacks. When we were about to say goodbye, God gave him a word for me. Russell told me that the Lord wanted me to go off that night and find a place to pray, away from my home and stay outside until midnight. He said that God wanted to give me a revelation on this first night of the blood moons. Not being one to miss what God wants to show me, I figured I would find my place of prayer and wait and see what God wanted to reveal to me.

I went out to the back field where we do our target practicing. I pulled up a chair and soon realized it was too cold on this desert evening for just my sweat shirt, so I went back to the house to get a warm jacket. I picked out a jacket from the closet that I had not worn in a year. While I was waiting for the Blood Moon to happen, I had a time of prayer with my wife. When she went off to the house, I stayed longer to have a private time of prayer with God. I prayed, I watched the lunar eclipse and the Blood Moon come together, and I just stared off into the heavens imagining how the creator of the universe cares for and loves each one of us. It was about 12:30 when and I figured that nothing special was going to happen, so I decided to head for the house.

When I went inside, I took my jacket off and was about to hang it up in the closet when I noticed there was a paperback book in the inside pocket of this jacket, (I had not used this jacket in a year). I pulled out the book to see what the title was, and I was surprised to see it was a prophetic book by David Wilkerson called <u>Set the Trumpet to Thy Mouth</u>, printed in 1985. The first thought I had was, "Could God have a revelation in this book that he wants me to read?" So I fanned through the pages of this book, and I noticed that there was one dog-eared page in the whole book, marking page 14.

When I read the subtitle on this page, it really caught my attention. It was called, "Warning Signs". When I read the page and a half that went with this subtitle, it blew my mind. This page starts talking about two holocausts, a smaller one and a larger one. The first holocaust describes the destruction of the oil fields in Saudi Arabia and Kuwait during the first Gulf war in the early 90's. The second coming holocaust is describing a coming economic collapse, famine, and the destruction of America. This destruction is followed by a future invasion of America.

Read it for yourself, and see what you think. (I have typed out this page and a half below for your reading.) I believe God is showing us that we are now entering the time for the fulfillment of what David Wilkerson was shown 30 years ago and also shown to the prophets over two thousand years ago. The portion about the invasion of America ties into what I see as part of the Five End Time Wars.

Warning Signs By David Wilkerson 1985

"Before the great holocaust there will be smaller holocausts---the oil fields of the Middle East will be ablaze, and the smoke will rise night and day as a warning of the greater holocaust yet to come. There will be bombs falling on oil fields, on shipping docks and storage tanks. There will be panic among all oil producers, and shippers, and upon all nations dependent on that oil."

"Soon, very soon, an economic **nightmare** will explode into reality. What frightful news it will be! *"O thou that dwellest upon many waters, abundant in treasures, thine end is come, and the measure of thy coveteousness, (Jeremiah 51:13)"* America is about to face a time of mass hysteria, as banks close and financial institutions crumble and our economy spins totally out of control. Gold and silver will also lose their value. *"they shall cast their silver in the streets, and their gold shall be removed: their silver and their gold shall not be able to deliver them in a day of the wrath of the Lord: they shall not satisfy their souls, neither fill their bowels: because it is a stumbling block of their iniquity, (Ezekiel 7:19)"* The chaos that is coming cannot be stopped by our government. Ezekiel warned, *"The hands of the people of the land shall be troubled: I will do unto them after their way, and according to their deserts will I judge them. (Ezekiel7:27)"* These prophecies once again reveal God's judgmental decrees to wicked nations."*

"Scoff if you choose, but the underlying fears about a collapse will soon become a tragic reality. Numerous cracks will appear in our fragile prosperity, and soon even the most pessimistic will know in their hearts that a total collapse is certain. Senators and congressmen will sit in stunned silence as they realize no one can stop the tailspin into chaos. Business, political, and economic leaders will be terrorized by its sudden-ness and its far-reaching effects. *"Son of man, when the land sinneth against me by trespassing grievously, then will I stretch out mine hand upon it, and will break the staff of the bread thereof, and will send famine upon it, and will cut off man and beast from it. (Ezekiel 14:13)"* The great holocaust follows an economic collapse in America. The enemy will make its move when we are weak and helpless." Davis Wilkerson's book, Set the Trumpet to Thy Mouth," pages 14,15.

What I will share below is the revelation God gave me on the night of the first Blood Moon. It has just dawned on me that God brought this to me on this night because I believe these warning signs will start before the end of the four Blood Moons.

David Wilkerson warns of three events that are coming to America. These three events are outlined in the last two sentences from what he wrote in his book under the subtitle called warning signs. "The Great holocaust follows an economic collapse in America. The enemy will make its move when we are weak and helpless."

1. An economic collapse

2. The great destruction.

This great destruction has been outlined in David Wilkerson's books as coming judgments on America and will include the greatest earthquake event in history.

3. An Invasion is coming. "The enemy will make its move when we are weak and helpless."

The first event covered in the warning was the coming economic collapse. If this were to happen before the end of the four Blood Moons, does it not make sense that this event will be timed to happen at the end of the current Shemittah cycle that ends September 13, 2015? I believe the second and third events included in this warning will follow in a timely manner after this first coming event.

DO WE NEED TO FEAR THESE COMING EVENTS?

The answer to this question is found on page 17 of his book, Set the Trumpet to thy Mouth.

"Are Christians going to suffer when God shakes this nation with earthquakes and economic disasters? Yes! There will be much suffering and hardship, but God will meet the necessities of His overcomers. He will comfort their hearts, and as they see these frightful things coming upon the nation and the world, they will be at peace, saying "God warned us! We are prepared! We knew it all along, and we are not afraid. Our blessed Savior will go with us through it all."

In Conclusion

On page 14 and 15 of Dave Wilkerson's book, <u>Set the Trumpet to thy Mouth</u>, God gave him four warning signs, with the first being the oil fields in the Middle East. This first warning was really the first warning to the coming destruction of America and New York City. I will quote from David's book, "<u>Set the Trumpet to Thy Mouth</u>", under " Warning signs,"

"Before the great holocaust (destruction) there will be smaller holocausts (destructions)--The oil fields of the Middle East will be ablaze, and the smoke will rise night and day as **a warning of the greater holocaust yet to come**."

There are two points here to look at, first it says there will be smaller destructions and second the smoke of the oil fields burning is a warning of the future holocaust coming to America and New York City.

I see the first warning sign of the burning oil fields as an alert to what was coming to America. This first paragraph talks of coming smaller destructions. The first smaller destruction was the destruction of the twin towers in New York City, with the towers ablaze and the smoke or her burning. This was one of the smaller destructions that would come as a warning to America of the greater holocaust yet to come perhaps the destruction of New York City.

This sentence I quoted above also talks of other smaller holocausts to come. I believe we will see other 911 like events that will be other smaller destructions that will come to America before the big destruction that David Wilkerson has predicted that will include the burning of New York City and the greatest earthquake event in history.

Chapter sixteen will cover the coming judgment of America and the instruments of judgments that God will use.

— CHAPTER SIXTEEN —

GOD'S WARNING OF COMING JUDGMENT

In this chapter, what I would like to do is lay out a case for the soon coming judgment of America. God has twice shown me beyond any doubt that judgment is coming to America and not just to America but to the nations. I will go into greater detail on these two instances that the time of Grace is running out.

The first of these two encounters, was three days before the presidential election of 2012. As we approached the election, I wondered about its outcome. I was considering putting my analysis on why Mitt Romney could not win this election in the reprinting of my book. I was talking to my publisher about adding these thoughts to my book, and he said "You can do what you want, but let's talk about it this afternoon because I don't want you to put things in your book that will date it and cause it to become irrelevant."

As I was waiting for the publisher to call me back, I was questioning God, asking if my book would become irrelevant. I thought I should spend some time in prayer and reading the Bible. After some time in prayer, I was getting ready to read my Bible and I said, "Lord, I sure wish I knew what was going on. I know you called me to write this book; will my book become irrelevant?". Then I said to the Lord, "It would sure be nice if you would speak to me with a special word from the Bible, It would be nice if I could just open my Bible and you would show me a special verse that would tell me what is going on." However, I then said, "Lord, I know that it is not right for me to ask for that kind of favor, so I won't ask." I still needed to read my Bible, and when I opened my Bible to a random page, it opened to Ezekiel 30. I read the first three verses, and it set me back. I could not believe what I was reading. It seemed the Lord was showing me that He would reveal to me what is going on, and this Word was God's answer to my prayer. Below are the first three verses I read from Ezekiel 30: 1-3:

"The Word of the Lord came to me: Son of man, prophesy and say; this is what the Sovereign Lord says; Wail and say, "Alas for that day! for the day is near, the day of the Lord is near-- A day of clouds, a time of doom for the nations."

When I read this, it was as if God appeared in my office and answered my prayer, telling me that the Day of the Lord is near and my book would not become irrelevant. This was three days before the election, and I knew that no matter the outcome of the election, God's outcome and the timing of his coming will not be changed.

The last portion of the verse is addressing the subject of this chapter, "**A day of clouds, a time of doom for the nations.**" Clouds denote storms, and "doom for the nations" is speaking of God's judgment. The Bible teaches that God decides who will be placed in leadership to the nations of the world. When I first published the first edition of my book in 2010, I felt I heard the Lord tell me that the president at that time would lead America into the Great Tribulation. So when we were three days out from the presidential election of 2012 and it was looking like Mitt Romney was going to win, I was wondering if I had really heard from God. Now as we are approaching the middle of 2015, many Christian leaders are saying we can pray ourselves back into the blessing of God as a Christian nation.

I believe a nation can get to a point of no return. In America's case, our leaders are taking a very dangerous position concerning the nation of Israel. This alone is enough to bring God's judgment on America. When you look at what is happening in our courts, where evil is called good and good is called evil, we are heading in a direction that requires that God bring judgment on our nation. If God loves the people of this nation, it must require that God bring judgment to turn the people of America back to God.

Many people in our nation are upset at the direction the leadership of our nation is taking us. I believe God has allowed the leaders of our nation to come to power as part of his judgment on this nation. I believe we are in the window of time that will be the time of the Lord's Return. If I am right, as so many other prophetic teachers also believe, then It would require that we would have leadership in place that would make poor decisions that would ultimately lead to our collapse as a nation and force America to accept the joining of a Global One-World Government. This must happen for the fulfillment of the prophecies of the last days to come to pass.

I have been reading a book called, The Science of Judgment, by Johnathan Hansen. He brought many Old Testament verses to me that reinforces that a nation or people can get to the place of no return. I will share a couple of these verses.

Jeremiah 7:16 (NIV) *"So do not pray for this people nor offer any plea or petition for them; do not plead with me, for I will not listen to you."*

Jeremiah 11:11 (NIV) *"Therefore this is what the Lord says: 'I will bring on them a disaster they cannot escape. Although they cry out to me, I will not listen to them.'"*

I believe the end of 2015 and the beginning of 2016 will be the striking of midnight on the prophetic time clock. I believe time is running out. A new day is about to dawn, and that day will bring great storms and the judgment of God.

The second encounter I had where God spoke to me that judgment was coming to America was when I had a dream on May 11, 2013. This dream had caused me much concern; I wanted to know if this was a revelation from God. God has called me into the prophetic ministry and as a watchman on the wall, I didn't want to stick my neck out on a pizza dream.

I labored several days over whether I should send the message of this dream to my Facebook friends and the contacts from the sale of my book. I firmly believe that God has not given me light to hide it under a bushel. I was willing to accept that some of my friends would pass this off lightly; some would defriend me. I am willing to accept any criticism from man in my efforts to be obedient to God. Below I will explain and share this dream.

It was now Tuesday evening, May 14th. On Saturday, May 11th, I woke up from just having a dream that was not like my normal dreams. I could remember every detail and conversation concerning this dream.

In this dream, I was with people I knew from the Northwest Seattle area. It was about an earthquake that would hit the Northwest. It had not yet happened, but we were discussing it as if it had already happened. In the dream, we knew this quake was of the same magnitude as the earthquake that hit Alaska in 1964, which is said to have been a magnitude 9.2. Like I said, we were discussing it as if it had happened but it had not yet happened. It was like I was warning the people I knew, but they would not take it seriously. However, they seemed to know it was going to happen.

I felt it would happen soon, because in the dream we were talking as if we knew it was about to happen. I prayed for three days that God would let me know if this dream was really going to happen. I even asked if God would give this dream to me a second time, but this did not happen. On the morning of my third day, I felt compelled to find a place to pray. I continued to ask for God to confirm if this dream were from him. After a time of earnest prayer, I then went to my office to read my Bible. As I was reading my Bible, I just happened to be reading from the book of Psalms, and into my second page of Bible reading, this verse jumped out at me.

Psalms 18:6-7 (NIV) "In my distress I called to the Lord: I cried to my God for help. From his temple he heard my voice; my cry came before him, into his ears. The earth trembled and quaked, and the foundations of the mountains shook; they trembled because he was angry."

This verse from Psalms was the answer to my prayers. Yes, this dream was from God. The portion of this verse that says, *"In my distress I called to the Lord: I cried to my God for help"*, this was me in earnest prayer just minutes before. Then the verse goes on to say *"From his temple he heard my voice; my cry came before him, into his ears."* Then the verse talks about the earth shaking and that God was angry. *"The earth trembled and quaked, and the foundations of the mountains shook; they trembled because he was angry"*. The bottom line is God was confirming that the Northwest quake will be part of God's judgment on America.

It has dawned on me that this dream has a very interesting parallel to Christ's return. My Christian friends and the church in general know that Jesus is coming soon; they talk about His coming as if it were happening very soon, but they are not taking it seriously. They are not preparing for this event. I recently realized that there is a parallel to the church of our day and to the people living at the time of Noah's day.

To show how I see an application to this generation, I will start by sharing this verse from Matthew 24:37-39, *"As it was in the days of Noah, so it will be at the coming of the Son of Man. For in the days before the flood, people were eating and drinking and marrying and giving in marriage, up to the day Noah entered the ark:* **and they knew nothing** *about what would happen until the flood came and took them all away. That is how it will be at the coming of the Son of Man."*

I propose that the generation of Noah's day was like the lukewarm church of today which lacks the discernment needed to recognize its sinful condition and hear the warning of judgment being preached by God's men and women of today.

When you study the generations of Noah's day, you learn that Methuselah, who was a godly man, lived up to two years before the flood. When you consider that it took Noah a hundred years to build the ark, it would not be surprising if Methuselah actually helped Noah and his families build the ark. Now Methuselah lived to about 1000 years old, and he actually knew Adam and Eve. When I first thought of this, I realized that the generation of Noah was only one generation removed from the time of Adam and God's creation. When you realize this you have to consider that Noah's generation was not atheists. They did not question that there was a God, but the people of Noah's generation were the lukewarm, backslidden church of their day. In their backslidden condition, they lacked any discernment to recognize that judgment was coming. Read this verse again. *"And they knew nothing about what would happen until the flood came and took then all away".* Noah was preaching to his generation, but they were not listening. This verse is saying, *"As it was in Noah's day, so shall it be in our day."*

In our recent time, you can look back to the great Pentecostal revivals of Evan Roberts and the Welsh Revival, this great revival spread to America to the Azusa Street Revival and from these and other early fires of revival, a great Pentecostal revival with miracles, signs and wonders spread around the world. Today, many churches with this great spiritual heritage are absent of the miracles, signs, and wonders. Often the churches of today have substituted the miracles, signs and wonders for great entertainment.

As it was in Noah's day, God is again sending out his prophets with a warning message that the Lord is coming soon, but the lukewarm church does not want to hear it. Jesus told us that we would see hard times and tribulation before he returns. In fact, Matthew, chapter 24 lays out a great list of what is to come, but the warning from

God's Word and from the prophets of our day are not being heard or acknowledged. We have set ourselves up for a great surprise. God will soon be sending earth shaking events, and it will catch the church totally by surprise just as it says in Matthew 24:39, (NIV) *"and they knew nothing about what would happen until the flood came and took then all away. That is how it will be at the coming of the Son of Man."*

In fact, much of the church today is lukewarm and lacks spiritual discernment. We are one generation removed from the miracles of our heritage, just as Noah's generation was one generation removed from their spiritual heritage. The church of today is so lacking in discernment, that the church is being warned of coming judgment and the soon coming of the Lord, but as it was in Noah's day, the discernment is lacking to see it coming.

I will be sharing what God revealed to David Wilkerson decades ago and how God is bringing these prophecies back to our attention for such a time as this. It was David Wilkerson's three most important prophetic books, (The Vision, 1974, Racing Toward Judgment, 1976, and Set the Trumpet to Thy Mouth, 1985.) writers over the course of twelve years, warning America to repent and turn back to God. Instead of repenting, America has pushed God's grace to the outer limits. There comes a time when a people can drift so far from God that God has no choice but to bring judgment on a nation or, as in the case of Noah's day, his judgment was brought on the whole world with the exception of one family.

America and Israel are like cousin nations. We were both established as covenant nations before God. Israel became a harlot nation and broke its marriage covenant with God. God had to bring judgement on them in order to save them from becoming a totally polluted nation and people. Basically the judgment God brought on Israel was, **famine**, **destruction**, **invasion** and **captivity**. Israel saw great droughts and famines as part of God's judgment to bring Israel back to himself. For Israel, famine would be like the United States seeing famine brought on by economic collapse. Economic collapse is one of the first warning signs God gave to David Wilkerson for what is coming to America.

When God brought judgment on Israel, a great part of God's judgment was in the form of destruction. Many of its cities were conquered and destroyed and ultimately the destruction of the Jewish Temple. The Jewish Temple was the seat of both Israel's religion and government. In <u>Set the Trumpet to Thy Mouth</u> Wilkerson says that the destruction of America will follow the economic collapse. I see the destruction of our twin towers as a warning of the greater destruction of New York City that is the center of our economic strength and the heart of America.

Next, Israel was judged by invasion, captivity, and later the Jews would go through a great holocaust in the Second World War, I believe these judgments ultimately kept Israel from losing its identity, and I believe these events will lead to ever increasing revivals-bringing God's people back to himself in our day.

On page 14, he discusses four warning signs of coming judgment to America. The third warning would be the coming destruction to America. He then made the statement that "The enemy will make its move when we are weak and helpless." It appears to me that America will be facing invasion and captivity just as Israel did; I believe that these coming judgments on our country are our due for our turning away from God, even as Israel did.

A series of smaller destructions first. As discussed earlier, one has already happened, the destruction of the two towers of the World Trade Center. I believe just as the Jews faced a holocaust in Germany under Hitler, there is a strong possibility that America will face a similar holocaust on our soil at the hands of ISIS, and from a future invasion on our soil. I see these coming times as a time that will bring the church in America to its knees in true repentance to God, giving birth to great revivals in our land.

The first domino event that I believe can happen in the coming year is the collapse of the stock market. This will cascade into other events that will lead to the collapse of the dollar and the total collapse of our economy, and than our country.

When I dreamed of the Northwest quake, God strongly confirmed it was from Him from His Word. Shortly after posting it on my website and Facebook page, I was sent a link to Rev. Jonathan Hanson's website. He has had many prophetic dreams concerning America. After searching his name to get a feel for who he is, I saw evidence that he has been quite accurate in his prophecies.

Around 1995, God revealed to him that a great earthquake would hit the Northwest, bringing great devastation to the land. As a result of this tragic earthquake, he saw the 520 floating bridge destroyed and the stock market collapsing. He has been interviewed on TruNews, as well as the Sid Roth program, where he stated that civil unrest would follow this quake.

When I began reading, Set the Trumpet to thy Mouth and The Vision, I noticed David Wilkerson connecting coming earthquakes to a coming economic collapse. "Are Christians going to suffer when **God shakes this nation with earthquakes and economic disasters**? Yes! There will be much suffering and hardship, but God will meet the necessities of His overcomers. He will comfort their hearts, and as they see these frightful things coming upon the nation and the world, they will be at peace, saying, "God warned us! We are prepared! We knew it all along, and we are not afraid. Our blessed Savior will go with us through it all."

These prophecies from both Wilkerson and Hansen, are both clearly in agreement. If God were speaking and revealing the future to both of these prophets of God, then you would expect them to be in agreement. When you read the Wilkerson's prediction of the most devastating earthquake in American history, it does not give any indication that any similar type of devastating event has already affected America.

Here is another short excerpt from Wilkerson's 1974 book, The Vision, about this coming devastating earthquake. "The United States is going to experience, in the not-too-distant future, the most tragic earthquake in its history. One day soon this nation will be reeling under the impact of the biggest news story of modern times. It will be coverage of the biggest most disastrous earthquake in history. It will cause widespread panic and fear. Without a doubt, it will become one of the most completely reported earthquakes ever. Television networks will suspend all programming and carry all-day coverage. Another earthquake, possibly in Japan, may precede the one that I see coming here. There is not the slightest doubt in my mind about this forthcoming massive earthquake on our continent. I believe it will be many times more severe than the San Francisco quake. I am not at all convinced that this earthquake will take place in California".

In the following paragraph of this epic earthquake event, he makes a strong connection that this coming earthquake will be the hand of God's judgment:

"The Punishment of America, by David Wilkerson"

"I believe God has appointed the instrument of killer earthquakes as His most ominous weapon of judgment. Our nation will undoubtedly suffer the most severe judgment of all. It will strike suddenly, without warning. God has forewarned through many prophetic messages. Even scientists have been warning that major quakes are coming. It will not come as a surprise. **The very first tremor will send forth the judgment message loud and clear to all – THIS IS IT!** A day of judgment has come! There are no words in our language to describe the horror and the suffering. There will be no way of escape. The worst that man feared will suddenly come upon him.

God will literally shake our nation with this instrument of judgment. The mountains will tremble and the cities will fall. "Quakeproof" buildings will crumble like toothpicks. The earth will heave, split apart, and tremble."

"Hundreds of square miles affected. In less than two minutes on God's judgment clock, the death angel will claim the lives of multiplied thousands, over a radius of hundreds of miles. Mountain pass roads of escape will be blocked. Water mains will crumble and break. Cars and houses will sway like toys tossed about. Dams will burst and flood tides will carry many to their doom.

A series of minor earthquakes will precede the major killer quakes. One of moderate magnitude will strike, with moderate damage, and many will be relieved that a massive quake did not happen. But it will follow, most assuredly." David Wilkerson's book, <u>Racing Toward Judgment</u>, pages 65,66

JUDGMENT BEGINS AT THE COASTS

"God's judgments have always begun at the "entrance gates" of nations, cities and empires: "A cry of alarm will begin at the farthest gate ...." Zephaniah 1:10. This is representative of the seaports, harbors, and centers of influx. It is significant that most of the Old Testament prophets warned of judgment beginning at the coasts. Zephaniah warned the Philistine cities:"... Woe to you.....living on the coast....The Lord will destroy you ....The coastland will become pasture..." (Zephaniah 2:5,6)

"Many will survive. Among the survivors will be those who were prepared and who had humbled themselves before God. Those who heard the warnings and who began to trust God for deliverance will survive. Many unconcerned Christians will be lost, along with the thousands of unbelievers." David Wilkerson's book, <u>Racing Toward Judgment</u>, pages 67-69

In closing this chapter concerning the prophecies of David Wilkerson, I want to point out that my studies of God's Word and my listening to the prophecies of God's prophets has led me to the conclusion that the identity of first domino triggering the fall of all the other for coming dominoes will be a coming economic collapse to America and the world. A few weeks ago, someone sent me a prophecy David Wilkerson delivered in 2008. I believe it is quite possible that a great earthquake event may create the first domino of collapse that triggers the coming economic collapse.

2008 PROPHECY by DAVID WILKERSON

"The Most Important Issue of This Hour"

"Ten years ago, I wrote a book entitled, <u>America's Last Call: On the Brink of a Financial Holocaust</u>. In that book, I warned of the following events:"

"There would be a meltdown of the bond market. God's judgment would strike suddenly on the U.S. economy. A brief, false sense of prosperity would precede the coming economic collapse. (This short flicker of prosperity would be God's final mercy call before the chastening to come.) There would be a real estate meltdown, with a market made up of mostly sellers and very few buyers. Multitudes would lose their homes to repossession. There would be an ominous rise of homosexual power. A sudden storm of confusion would take place on Wall Street. God's watchmen and prophets would be silenced. The U.S. dollar would collapse. America would lose control of its economy. To date, China has loaned America hundreds of billions of dollars. We have become the world's number one debtor nation, no longer in control of our finances. Along with many other watchmen, I see that the greatest shaking of all is still to come. What we are about to witness upon the earth will affect every person living. The world is going to see a temporary calm, with relative stability, causing many to say, "The crisis has passed." But in truth, the real panic will still be ahead of us."

WHO WILL LISTEN

"We don't like to hear these words. They are too hard, too incredible. Too much to comprehend. How can this nation, now so proud, powerful, and prosperous, suddenly fall and become a place of slaughter and plagues? Who wants to believe it? Who is close enough to God to hear this sounding of His trumpet? Certainly not the false prophets like Pashur, the chief leader in the house of the Lord. He slapped Jeremiah's face and threw him in jail for prophesying such gloom and doom. "The religious leaders, priests, and prophets were all telling the people that good days were ahead, a time of national glory, success, peace, and endless prosperity. And they borrowed their soothing messages from one another, encouraging thousands with their lies. They went about prophesying their nation and people would not suffer destruction." David Wilkerson's book, <u>Set the Trumpet to Thy Mouth</u>, page22

"Prophecy of Coming Judgment" Rev. Jonathan Hansen

In closing, I will share a word of prophecy that was given to Rev. Jonathan Hansen in 1995 concerning coming judgment upon America, a judgment that would be a wakeup call to the church. Again I believe we are at the midnight hour and the unfulfilled prophecies of the past few decades are about to come to pass.

"The Lord is saying that he will exhort the American people to look to him. He will cause an incident to happen in America so great so as to get their attention. This could possibly be through the weather, food, disease, economy (although it would have to be a much greater degree than we have yet experienced), etc., or nuclear war at a national level.

God is saying that the people of America are guilty of intense pride, intense self-exaltation and self-satisfaction. In all areas of life in America, including the Church, most of the people are filled with pleasing themselves. The leaders in America, even in the Church for the most part, are filled with self-glorification and self-attainment. Many of their leaders not only have a gluttonous appetite for glory and "the things of the world," but some are guilty of immorality and amorality. Many church leaders do not know right from wrong any longer. Many are guilty of lying, cheating, fornication and adultery. Because so many of the pastors have become amoral and are no longer either capable or bold enough to counsel truth, the American people are turned over to the philosophies of evil men and satanic spirits. The psychic, the philosopher, the professor, and even eastern religions take the place of the truth of Jesus Christ that should be taught fundamentally, doctrinally sound and without error. But the message is not popular with people of America, nor with many deceived pastors within the Church. So, the people of America turn to the lies of the cult and occult because a true servant of the Lord is not popular even within his own denomination. They dance to the fiddle of the majority who are intrigued by the psychics' predictions, but are deaf to the words and warnings of a true prophet. Thus, the people of America and members of the church are conned by false doctrine. They are inept to scripturally and spiritually deal with the deceptions, lies, lusts, lifestyles, values, behaviors, sins and spirits that are in our society and church. God is saying that he will bring down (humble, shame) the American people, including many church leaders. Many people in America and members of churches feel immune from the catastrophes that have struck other countries such as war, famine, disease, persecution, etc. But, God is warning that the people, both in society and the Church, will not escape his dealings with them. There are hard times ahead for both the Church and people of America. Great trouble, plagues and persecution lie ahead. This is needed out of God's deep eternal love to give every opportunity for people to repent and prepare themselves for the coming of the Lord.

When there is a lack of righteousness and holiness in peoples' lives, they compromise. They are afraid to speak the truth to others. They lie and give excuses for their unfaithfulness by saying they do not want to hurt people's feelings. You can say it another way, but the truth is, their own relationship with God is lacking. In reality, they do not have the spiritual strength to obey the spirit; nor are they led by the Spirit, but by their own understanding, mentality and flesh. They find it difficult to give godly counsel because, according to his Word, they do not have an intimate relationship with the Author of Truth. Thus, they do not know what the truth is, or if they do, they do not have the spirit (strength) to do or say what he asks of them.

The majority of the Church in America lacks holiness and righteousness. God must and will prepare them for his return. For he will not allow his New Jerusalem to be polluted, corrupt, diseased, poverty stricken, ruled by the vain, immoral or amoral, again. Before his final judgment when people are sentenced to eternal separation or eternal life with him in the New Jerusalem, Jesus will give more opportunity for a change of heart. The American "born again Christian" will be chastened by the Lord and tried by the fire. God will force events to deal with their spiritually weak condition until the American Christian (true believer) will look to the Lord for their strength and call upon the Lord earnestly, not out of some mythical explanation or prayer. Through the changing events and new laws in society, the American believer will be forced of God to take his stand on spiritual and moral truths until they are hated and persecuted by society. The American Christian will not escape having to take his stand and position in the Lord!

Wrong doctrine taught by denominations and pastors will be exposed by time itself, by the Holy Spirit, by the Scriptures, which will finally be studied studiously by the elect instead of just accepted from the pulpit. Many large churches, denominations, church leaders and pastors will fall. They will be rejected both by society and by the believer, for their vain lifestyle and teaching of God's Word. Eventually all godly organized churches and ministries will be shut down as persecution of the true believer takes its full course. As believers have suffered in many countries throughout the world for their faith, so many will now suffer in America.

The Lord Jesus is warning the American Christians that he is preparing to return to earth. Before he returns, he will give more opportunities for both the unbeliever and believer to prepare for his coming. Great trouble will fall on America along with a major Crisis that will change the American lifestyle. He warns that the born again believer will also be challenged by the Lord through the change of events in American lifestyle, calamities and persecution. But through it all the true Church will become holy without spot or wrinkle and learn to trust in Jesus. Amen and amen! "

Rev. Jonathan Hansen, 1995

— CHAPTER SEVENTEEN —

THERE WILL BE SIGNS IN THE SUN, MOON, AND STARS

T he title to this chapter comes from the very words that Jesus spoke to his disciples when three of them met with him on the Mount of Olives. As I mentioned earlier in a study from Matthew 24, Jesus' disciples asked him, *"What will be the sign of your coming and the end of the age?"* Jesus gave them the answer in Matthew 24:4-31. The Gospel of Mark and Luke both share this account of Jesus on the Mount of Olives, and each of these gospel accounts sheds a little different perspective that collectively helps us understand all that Jesus shared with his disciples. He basically told them all of the things that would happen and what the followers of Jesus would have to go through before he would return in the clouds for his saints in the Rapture as described in Matthew 24:29-31.

He basically told them all of the things that would happen and what his followers would have to go through before his return in the clouds for his saints in the Rapture as described in Matthew 24:29-31. It is from the account of Luke that I am writing this chapter. Some of what Luke describes, in Luke 21: 25-27, is not mentioned in Matthew 24, and what is described in Luke is both frightening and important. Luke 21:25-27 (NIV) *"There will be signs in the sun, moon and stars. On the earth, nations will be in anguish and perplexity at the roaring and tossing of the sea. Men will faint from terror, apprehensive of what is coming on the world, for heavenly bodies will be shaken."*

On my last recent visit to the Jim Bakker program, we were discussing the coming solar eclipse in March of 2015 and the last two of the four Blood Moons coming this

April and September of 2015. I mentioned this verse from Luke 21, quoting how Jesus said that there would be signs in the sun, moon, and stars. I said on the program that I would not be surprised if, during this year of 2015, we would see events from all three of these key words. We know that a solar eclipse will be coming March 20, 2015 in the middle of four blood moons, (According to Jewish Rabbis, this solar event signifies the judgment of the Gentile nations).

We know that we will see the last of the four blood moons happening this April and September of 2015. The thought that occurred to me was maybe we might see a major event tied to the last of these three words, signs in the stars. If you look up the word star in the Greek, it means astor or asteroid, or what we know as a large meteor. In Bible days, when a meteor was spotted, it was looked on as a falling star, thus the word star was used in the translation of this word found in Luke 21. The word, star, would have been recognized to be a falling star or asteroid- "You will see signs in the sun, moon and stars." As I have continued the study of this chapter, I have discovered some incredible insights on the timing of great meteor events which has caused me to adjust my thinking and make me wonder if we will see book-end events concerning the Sun, moon and stars, both possibly this year and again at Christ's coming for his saints at The Rapture. I say this because when you get to the end of this chapter, you will see events again unfolding at the time of the Lord's coming that will deal with the sun, moon and stars.

A week after arriving home from the Jim Bakker show, I received an email from a friend who was sending me a prophecy from Efrain Rodriguez, a prophet from Puerto Rico. This prophecy concerned a coming meteor event that would be of epic proportion. When I read it, I remembered seeing this described on YouTube, several months before, and I remember dismissing it as just way over the top and not possible.

Because I received this recent email from someone I trusted, I decided to look into it with greater detail. The first thing I did was to google the name of Prophet Efrain Rodriguez to see what I could find on him. I found one account that labeled him as a false prophet, but after reading this assessment it turned out he was labeled such because this person does not believe prophets are on the earth today. I dismissed this assessment. I then saw accounts where he was labeled as a false prophet because this event did not happen when Efrain had predicted it would. But when I consider many prophets I have known over the years, I have learned that when God gives a prophecy, the prophet will often have such an urgency to get the message out in time that they often believe it is coming sooner than it is. This was true of David Wilkerson who was also labeled as a false prophet. Over the test of time, he has been proven to be a true prophet of God.

I then called a couple of prophet friends to see if they had any word on this prophecy. Friends in Canada had heard of this prophecy several months before, and the Lord told them that this event was really coming. Since discussing this with them, they have made contact with Efrain and his staff and had several conversations. Now they are convinced more than before that this prophecy is true and will happen soon. I called another prophet friend, and after reading the prophecy and staying up all night in prayer, this prophet friend came to the same conclusion of this being true and a warning from God. I have tried to find valid reasons for labeling Efrain Rodriguez a false prophet, but I have found none.

Before I go any further in describing what I am about to share, I want to say that this event is so scary and epic in size that I have been very hesitant in sharing this. I realize that if this event does not happen in a timely schedule, it could make many question my predictions. You will see why I have concluded that this event may not happen soon, but it will happen before the rapture. **I have to add as a warning, that after fully studying this, I have concluded that a similar meteor event could also happen sooner. As I mentioned earlier, I am wondering if we will see book-end events concerning the sun, moon and stars.**

From the mouth of other witnesses, I believe God is sending us a warning of this coming event. Does not God's word say, "By the mouth of two or three witnesses let the word be established?"

If I believed there were the remotest possibility that this event were going to happen, I have put my reputation on the line rather than take the chance of its happening and of not warning the body of Christ.

There is a powerful connection to the prophecy given to Efrain Rodriguez and a prophecy given to David Wilkerson and published in his book, called <u>The Vision</u> in 1974. It is very interesting that Efrain Rodriguez at the age of sixteen was given his prophecy in 1974 as well. The prophecy is very long; I imagine God has given Efrain more information concerning this coming event over time. David Wilkerson's prophecy concerning the greatest earthquake event in history was also very detailed, and parts of his prophecy were given in different books over a twelve year period of time.

Below is a brief summary of Efrain Rodriguez's prophecy

Full text can be found online at, http://www.profeta-de-dios-efrain.com/399377031.

"We all have a duty to ask the Holy Spirit to confirm this message. To receive this message, you must have The Presence of the Holy Spirit. He is the main basis of this message, not Efrain or his team. Ask Him, with sincerity and humility of heart, if this message comes from Him. If you are sincere, He will answer you.

Jehovah God will touch the Earth with His Feet at two in the morning. This chastisement, even if some think otherwise, is because of the Church, both here in Puerto Rico as in the rest of the world. The Church today day left aside all the tenets by which Jesus died on the cross, to provide the Way to be able to see Him and the Father. Everything comes down to holiness, without which no one will see the Lord.

The Rapture will occur after the events that are approaching. It will occur when the resulting gigantic worldwide Soul Harvest, of which the Holy Spirit has spoken for many years, is ready to be reaped. If the God of Heaven did not do this, many would be lost. These events are part of the Beginning of Sorrows, signs that the Bible indicates will occur before The Great Tribulation. It is the preamble, the necessary brokenness needed to raise the new Church of Christ worldwide.

The Reason for this Approaching Judgment is the Apostasy of the Church

Those congregations that seek Holiness and the true Word have little attendance, but churches where prosperity and an empty Gospel is preached, are packed. Sin walks through the altars and churches: homosexuality, adultery, fornication, promiscuity, lust, lies, theft, jealousy, envy, murmuring, abuses against women and children, profanity; Pastors, Apostles, evangelists and members living double lives: living as the world and then, from the altar, shouting Hallelujah and speaking in tongues, as if they could fool God All this is a mockery, an insult to the Lord of Heaven

Puerto Rico will be the epicenter of the Wrath of the Lord in this particular Judgment. The island is contaminated. Only tithes and offerings are of interest to the majority of pastors. They do not desire nor seek the Presence of the Holy Spirit. They say that they cannot speak about this judgment to the people, so that they will not panic, and hide behind the excuse that: "God is love and He would never do such a thing." But they seem to forget the Consuming Fire that also is God, Who destroyed the generation of the time of Noah, Sodom and Gomorrah, and they forget the announcement of Jonah to Nineveh.

DESCRIPTION of the Chastisement: God showed me a large rock, an asteroid, entering the airspace of the municipality of Arecibo and exiting through the airspace of Mayagüez, in Puerto Rico. This will be at 2 a.m. This Rock will be making impact on the sea, between the island of Mona and Mayagüez, hitting the active seismic fault located in that part of the Caribbean. This impact will unleash a 12 point earthquake, something that has never been. The impact at sea will raise a giant wave, more than 1,000 feet high. The wave will be entering the island of Puerto Rico immediately.

It is important that you ask the Holy Spirit what are His plans for you and your loved ones before, and through this event. Multitudes will depart with Jesus that night. Some will have a last minute to repent before the Lord, for not having believed His warning. Our Lord Jesus comes with His Book, to claim before the Father, the souls of multitudes of people who will die that night; to take them to Heaven. Many others, who will die will not depart with the Lord, including many pastors.

The impact of the asteroid will be identical to a nuclear explosion. It will create a shock wave with winds of 300 mph. It will travel the whole world. Then, the tsunami will come. The gigantic wave will travel in all directions: toward the Gulf of Mexico, South America, United States and all the islands of the Caribbean: They will all receive the wave. There will be millions of deaths that night. The wave will be entering Miami at 5:00 in the morning and will continue its course towards the Eastern area of the United States, the Gulf of Mexico and South America. Besides the sea entering 50 to 100 miles inland from the coasts, all rivers will overflow, having no outlet into the oceans due to the rise of the sea level.

The 12 point earthquake caused by the impact of the asteroid in the seismic area between the Western part of Puerto Rico and the island of Mona, will be felt practically all over the world. This seismic fault has ramifications throughout the whole planet.

The impact of the asteroid will stop the rotation of the Earth and will produce three days of darkness on this side of the planet. In the dark, it will make burying and disposing of the bodies very difficult. Bodies will start to decompose in the water and on land, giving way to the last and worst of the events of this trial: the pestilence.

THE SPIRITUAL CONDITION OF THE WORLD TODAY IS WORSE THAN IN THE DAYS OF SODOM AND GOMORRAH. AND THE CHURCH, IN ITS VAST MAJORITY, HAS ALLOWED IT BY KEEPING SILENT. The pastors, who have been preaching and deceiving their flock with the Gospel of wealth and prosperity, will see scarcity like never before.

Christian people of Puerto Rico and everywhere: remember that the Lord wants that before this judgment, all the backslidden will return to Him as soon as possible. Urgently! They have to run to His feet immediately. Please, do not think twice. Run, because you will have no excuse before the Lord. It is a call with tears from the Most High God, because a multitude of backslidden will die that night. They live and are around the churches; what is the church doing to go look for them, warn them and bring them back to The Lord? Also a multitude of those who are within the churches will die. All this is because of the rebellion against the tenets of holiness that our Lord demands.

ALL, ABSOLUTELY ALL COUNTRIES WILL BE AFFECTED, ESPECIALLY IF THEY ARE PART OF LATIN AMERICA, CANADA AND THE UNITED STATES. THE EUROPEAN COUNTRIES WILL ALSO RECEIVE THE EFFECT OF THE SHOCK WAVE, TSUNAMI AND THE AFTERMATH EFFECTS. THE MESSAGE IS THE SAME FOR ALL: PREPARE, COMING TO THE LORD JESUS CHRIST AS OUR ONLY ARK OF SALVATION; AND

STORE WATER, MEDICATION AND FOOD TO THE EXTENT THAT YOU CAN. IF YOU ARE BOUND TO CHRIST, HE WILL PROVIDE WHAT YOU LACK.

No plan of the Lord can be stopped by hell. This chastisement has to happen, to awaken Christ's Church on Earth. Little time remains. Be prepared in South America and Central America. The churches must bend their knees, pray, ask for signs from Heaven.

The fact that a country or a country area has no coasts does not mean that it will not be affected. In addition to the tsunami, the other events mentioned before will follow the impact of the asteroid: the shock wave, the earthquake, and the three days of darkness, the overflow of all rivers, the pestilence, and the resulting shortages of food, drinking water and medications. All of these events will claim many lives, especially the resulting pestilence due to the decomposing bodies in the waters, and unburied bodies on land. It will be very difficult to get rid of the bodies due to the 3 days of darkness and flooding.

The United States will be shaken by the 12 degree earthquake at the time of the asteroid impact. At 5 in the morning, the nation will start facing chastisement when 500 feet waves enter Miami. The waves will move onwards throughout the nation's coastlines. There will be a shock wave produced by the blast of the asteroid impact. Very strong hurricane winds, without rain will be received. Then the tsunami will come. The wind will come first, and then the wave. Rivers will have no outlet to the ocean due to the increase of the level of the sea. All rivers will overflow. Many will die because of this.

When the asteroid impacts, we will feel the shock wave as a very strong wind. Ask the Holy Spirit, where and if you should move, and what to do. Requirement: Being bound to Jehovah God. Stay away from sin, so you can hear His Voice. More than 35 million deaths are expected in the United States. Authorities remain silent.

Martial law is ready to be implemented in the United States and around the world, to deal with the catastrophe and its aftermath. The United States is prepared for 15 months of scarcity, shortages and national emergency. They have stored millions of boxes of dry food, among other resources, in the middle of the nation. Civil war will be unleashed due to the scarcity of food and resources. Martial law will be implemented, due to the need to maintain control.

The events described in this message will come to pass, and you shall respect God. The entire nation will respect God. There will be more than 70 million dead on this side of the Earth.

IMPORTANT!!! This is not the End of the World. The Covenant that God made with Noah will not be broken. The Earth will not be completely destroyed with water. The Lord will have absolute control of this event and will protect His people, even in situations that seem humanly and scientifically impossible to us. God makes "the impossible" possible.

The game of pretending to be a Christian is over. BE ONE! No more games with the Lord. Brothers: Where ever you go, give testimony, as a Christian and watchman. Go rescue souls, before, during and after these events. Be active watchmen. Sound the alarm! Point to the safe place: our Ark, our shelter and strength is Jesus Christ. After the event, the whole world will seek answers. We will present them the true God, The One who spoke prior to the event and prophesied everything that took place. The One Who fulfilled His sentence of judgment and protected His true flock, as He promised, The One who performed miracles through His spirit, during the time of shortage, mortality and pestilence. What a great testimony to the rest of the world!

The Lord promised Abraham that the righteous and the wicked would not die together. The same promise applies to us, if we are bound to our Lord and Master Jesus Christ, in our hearts and in our behavior.

"May The Lord keep You"

Efrain Rodriguez

A couple of comments I would like to make concerning what Efrain Rodriguez has predicted concerns the first statement regarding the earth stopping its rotation for three days. "The impact of the asteroid will stop the rotation of the Earth and will produce three days of darkness on this side of the planet."

This was initially a real stumbling block for me. I have even heard critics of Prophet Efrain say that this is scientifically impossible, and that if the earth suddenly came to a stop it would cause everything on the planet to fly from its place. But when I really thought about this, I had to remind myself that God turned back the sundial and stopped the sun from setting on two occasions in the Bible when the Israelites needed more time to win the battles over their enemies. On both of these occasions, things did not fly all over the place. The God who put the laws of physics in place is quite capable of working around what we may see as an impossibility.

As I was considering what would happen when a great meteor hits our planet, I went to my globe and looked at the direction from which the meteor would be coming. Then I looked at the direction that the earth is rotating and discovered that the rotation of the earth will be rotating into the direction of the coming meteor. This would create what will be like a head-on collision. For this reason, it makes sense that a big enough meteor hitting the earth just right could stop the earth's rotation. In Isaiah it says that *"the earth will reel like a drunkard"*!

If half of the earth would be in darkness for three days, I do not believe this would be long enough for half of the planet to go into a deep freeze? What I have been able to calculate is that all of North America will be dark for three days. Will this period of darkness make some believe that the rapture is about to happen, because of the Bible verse in Matthew 24:29-31 that says, "The sun will go dark", just before the rapture? Later in this study I will show that a great meteor event will happen just before the rapture.

The last comment I will make concerning this prophecy is about the high number of those who will die. Efrain Rodriguez said God told him thirty five million would die in South America and thirty five million in North America. These numbers seem just too high and over the top to be possible. After giving much thought to this, I have concluded that this is not really that far over the top when you consider the large numbers who will die during the time of the wrath of God. **Please don't think I am taking the large number of dying lightly, death is very sorrowful whether we are looking at small or large numbers.**

In Revelation, chapter nine at the time of the sixth trumpet, one third of mankind will die in what I call the Six Trumpet War. Revelation 9:18 (NIV) *"A third of mankind was killed by the three plagues of fire, smoke and sulfur that came out of their mouths.*" One third of mankind at this time would be 1/3 of 7.244 billion people on the planet today, or over 2,400 million will die in this war. When you realize that we are now entering the birth pains of the End-Times, 70 million dying, in what I see as God's judgment to bring man to repentance and the church to awakening, is only a small fraction of the numbers of those who will die when God pours his wrath on the unrepentant. Read what Revelation says will happen when 1/3 of mankind dies under the hand of God's wrath. Revelation 9:20,21 (NIV) *"The rest of mankind that were not killed by these plagues still did not repent of the work of their hands; they did not stop worshipping demons, and idols of gold, silver, bronze, stone and wood – idols that cannot see or hear or walk. Nor did they repent of their murders, their magic arts, their sexual immorality or their thefts."*

Now let us read and examine what David Wilkerson saw in his Vision

(What I am going to share here will be a prophetic message that David Wilkerson delivered over a twelve year period contained in the writings of three of his books.)

Earthquakes coming to the United States

As you read about these predicted earthquakes coming to America, I want to propose that part of what David Wilkerson saw may have been caused by a great meteor event.

"The United States is going to experience, in the not-too-distant future, the most tragic earthquake in its history. One day soon this nation will be reeling under the impact of the biggest news story of modern times. It will be coverage of the biggest, most disastrous earthquake in history.

It will cause wide spread panic and fear. Without a doubt, it will become one of the most completely reported earthquakes ever. Television networks will suspend all programing and carry all day coverage.

It will be so high on the Richter scale that it will trigger two other major earthquakes. The earth is actually going to shake, and there will be numerous other earthquakes in various places throughout the world. This is one kind of judgment that cannot be explained by the scientists. It is supernatural intervention into the affairs of men. It is an act of God causing havoc and judgment, calling men to repentance and reverence. It can strike at any time, and there is no way to deter it. Men will just have to stand back in awe and terror as the power of God is demonstrated in the earthquake." David Wilkerson's book <u>The Vision</u>, page 32,33

EXAMINING THE SIMILARITIES

After reading and studying the prophecies of these two prophets of God, I am seeing some undeniable similarities. As I mentioned earlier, both Efrain Rodriguez and David Wilkerson received similar prophecies around the same time, in 1974. I am open to the possibility that these two prophecies are two independent prophetic events, one coming before the other. Later as I share the other similarities of these prophecies, you may agree with me that these two prophetic events may be one and the same.

David Wilkerson was labeled a false prophet for bringing out these prophesies. Efrain Rodriguez took many years and chastisement from the Lord before going public with his prophecy because he did not want this to ruin his ministry.

Both David Wilkerson and Efrain Rodriguez are holiness preachers. I believe the teaching of holiness is greatly lacking in our churches today. I don't mean the legalistic form that judges you from your outward appearance. No! I am talking about a holiness that is in ones heart and manifests in ones actions and daily lives.

David Wilkerson predicted the largest earthquake event in history would take place and said the whole planet would shake. He said there would be numerous earthquakes around the world. Efrain Rodriguez said the earth would shake from the collision of a meteor and it would create the largest earthquake event in history. Both of these prophets of God said that these events were coming as judgment on the church to wake up the church and bring us back to a place of repentance and reverence towards God. Both David Wilkerson and Efrain Rodriguez have been called false prophets for delivering these prophecies.

Before I move on to the third witness, I have to say that I now believe that what Wilkerson wrote about over the period of twelve years was covering possibly two similar events-one dealing with a great earthquake event that will come before a second devastating earthquake and meteor event. I believe my later chapter 19 called "A Possible Scenario Story leading up to the Rapture" will show why I see two events coming from his prophecies.

Now, I want to look at the writings of the third witness to these coming events, God's Word, the Bible

I started my study with Luke 21:25-27. Now we need to look at it again, a little closer this time. Luke 21:25-27 (NIV) *"There will be signs in the sun, moon and stars. On the earth, nations will be in anguish and perplexity at the roaring and tossing of the sea. Men will faint from terror, apprehensive of what is coming on the world, for heavenly bodies will be shaken."*

When I read this and see that there will be signs in the sun, moon and the stars, what comes to mind is that this is the year 2015 where we have a solar eclipse in the middle of four blood moons that started last year. It is interesting that books have recently been written concerning the solar eclipse and Blood Moon events, but not much has been said concerning the signs in the stars.

When I was recently thinking about these three signs, a thought came to me that I will mention. Time will tell if it really makes sense. It has been said that Jewish Rabbis see a significant connection between the solar eclipse in the middle of four blood moons and the judgment of the gentile nations. The four Blood Moons happening on Jewish holy days has historically signaled major events connected to the deliverance of the Jews and Israel. This year, we also have to factor in the fact that we are in the last year of a seven year Shemittah cycle, and this event can also coincide with large economic downturns. I believe other events connected to the nation of Israel will follow the event of the fourth Blood Moon as much as a year or two after the fourth Blood Moon comes this September 28, 2015.

Now moving to the next portion of Luke 21:25-27, it says, "On the earth, nations will be in anguish and perplexity at the roaring and tossing of the sea". This is saying that this coming event will affect nations! The word anguish is a strong word that would indicate great loss of life. The roaring and tossing of the seas could easily mean tidal waves.

The next portion says, *"Men will faint from terror, apprehensive of what is coming on the world,"* Again, this sounds like great loss of life has happened, and those who are in the way of this event will be terrified. Where it says, "apprehensive of what is coming on the world," to me, this is pointing to an event that may come from outer space and hitting our world.

The last portion of this verse says, *"For heavenly bodies will be shaken".* The Earth is a heavenly body and the prophecies of both Dave Wilkerson and Efrain Rodriguez are saying that the whole earth will shake at this time. These verses found in Luke 21:25-27 make a strong case for a coming epic meteor event. I also see there is even more scriptural evidence that something big is coming.

The first verse that makes a strong case for this coming meteor hitting the Atlantic Ocean and the resulting tidal wave hitting the USA is Revelation 18:21. I base this on my belief that Mystery Babylon is the USA.

Read Revelation 18:21 NIV, *"Then a mighty angel picked up a boulder the size of a great millstone and threw it into the sea, and said: "With such violence the great city of Babylon will be thrown down, never to be found again."*

Another passage is Isaiah 24:18b-20a (NIV) *"The floodgates of the heavens are opened, the foundations of the earth shake. The earth is broken up, the earth is split asunder, the earth is thoroughly shaken, the earth reels like a drunkard".*

When floodgates are opened, something pours out. This could be a huge asteroid because it says the earth is shaken and split asunder. Could a huge meteor event trigger the New Madrid fault that would cause the United States to be split in two?

Follow those verses with Isaiah 26:9b-10 (NIV). "When your judgments come upon the earth, the people of the world learn righteousness. Though grace is shown to the wicked, they do not learn righteousness, even in a land of uprightness they go on doing evil and regard not the majesty of the Lord."

In other words, God gives man plenty of grace, but as we sin and ignore God and all that he does for us, the day comes when the day of grace is over and judgment falls. It takes judgment for man to learn righteousness.

Many prophetic teachers are in agreement that we are not only in the last days, but we are in the birth pains leading to the Lord's Return. We really don't know when we will enter the final countdown. It's like we are watching the fuse burning its way to trigger events that will lead to the forming of a One World Government and the last seven years of the Great Tribulation.

After further study of the warning signs from David Wilkerson's book, Set the Trumpet to Thy Mouth, I saw that he gave us an order of events. Economic collapse would come first, followed by destruction, and finally, we would see an invasion of America by our enemies. I believe we need to closely watch what happens to our economy around September 13, 2015, which is the end of the current seventh, seven year Shemittah cycle. If the first of David Wilkerson's warnings take place at this time, then the next two events will follow. We may not know exactly how soon they will follow, but I believe my chapter on the sequence of events will give us some valid clues.

The quote below From Wilkerson's book, Set the Trumpet to Thy mouth, best describes the first Warning Sign. He told us what for what to look, and this will let us know that the final countdown has begun.

"Scoff if you choose, but the underlying fears about a collapse will soon become a tragic reality. Numerous cracks will appear in our fragile prosperity, and soon even the most pessimistic will know in their hearts that a total collapse is certain. Senators and Congressmen will sit in stunned silence as they realize no one can stop the tailspin into chaos. Business, political, and economic leaders will be terrorized by its suddenness and it's far – reaching effect." David Wilkerson, Set the Trumpet to Thy Mouth, page, 15.

It was only recently that I made a Biblical connection to a large meteor event described in Revelation 18:21, *"Then a mighty angel picked up a boulder the size of a great millstone and threw it into the sea, and said: "With such violence the great city of Babylon will be thrown down, never to be found again."* (This verse is describing a great meteor and tidal wave hitting the heart of Mystery Babylon).

The connection I did not make until recently was that the final destruction of mystery Babylon does not happen until the anti-christ is on the scene, and the global one world government is in place. I also concluded that there can be other destructions hitting America before its final death blow. This being the case, it would mean that from the start of the first warning judgment noted by David Wilkerson, **(Economic collapse)** we could have a few months to even a year from this first judgment until the other judgments of destruction that will come from many forms and conclude with a great meteor event. The timing of this event is becoming clearer, and I will share this facet toward the end of this chapter.

David Wilkerson said that before this big destruction, we will see smaller destructions such as moderate to large earthquake events as a warning of the greater judgments to come. I believe we will see the destruction of America coming in a variety of smaller hits. Smaller destructions will hit in the form of terrorist events. I already pointed out in a previous chapter why I believe the destruction of the Twin Towers was one of these smaller destructions.

Other similar events could happen any time, and these events will come with increasing intensity, similar to birth pains. Finally, once the global government is in place and the antichrist has been revealed, then the major destruction, as described in Revelation chapters 17 and 18, will be done at the hands of God and the help of the antichrist. Read Revelation 17:15,16. (NIV) *"Then the angel said to me, "The waters you saw, where the prostitute sits, are peoples, multitudes, nations and languages. The beast and the ten horns you saw will hate the prostitute. They will bring her to ruin and leave her naked: they will eat her flesh and burn her with fire."*

A study of these chapters 17 and 18 in Revelation, will give further confirmation to the players of this final destruction of America. It behooves us to understand the timeline of these coming judgments, for the first warning sign will give us a heads-up and time to make our decisions to move out of harm's way without being moved prematurely by fear. God does not want us to fear, but He is all about warning us. In spite of what looks like horrific events coming, God has been giving me a greater sense of peace as I study His Word.

As I continue to search for other witnesses to this event, I am finding further confirmations to future events. I am seeing many witnesses to these events from both known and unknown prophetic voices who have been warned of a coming tsunamis on both the east and west coasts. The first one I will share is from the late John Paul

Jackson.

John Paul Jackson had a vision from the Lord in 2012, and he saw large tsunamis devastating the east and west coast of America in the near future. They would hit New York City and Los Angeles; he saw seven to ten story buildings in LA underwater. John Paul Jackson said, **"These tsunamis were caused by an unusual event that he could not explain."**

I recently found David Wilkerson's last prophetic message to America before he died, on YouTube. In this last message before he died, he said many prophetic friends who have been warned by God of a coming catastrophe, had asked David Wilkerson to use his platform to warn the church. They were telling him, "A great catastrophe that will change the way we live forever is coming." Wilkerson said that news people are also saying in essence, "Something is telling the whole world that we are on the brink of a catastrophe. These are secular people."

It was about two weeks ago, March of 2015, that I watched an interview on the Sid Roth program with Perry Stone. At the time, I thought I had finished this chapter; I was wrong, as God has continued to reveal more and more as I wait on Him. What I heard on this interview was like a great shock and great confirmation at the same time. Perry Stone was sharing about a dream he has been having every two weeks in vivid color. In this dream he described a tsunami hitting both the East and West coasts of the United States. He said the largest Tsunami hit the East Coast and described events connecting this larger tsunami to New York City. Both Sid Roth and Perry Stone seemed to be in agreement that the close repetitive nature to these dreams was an indicator that this event would happen soon. I have shared this study with a number of close friends, and they have all come back and agreed that this event will happen, but when, is the question.

Below is a letter I received 4-11-2015 from a good friend from Facebook. His name is John, a retired JAG lawyer for the Air Force. He understands who a credible witness is. He has had three friends recently contact him concerning dreams about meteor or tidal wave events. Below is one of the dreams his friends sent him.

Pastor John Shorey,

I just received this message from a Facebook friend who lives in Florida. It seems God is continuing to confirm Efrain Rodriguez prophecy. Below is the dream God gave to my friend.

"My dream occurred June 30, 2014. The day before that on the 29th I prayed to receive Baptism of the Holy Ghost and I asked God to give me any and all gifts of the Spirit that He wanted to give me.

I was at my mom's house in North Carolina at the time and I drove that day back to Florida where I live. The next morning on June 30th when I woke up I was shaking for three hours from a prophetic dream of the future. In my dream I was in the mountains of the Carolinas. The Lord was standing next to me and He all of a sudden told me to look down toward Florida. I said ok father, so I looked down and I see all the major highways in Florida jam packed with cars like people were trying to escape something coming but they couldn't move because there were too many cars.

The next thing I know the Lord told me to look toward the ocean surrounding all sides of Florida, so I did and then I see an asteroid, meteor shower, hit the ocean which caused 1,000 feet tsunami waves to come at Florida from all three sides of the state. Then I realized the people were trapped, no escape. Then the whole state was underwater.

I grew up in Florida, so this dream was devastating. The last thing the Lord showed me was, He told me to stay in Florida where He would use me to further his kingdom for a short time then I am to prepare and wait for His Word to leave before the event happens. So I haven't questioned Him since and now I'm trying to reach people however possible and just wait on my father God to speak.

The Lord showed me that the Four Horseman of the Apocalypse are riding now. After diving deeper into prophecy and speaking to other prophets it all makes sense what's happening in the world now."

Javonna

She knew nothing about the Efrain Rodriguez prophecy.

I spoke to a friend from Maine about this study, and she shared with me about a friend of hers who, over a year ago, had a dream of a great tidal wave hitting the coast of Maine. This tidal wave went many miles inland, and she was shown that she would have to leave to escape harm's way. Checking online, I found many accounts where God has given dreams to many about this coming judgment. Below I have the links to two of these accounts on YouTube. If you copy these links into your computer browser, you should be able to watch them.

https://www.youtube.com/watch?v=LMHLmv8-DjU&feature=youtu.be

https://www.youtube.com/watch?v=kIKhvZiySz0

Concluding thoughts continue to come to me on this coming epic event. I see God revealing his truths line upon line. Recently, while writing chapter 19, covering the scenario timeline of sorts, placing events in chronological order, and linking events to scripture, it has caused me to see the picture come into focus like what happens when you put a puzzle together. I believe the clarity that is now coming is being guided by the Holy Spirit.

I now believe an epic meteor event will happen just before the rapture. The scriptural basis for the order of this event can be found in Matthew 24:29-31, Mark 13:24-27 and Luke 21:25-27. I will write out these verses that show the Lord Jesus coming to gather his elect following this event. In fact, as you will see, each of these verses describes the Lord coming in the clouds just following the description of the meteor event.

Matthew 24:29-31 (NIV) *"Immediately after the distress of those days, 'The sun will be darkened and the moon will not give its light;* **the stars will fall from the sky,** *and heavenly bodies will be shaken'* **'At that time the sign of the Son of Man will appear in the sky, and all the nations of the earth will mourn. They will see the Son of Man coming on the clouds of the sky, with power and great glory. And he will send his angels with a loud trumpet call, and they will gather his elect from the four winds, from one end of the heavens to the other."**

Mark 13:24-27 (NIV) *"But in those days following that distress, 'the sun will be darkened, and the moon will not give its light:* **the stars will fall from the sky,** *and heavenly bodies* *will be shaken.'* **"At that time men will see the Son of Man coming in clouds with great power and glory. And he will send his angels and gather his elect from the four winds, from the ends of the earth to the ends of the heavens."**

Luke 21:25-27 (NIV) *"There will be signs in the sun, moon and stars. On the earth, nations will be in anguish and perplexity at the roaring and tossing of the sea.* **Men will faint from terror, apprehensive of what is coming on the world,** *for heavenly bodies will be shaken.* **At that time they will see the Son of Man coming in a cloud with power and great glory."**

When I shared these Bible verses with a friend, telling her that I now see from scripture that this event will happen just before the rapture, her response after reading these verses was, " It was right in front of us, and we just didn't see it."

Now I will share the next piece of the puzzle that I know the Holy Spirit allowed me to see. This next verse will show us when this event will happen in the order of events found in the book of Revelation.

Revelation 6:12-14 (NIV) *"I watched as he opened the sixth seal. There was a great earthquake. The sun turned black like sackcloth made of goat hair, the whole moon turned blood red, and* **the stars in the sky fell to earth, as late figs drop from a fig tree when shaken by a strong wind.** *The sky receded like a scroll, rolling up, and every mountain and island was removed from its place."*

This verse in Revelation chapter six is rich in evidence that ties the meteor event to the verses in Matthew, Mark and Luke. The quote above contains the signs Jesus gave to his disciples when they asked Him "what will be the sign of your coming and the end of the age." Realize Jesus was talking to his disciples regarding the things that would happen before the Rapture of the elect.

By contemplating Matthew 24, you will see much of what Jesus told his disciples is the outline of the Seals of Revelation, chapter six. The verses from Matthew, Mark, and Luke all describe a coming meteor event. Revelation chapter six reads, *"the stars in the sky fell to earth, as late figs drop from a fig tree when shaken by a strong wind."* This is describing a meteor event. When you read of a great earthquake, it says *"every mountain and island was removed from its place."* This is what would happen when a great meteor hits the earth, causing earthquakes and volcano eruptions around the earth. When you have large volcano eruptions you will not only have ash circling the globe but it will cause the sun to turn black. It will affect the light of the moon. I have seen pictures from Mount Saint Helens, where the eruption generated two hundred mile an hour winds, and the effect made the ash cloud appear as rolling clouds. Again the verse above in Revelation, chapter six, supports this, *"The sky receded like a scroll, rolling up."*

Now, I want to propose a question that some will ask, "Could this be pointing to a pre-tribulation rapture during the coming fourth blood moon?" The verse above says the sun turned black and the whole moon turned blood red. There are those who are saying that the Great Tribulation will start this September following the end of the Shemittah cycle. I should also point out that if you take the position of a Post-Tribulation rapture, the Great Tribulation has to start in September in order for the Rapture to occur in September at the time of the Feast of Trumpets seven years later. If you take the pre-tribulation position, then it would make sense for the Rapture to start in September during the feast of trumpets for this to be the beginning of the Great Tribulation.

Those who hold to the Pre-trib or Post – trib position are also saying, " If the Great Tribulation does not start at the end of this year, at the end of the Shemittah cycle, then the Great Tribulation and The Rapture will have to wait for another seven years." I have covered why I believe we cannot kick the can down the road for another seven year cycle. I will also point out that this is the last blood moon Tetrad event for 400 or more years. We are also approaching the year of Jubilee that will not be repeated for another fifty years.

This is why I believe it is not possible for the Great Tribulation to start in September of 2015. From what I see clearly from Scripture, before the Great Tribulation can start, the antichrist must be revealed. I have shown from Scripture that this event cannot happen until a global government is in place and one of the ten regional leaders is fatally wounded but comes back from his death bed to become the antichrist. Once the antichrist is revealed, he must negotiate a peace treaty with Israel and the Middle East countries. The fact that the end of the Shemittah cycle that ends this September 13th could be the time that the economies of the world start to crumble, I just don't see how all these other events, (a global economic collapse, the forming of a new global government and the revealing of the antichrist), can come together by the end of September of 2015.

It makes more sense to me that the dominoes will start to fall this September - leading us to the signing of a peace treaty with Israel by March of 2016 and this being the beginning of the Great Tribulation. Then when the saints go through forty-two months of War on the Saints, as described in both Daniel and the book of Revelation, this will bring us to the time of the Feast of Trumpets in September of 2019. This is seventy years from the signing of the peace armistice in Israel in 1949.

I, personally, hold to a mid-tribulation Rapture, and the verse in Revelation chapter six above, shows the meteor event happening after the opening of the Sixth Seal. When this verse is studied with the meteor verses in Matthew, Mark and Luke, I see the combination of these verses supporting my position of a Mid-tribulation Rapture. My position of a Mid-tribulation Rapture would require that the Great Tribulation start in the spring, around the end of March, in order for the three and a half years of war on the saints to end in September during the time of the feast of trumpets. This is where I believe we will see the Rapture happening at the last trumpet of this Jewish festival.

I must interject that many great Bible scholars, for legitimate reasons, hold to three common positions for the timing of the Rapture, Pre, Mid or Post-Tribulation. We all hold dearly to our chosen position. This is not about who is right and who is wrong. No! This is all about our coming together and looking at all the pieces of the puzzle as they are revealed to us and eventually we will come to a common conclusion. I would love to be wrong in my position and find out the Rapture is a Pre-Tribulation event.

I have recently realized that it could become evident to all of us this coming September of 2015, which position on the timing of the Rapture, is the correct position! If this September brings a spiraling collapse to the economies of the World, that would pressure all the countries of the world to accept a global solution and the forming of a One World Government. Then, from the Pre-tribulation position, the Rapture will happen before things get too bad. Now realize, if we go into a global meltdown, and we see the imminent forming of a One World Government, but the Rapture does not happen, then those who hold to the Pre-tribulation position will have to realize that we cannot kick the can down the road for another seven years because the falling dominoes will not allow the holding off of the beginning of the Great Tribulation for another seven years. At this point, I believe we could see a great falling away because so many will realize they had been taught wrong.

Now; let's look at how events this September will play out from the Mid-tribulation position. When September 13, 2015 arrives, which is the end of the seventh, seven year Shemittah cycle, this is when, from a Mid-tribulation position, we would need to see the economies of the world start to spiral out of control. This would be the first domino that will leap frog the world into a series of events that could include major breakdowns of infrastructure and the use of martial law and other events over the course of the next six months that will see the world accepting a global solution of a new One World Government. These events would lead to the revealing of the antichrist and the beginning of the seven years Great Tribulation by March of 2016. If we don't see these events happening over the course of a six month period of time, then the Mid-Tribulation position will look to be flawed. Yet, if we do see events happening that will lead to the signing of a peace treaty in the Middle East by March of 2016, this would give credence to the Mid-tribulation position because 42 months of war on the saints will conclude in September around the time of the Feast of Trumpets. Seven years from a March start of the Great Tribulation would end the Tribulation in March, and it would not line up with the Feast of Trumpets.

This brings us to the Post-tribulation position through the glasses of the coming end of the current Shemittah cycle that is coming in September of 2015. If this position is correct and the Great Tribulation is to start this September so that after a seven year Great Tribulation the rapture will occur during the Feast of Trumpets at the end of September of that year, then for this position to prove itself to be the correct position, the events I have outlined above that would include an economic collapse, the forming of a One World Government, and the revealing of the antichrist will have to start before September of 2015 so that everything will be in place soon enough for the arriving antichrist to broker a peace treaty with Israel and the Middle East by the end of September of 2015. As we approach this September, if we do see the economies of the world spiraling out of control but a One World Government is not being formed by the end of September and the anti-christ has not arrived by this time, then the accuracy of this position will come into question.

The wild card to all of these scenarios is "What if nothing happened this September of 2015?" I would say that if we make it to Christmas of 2015 and we do not see the economies of the world in a tailspin, then I and numerous prophetic teachers will be in a state of confusion. We will have more questions than answers, and the question I would ask is, "If Jesus told us to watch for the signs of his coming because he did not want us to be caught unaware, then if nothing happens, then why would Jesus ask us to watch?" I really don't personally see any way for us to get into the spring of 2016 without these events that I have outlined coming to pass.

— CHAPTER EIGHTEEN —

THE FIVE END-TIME'S WARS

W hat I have assembled below is a collection of studies related to the five wars of the End-Times that I have written about in the last year. I am now seeing that these separate studies all tie together, and I am arranging them together to see if I can connect the dots to reveal a greater revelation than what was seen when studying them separately.

I am starting this chapter with a study I did concerning what I see as five End-Times Wars. Up until recently, I have thought that there were only three End-Times Wars. **The first war is the Psalms 83 war** that would happen before the Great Tribulation starts. This war would leave the Middle East in an explosive state, with more war threatening to erupt at any time, thus setting the stage for the antichrist to show up and broker a seven year peace agreement.

The second war I had seen coming was **the war of Gog and Magog.** I had always said that this war could not happen before the antichrist arrives. The reason I said this was, if this war were to happen before the antichrist arrived, and as the Bible says in Ezekiel 38, God will intervene, this intervention of God is so powerful that the Bible says the nations would recognize that it was the hand of God saving Israel. Ezekiel 38:22-23 (NIV) *"I will execute judgment upon him with plague and bloodshed; I will pour down torrents of rain, hailstones and burning sulfur on him and on his troops and on the many nations with him. And so I will show my greatness and my holiness, and I will make myself known in the sight of many nations. Then they will know that I am the LORD."* If this intervention were to happen before the antichrist arrived, Israel would not need to accept a peace treaty brokered by the antichrist. The back of their enemies would have been broken by this defeat, and Israel would know that God was watching their backs.

I believe the war of Gog and Magog happens close to the middle of the seven year Great Tribulation. It makes sense to me that it would happen just before the desecration of the temple by the antichrist and the soon to follow Rapture of God's elect. I think it also makes sense that after God intervenes during this battle that the antichrist will take credit for this victory by saying that he is God and taking over the temple.

Previously, **the third war** I had seen coming would be the last war, **the battle of Armageddon**. This would be the War when Israel is again surrounded by her enemies and without God's intervention, Israel would be destroyed. But Revelation 19: 11-18 says that Jesus comes riding a white horse with his armies following him, and Jude 14 b, (NIV) says *"See the Lord is coming with thousands upon thousands of His holy ones."* This is when the saints will be coming back with Christ when he returns at his Second Coming.

Now, I will come to the point of this chapter. I recently finished a second book, <u>Unlocking the Mystery of the Book of Revelation</u>. It shows how the book of Revelation came to be written out of chronological order and how it could be sorted out when read in order. Many truths not previously seen have been jumping out now that I can read the book of Revelation in chronological order. One of the biggest revelations coming to me was concerning the destruction of Mystery Babylon. I had always seen this event happening after the Rapture and during the wrath of God. Now my studies strongly show that Mystery Babylon, (America) is destroyed in the first half of the seven years Great Tribulation and before the Rapture. Recently my studies have opened my eyes to the possibilities that the destruction of mystery Babylon,(America) could happen even before the Great Tribulation begins. It was my studies and the leading of the Holy Spirit into the prophecies of David Wilkerson that rerouted my thoughts on the timing of this coming destruction.

I also see the destruction of Mystery Babylon as a war, (**The first or the Second war**). Later I will show what makes sense to me from scripture as to the timing of this war. Concerning the destruction of America, it is a toss-up as to which of the first two wars will happen first. The first step in the destruction of America could very well be the destruction of our economic system. When countries try to hurt another country's economy, this can be called an act of war. Our country has brought down major economic sanctions against Russia because of its aggression against the country of Ukraine. In fact, Russia has warned America that our economic sanctions against Russia would be looked at as an act of war.

I discovered another war, (**the fourth war**). This observation came from one of the closing chapters of <u>Unlocking the Mystery of the Book of Revelation</u>. This chapter is a running commentary showing the order of key events from the book of Revelation. While I was writing that chapter, I noticed a key war showing itself at the Sixth Trumpet. I had previously connected this war with the Battle of Armageddon, but after further study, I see it is a separate war. I will be going into greater detail later as to why this is a separate, significant war of the Last Days.

The last five wars unfolding in the Last Days. The last five wars unfold in the Last Days as three wars happening before The Rapture, of which two will greatly affect the United States. If this is true, I believe that two of these wars will greatly affect the United States, and if this is true, it should compel us to take whatever steps needed to equip ourselves and prepare for what is coming in the last days. The reason to be prepared for the last days is not so we can survive until the Rapture but for us to be prepared in order to share the Gospel with the lost. We need to be prepared by the Word and in supplies for a great harvest in the last days.

1. The Psalms 83 war.

This war, happens before the Great Tribulation starts. This is a coming war that we should be watching the current events of today unfolding in the Middle East. Iran is moving fast to having nuclear bombs, and, I believe, Israel will have to make its move to stop them from having this capability. I believe this is the war which will fulfill Bible prophecy concerning the destruction of Damascus. I believe for this prophecy to be fulfilled, to cause Damascus never to be lived in again, will require that this city be destroyed by a nuclear bomb. I have said before, and still believe, that when a nuclear bomb goes off in the Middle East, it will cause a global panic that could be one of the dominoes that will cause the collapse of global economies. Also, when

God wants the dominoes to fall in place, major economies around the world can start collapsing for <u>no</u> apparent reason.

Currently we are seeing much infighting among the nations of the Middle East. Saudi Arabia is fighting in Yemen. Iran is getting ready to attack Saudi Arabia. ISIS is trying to carve out its own territory. I don't see this infighting as one of the End-Times wars.

I am structuring the order of these five wars with the Psalms 83 war coming first. I now realize that the destruction of America could happen first. If the Psalms 83 war is the first war and America is still a super power, then I see the two super powers sitting it out, supplying arms and playing the referees on the side lines. We see Russia currently arming the key players in the Middle East, Syria and Iran. The United States has been a major source for arming and supporting Israel. What I see happening is the United States and Russia will be sort of referees on the sidelines making sure that each super power keeps its hands off when this war erupts. The two super powers will be at a stalemate watching to see who comes out on top as Israel and the Middle East battle it out. Below, I am including a recent study I did that shows what could be the effects to the world when the Psalms 83 War breaks loose.

IS SYRIA THE DOMINO THAT WILL TRIGGER A GLOBAL ECONOMIC COLLAPSE?

We have been seeing the possibility of a War in the Middle East since September of 2013. On September,4, 2013 the news was showing a great effort being made to gain the support from Congress for approval for attacking and punishing Syria for using chemical weapons on innocent civilians. The biggest argument I heard was, "If we do not act, we will appear weak to the world for not acting after the line in the sand has been crossed." So far, I question if the evidence presented is compelling enough to attack a sovereign nation. I have been praying and hoping that our leaders would stand down.

The United States has been acting as the world cop for some time now. This has been building up a great amount of resentment towards America, and the day has to come when America will be reduced from being the world's number one Super Power. According to a Bible Prophecy perspective, America is not going to be a major player in the coming tribulation years.

Because there was not enough support to build a coalition of support to attack Syria and Iran, the United States accepted terms set up by Russia to put off the inevitable. This stalling, of what could have been the start of a war in the Middle East, has basically bought time so Russia can further arm Syria and Iran to such a level that they will feel confident in attacking Israel.

There are many reports saying that Russia has equipped Syria and Iran with S200 and S300 cruise missiles. Since writing this article, I have read that Russia is now marketing even more advanced missile systems. I have studied these missiles for some time. They travel at almost subsonic speeds, they zig zag as they approach their targets, and they cruise close to the ground so not to be detected by radar. Then add to this what I learned later about a far more dangerous missile that Russia has supplied to Syria, the P-800 Yakhont anti-ship missiles. These missiles are one of the most advanced missiles in the Russian arsenal, and they could be fired at our ships if we make a move to attack Syria and Iran.

The second facet to all this is, I believe along with Russia supplying Syria and Iran with high tech missiles, Iran is aggressively moving toward developing and acquiring nuclear armed missiles to use against Israel. This fact convinces me that if Iran is months away from having nuclear weapons, then Israel would have to make a preemptive strike against both Syria and Iran to stop this war before it gets started in order to take out Iran's ability to finish developing these nuclear weapons. I believe it is possible that we could see the Psalms 83 war this year, 2015.

The current development with the USA and Iran currently in negotiations that would allow Iran to keep its nuclear program is insane. We know Iran wants nuclear weapons to destroy Israel, and we know we cannot trust Iran's words for the peaceful use of their nuclear program. If Iran and our government agree to allow Iran to continue to enrich uranium, then it is a given that Israel will have to make a strike to take out this program. I could not believe it when I heard that if Israel attempts to do an airstrike on Iran; our government has threatened to shoot down the Israeli planes.

Another option that comes to mind would be that when another state of war flares up and missiles are sent over the border into Israel, that Israel will take one of these events as a reason to do a full-blown retaliation strike against Syria and Iran. This could escalate into a major war event, and Israel could be pushed back against a wall far enough that they would use what is called the "Sampson Option", the use of nuclear weapons. This last ditch tactic would be used to push their adversary back far enough that the attacking enemy would have to stand down. I believe one of these nukes will be targeted at Damascus, and maybe one will target Iran's nuclear development facilities.

For those who are not versed in Bible Prophecy, the Bible predicts that the day will come when Damascus will be destroyed, never to be inhabited again. Damascus is the hub of all that is happening in Syria today. Isaiah 17:1 *"See, Damascus will no longer be a city, but will become a heap of ruins."* This prophecy is yet to be fulfilled. I believe the reason Damascus will no longer be a city and never rebuilt, will be because this city will be destroyed by a nuclear bomb and will be too contaminated to be inhabited.

The third facet to all of this is the most frightening. If the Bible prophecy that says Damascus will be destroyed is fulfilled in the near future, the effect this could have on the world will be devastating. When a nuclear bomb goes off in the Middle East, released by Israel, it will cause the world to believe that WW111 is about to start. What effect will this have? Based on my study of Bible prophecy, this will not be the timing for the Battle of Gog and Magog, nor will it be the timing for the Battle of Armageddon. What will happen is, people around the globe will believe it is the beginning of WWIII. Christians in America will start to wonder, "Where is the Rapture?" These same Christians and non-Christians alike will realize that a storm is coming and they need to stock up on food and supplies for what is soon coming. Think about what happens when a snow storm or even hurricanes are forecast. Your grocery stores are slammed with customers, and the shelves are emptied in hours. Imagine a line of customers lining up outside of Costco and Walmart stores waiting their turn to get in, hoping to find food still on the shelves. Something like this happened during the Cuban Missile crisis in the early Sixties, and a bomb was never detonated.

I have read that only 3% of Americans are what you would call preppers, getting ready for the hard times that could lie ahead. I have also heard that the prepping industry that is packaging long term storage food and supplies can only supply up to 5% of the American population. What will happen if all of a sudden 20 to 50% of Americans realize there is a huge storm for which to prepare. I believe the system that supplies all food to America would be overwhelmed in days. This would lead to food shortages, rationing, and rioting. This fear would cause people to watch where every dime was spent, and restaurants would close within days. Other businesses would soon follow and go out of business. All that I am describing would lead to rioting, anarchy and food rationing. Not only will the fifty million people on food stamps not be able to get food, but just average Americans will not be able to get food. With rioting happening in cities now over racial issues, what will happen when fifty million Americans can no longer get food from failing entitlement programs?

If what I am describing makes sense, then you will realize that it will not take long for all that we hold dear in America to collapse. If this event were to be timed with another crippling event like the Northwest quake that God showed me on May 11, 2013, panic could accelerate until every major city in America would be placed under curfew and Martial Law. This is a key domino to fall that will lead to other dominoes falling around the world. This could be key to bringing pressure to bear on all the countries to lead the world into joining a One World Government and a new global currency. This could lead us into the Great Tribulation and what I call in my book, The Window of the Lord's Return.

2. The Destruction of Mystery Babylon.

Up until 2014, I had thought that the destruction of Mystery Babylon would happen during the wrath of God in the second half of the seven years Great Tribulation. After reading and studying the book of Revelation in chronological order, I am convinced that this destruction will happen before the Rapture. I have recently concluded that the beginning stages of this destruction will begin with an economic collapse and other events before the Great Tribulation begins. In my timeline chart I show this period as the Birth Pains that we will go through before the Great Tribulation begins.

It has already been explained that Mystery Babylon is the United States. Some teach that Mystery Babylon is New York City, the center of finance for the world. It could go either way. If New York City were totally destroyed, as Revelation 18 describes, it would lead to a total collapse of all business and commerce in America. This would fulfill what is described in Revelation 18:11, *"The merchants of the earth will weep and mourn over her because no one buys their cargoes anymore."*

My next point concerning this second war happening in the last days will cover who, why, and when this will take place. First we will look at the who and the why.

Who will have a part in the destruction of Mystery Babylon and why? In the context of my study, I am referring to the destruction of America as we know it. America is the only significant Super Power on earth that did not exist when the Bible was written. Thus, she was a Super Power that was a mystery to the writer of the Book of Revelation. When the new global government comes to power as the solution to a global financial collapse, it is my belief that this new global, One World Government, being led by the antichrist, will not want to see the USA around to challenge its power over the nations of the world. I see the coming global economic collapse as the first blow that will lead to the destruction of America. Once America goes down, there will be many evil forces that will not want to see America attempt to rise up on her own and challenge the leadership of this new One World Government, (**this is the why**). I see the destruction of America coming from many directions. I believe the first blow will be the collapse of our economy.

Revelation 17:15-16 explains a part of the who will play a part in this coming destruction of America or Mystery Babylon. "Then the second angel said to me, *"The waters you saw, where the prostitute sits, are peoples, multitudes, nations and languages.* **The beast and the ten horns you saw will hate the prostitute.** *They will bring her to ruin and leave her naked: they will eat her flesh and burn her with fire."*

I also see a second player in the destruction of America. I see God's divine judgment coming that will include destruction by earthquakes and a meteor event that will bring destruction by a great tidal wave. I recently saw this event described in two places in God's Word. I covered this event in a previous chapter called, "There will be Signs in the Sun, Moon and Stars." Revelation 18:21 describes God using an angel to bring destruction to the queen city of America. Rev.18:21 (NIV) *"Then a mighty angel picked up a boulder the size of a large millstone and threw it into the sea, and said: "With such violence the great city of Babylon will be thrown down, never to be found again."*

I believe that a global financial collapse, natural disasters and terrorists attacks in our cities and possibly an attack on our electrical grid will have left America in a weakened state, making America an easy target to take out. I recently heard a guest on Fox News saying that within a year of America's grid going down, that as many as 90 percent of all Americans will have died. This weakened state would leave us wide open for a full blown attack on our soil. In a previous chapter entitled, "The night of the Blood Moons" it is shown God resurrected an important revelation prophecy given to David Wilkerson over thirty years ago showing that America would see destruction coming in multiple stages that will conclude with the invasion of America by our enemies.

If our enemies attack our grid at some opportune time, this would really bring America to her knees. What I see coming would be nothing less than an act of war against America. This attack will take America out of the world picture. There have been many recent prophecies saying that America would be attacked in the last days. One notable prophecy was from George Washington, giving a vivid description of this invasion. He saw cities and villages all across America burning. What was encouraging was his seeing America turning back to God and the tide of the war going in America's favor.

The last point I will cover on this second war of the last days will be when it will take place. I see the first stages of America's destruction happening with the collapse of our economy. I see later stages of this destruction coming at the hands of the antichrist, once he comes to power. If we agree that the antichrist coming to power is revealed at the First Seal, and if it is agreed that in order for the antichrist to consolidate his power, he would want to see the destruction of his greatest rival, then it makes sense to me that this second war that will see the final destruction of America will be part of what is described in the Second Seal. Revelation 6:3, 4 *"When the Lamb opened the Second Seal, I heard the second living creature say, "Come!" Then another horse came out, a fiery red one. Its rider was given power to take peace from the earth and to make men slay each other. To him was given a large sword."*

I was recently sent a copy of David Wilkerson's, Time Square Church Pulpit Series, this was dated 4-11-1994 and its title was, "The Red Horse of the Apocalypse" It is almost hard to believe how accurately David Wilkerson was seeing into the future by more than twenty years to describe what we are seeing unfolding before our eyes. I will share a few paragraphs from this prophetic document.

"Whoever thought we would live to see this day of violence and bloodshed? Yet what amazes me most is that so many Americans – Christians among them – react smugly, viewing America as an "Island of peace." We tell ourselves, "God will never come to America and snatch away our peace!"

"The Red Horse has been set loose – and He will not bypass Godless America as he takes peace from the World." He is galloping on the winds, headed for America's shores – and he is about to gallop through our cities, taking away all peace and order as he goes!"

"Now the red horse of the apocalypse is galloping! Our peace is about to be forever taken from us – and in its place will be a bloody sword! An increasing spirit of hate and murder will take over. Cities will be on fire, guns will blaze, rioting and bloodshed will fill the streets. America is going to become a bloody war zone!"

"Soon Christians won't be thinking about marital differences, the right dentist, the right schools, credit-card bills, hair styles, shopping malls, vacations, "How to cope" psychology. Instead, we'll be thinking, "Where can I send my children to spare then from all the bloodshed? Is some disenchanted madman coming to torch our building? Do we have enough food stored for the week? Please God – what am I to do?"

"All the false peace in America is going to come tumbling down! When the red horse gallops through America – when our cities are in flames, race riots break out, federal troops and tanks roll down our streets – all false hopes will vanish into thin air!"

"Preachers who stood in the pulpit and said, "Peace and safety," are going to see their churches fall apart! Desperate men and women will stand up in the middle of meetings, crying, "Pastor what's going on? This is not what you told us would happen. What does the Bible say?" But he won't know! And the people will turn on him, shouting. "You lied to us." Dave Wilkerson Time Square Church Pulpit

Series 1994

I will interject that at the time of the opening of the Second Seal, it says the rider of the second horse was given power to take peace from the earth. The Window of the Lord's Return, I mention that I believe that many small wars will break out around the world. Countries like Russia consolidating its power and taking back lands that had been lost in recent years. As I write this, we are seeing Russia making its move against lands that used to be under their power.

I believe it is possible that during this time that peace is taken from the earth, this could be the time that Mystery Babylon is destroyed. As events are currently playing out in the news, we see the Muslim faction called ISIS making its move to take peace from the earth. These wars would then lead into the third seal which will be global famine and starvation. This would be when it would be most important for the implementation of the mark of the beast as a solution to global financial collapse and global famine. If you will read the opening of the first four seals, it seems to describe a period of global turmoil that could all happen in a short period of time. At this time the man of peace, the antichrist, will consolidate his power.

As a further point of clarification, when I read the opening of the second, third and fourth seals, I see these seals connected as a series of events that are all connected. The second seal says peace is taken from the earth and that man will slay each other; this is war. The Third Seal describes famine, which is a byproduct of war. The Third Seal describes the scope of this war. This seal says that, *"They were given power over a fourth of the earth to kill with sword, famine and plague, and by the wild beasts of the earth."* (Revelation 6:8b) This description says this war will cover one fourth of the earth. It does not say one fourth of the earth will die. It shows me this is not a world war but limited to one fourth of the earth geographically.

It is not beyond the possibility that it will be at this time that the antichrist will institute the system of the Mark of the Beast. It could also be at this time after the opening of the first Four Seals that the antichrist will propose a number of peace treaties to bring about a period of peace on earth after this time of war. This could be the time that the seven year peace is signed with Israel, that would trigger the beginning of the Great Tribulation.

This scenario leaves me with an interesting thought to ponder. Could it be possible that the first few seals will open BEFORE the seven year peace is signed that starts the seven years of Jacobs trouble, (The Great Tribulation)? Current events happening in the Ukraine and Russia are certainly pointing to the fact that things are lining up and are actually happening to a degree. I have to wonder if the Second Seal is ISIS, and I wonder if this seal has already been opened. Revelation 6:3,4 *"When the Lamb opened the second seal, I heard the second living creature say, "Come!" Then another horse came out, A fiery red one. Its rider was given power to take peace from the earth and to make men slay each other. To him was given a large sword."*

3. The Battle of Gog and Magog

I have mentioned in the first paragraphs of this study why I believe this battle will happen just before the Rapture, in the middle of the seven year Great Tribulation. I will add a few more insights concerning this war. The Bible supports a teaching that at some point the ten region global government will be reduced to seven. This makes sense to me because two of the regions discussed in the last days wars have separate parts to play as opposed to the beast government of the antichrist. If I were to give my best guess as to who these three breakaway regions would be, it would include the region of Russia that is the key player of the battle of Gog and Magog. The second would include China because it has a separate role in the last days' wars, separate from the beast government. I am split between two choices for the third breakaway.

One of my choices for the third breakaway from the 10 is the region of Mystery Babylon. This region is somewhat destroyed and brought to its knees by the beast, and under these circumstances, it could remain separated from the rule of the beast. But I am not totally convinced of this reasoning because the destruction of the financial heart of America could be a way of forcing America into submission to the rule of the antichrist. To me it really does not seem possible that America would escape the system of the mark of the beast in the last days.

Probably a better option for the third breakaway would be the Middle East region. This would include Israel and the Arab countries. I have a few reasons for this choice. One reason is, I don't believe the mark of the beast will be forced on this region.

When the War on the Saints is happening, Israel and the Middle East are living in peace. Another reason is, if this region were forced to take the mark of the beast, it would result in God's judging them for taking the mark, and they would not go into the Millennial Reign of Christ. A third reason would be because the players of the battle of Gog and Magog include Arab nations in league with Russia acting outside of the authority of the antichrist.

Concluding my thoughts on this third war, (the battle of Gog and Magog), an important point to remember is how I described both super powers, the United States and Russia, remaining on the sidelines for the Psalms 83 war. With the destruction of Mystery Babylon (America), the United States has been taken out of the picture. This circumstance has given Russia the freedom to win the favor of the Arab nations by going into league with them to destroy Israel. Unfortunately, Russia was not counting on the intervention of God that will ultimately take out a second global superpower.

Some teach that the war of Gog and Magog could happen any day now. I have held my ground that this war will not happen until America is taken down. I also believe the peace treaty must be in place that is brokered by the antichrist before this battle takes place. I have already given my reason for this because when God takes down the enemies of Israel in this war, the Bible makes it plain that the world will recognize that it was the power of God that brought this victory. Israel will not need a brokered peace from the antichrist at this time. God will be watching the back of Israel. I may be wrong on this point, but I believe I see the possibility that the Rapture takes place after this war. I see this as a time when God's people, the Jews, will be in such awe at the victory God gives them that it will be a national revival of the Jews accepting Jesus at this time, just in time to be raptured as part of the Bride of Christ!

I will share Bible verses below that I see supporting this position. I believe this first verse from Ezekiel 38 ties into the timing of the opening of the Sixth Seal of Revelation. I will show this below. Ezekiel 38:18-23 (NIV) *"This is what will happen in that day: When Gog attacks the land of Israel, my hot anger will be aroused, declares the Sovereign Lord. **In my zeal and fiery wrath I declare that at that time there shall be a great earthquake in the land of Israel.** The fish of the sea, the birds of the air, the beasts of the field, every creature that moves along the ground, and all the people on the face of the earth will tremble at my presence. The mountains will be overturned, the cliffs* *will crumble and every wall will fall to the ground. I will summon a sword against Gog on all my mountains, declares the Sovereign Lord. Every man's sword will be against his brother. I will execute judgment upon him with plague and bloodshed: I will pour down torrents of rain, hailstones and burning sulfur on him and on his troops and on the many nations with him. And so I **will show my greatness and my holiness, and I will make myself** known in the sight of many nations. Then they will know that I am the Lord."*

The last sentence above makes my point. The nations will know God's greatness when this battle is over! The next verse is where I believe the timing of this battle takes place. At the time of a great earthquake in Israel that is shown after the opening of the Sixth Seal of Revelation. It is at this time, I believe, we will see the Rapture of God's elect. Revelation 6:12-16 (NIV) *"I watched **as he opened the sixth seal. There was a great earthquake.** The sun turned black like sackcloth made of goat hair, the whole moon turned blood red, and the stars in the sky fell to earth, as late figs drop from a fig tree when shaken by a strong wind. The sky receded like a scroll, rolling up, and every mountain and island was removed from its place. Then the kings of the earth, the princes, and generals, the rich, the mighty, and every slave and every free man hid in caves and among the rocks of the mountains. They called to the mountains and the rocks, "Fall on us **and hide us from the face of him who sits on the throne and from the wrath of the Lamb! For the great day of their wrath has come** and who can stand."* The last sentence I have marked in bold, supports that the Wrath of God will begin after the events of the Sixth Seal.

I will close my study on the Battle of Gog and Magog with a verse that appears to me to say that this time is the time of the "Day of the Lord", The Day of the Lord is generally recognized as the day of the Rapture. Ezekiel 39:7,8 (NIV) *"I will make known my holy name among my people Israel. I will no longer let my holy name be profaned, and the nations will know that I the Lord am the Holy One in Israel. **It is coming! It will surely take place, declares the Sovereign Lord. This is the day** I have spoken of."* This verse that says, *"This is the day I have spoken of"*, this can only be the Day of the Lord, and it is at this time that the Rapture takes place.

4. The Sixth Trumpet War (The fourth war)

I will write out the key verses that describe the event of the Sixth Trumpet.

Revelation 9:13-16, *"The sixth angel blew his trumpet, and I heard a voice coming from the horns of the golden altar that is before God. It said to the sixth angel who had the trumpet, "Release the four angels who are bound at the great river Euphrates." And the four angels who had been* **kept ready for this very hour and day** *and month and year were released to* **kill a third of mankind***. The number of* **the mounted troops was two hundred million***. I heard their number."*

The first thing about this war that made me realize that this was not part of the Battle of Armageddon, was when I noticed that this war could last a year, and it would result in the death of 1/3 of mankind. One Third of mankind based on the current population of the earth would amount to 2400 million dying in this war. Realize that the Battle of Armageddon will be very short. I believe that when God unleashes his battle plan, it will be over in a day. As you read this verse, you can see it is talking about an event that could take a year, **"And the four angels who had been kept ready for this very Year."** Some who read this may see this as just a point in time, pointing to a specific year. Further evidence to the thought that this war will take a year is the fact that it will be an army of two hundred million soldiers. It takes time to move this many men, and if this war were a nuclear war, it would not last very long, you would not need this many boots on the ground.

At the time of this war, two super powers have been destroyed. The United States and Russia have been taken out. This leaves only China and the global beast government led by the antichrist. This will empower China, possibly in league with North Korea to attack many Asian countries like Japan, South Korea, and Taiwan. This will be the time that China will take back lands taken from them in the Second World War by Russia. This could even be the time for China to attack the weakened nation of America and collect on the note it is holding on our debt. I see this war happening after the Rapture, but it affects many peoples and lands. It says a third of mankind will die in this war.

5. The Battle of Armageddon

This will be the last war for 1000 years. When this war breaks out, there will only be two major super powers left standing, the global government of the beast and the Asian coalition with China. At this time, these last two world powers will make their move to secure the Middle East and take out Israel. Again, the enemies of Israel don't realize that God will not allow destruction and conquest to come to the apple of his eye. It is hard to believe that after the outcome of the battle of Gog and Magog that any nation would try to bring harm to God's people.

At this time, Jesus will be seen coming back on his white horse and God's enemies will be destroyed in quick order. I believe, at this time, all who have taken the mark of the beast will be seen as an enemy of God and unredeemable. It will be a sad day when those who were deceived by the antichrist into taking the mark of the beast will call out to God for Mercy and as Jesus told the five foolish virgins, "I don't even know you". The beast and the false prophet will be thrown into the lake of fire, and satan will be bound for a thousand years. We won't win all the battles, but we will win the war.

— CHAPTER NINETEEN —

A POSSIBLE SCENARIO STORY
LEADING UP TO THE RAPTURE

L ast July of 2014, I wrote a scenario story based on the premise that The
Great Tribulation could start in March of 2015. This was based on a Mid-
tribulation view point that God's elect would go through three and a half
years of War on the Saints as described in both the book of Daniel and the book of
Revelation. A few months ago, God revealed to me what I call the Mystery of the
Fig Tree. This study is covered in detail in the introduction of my book. This study
explains that the prophecy of the fig tree in Matthew, chapter 24, was not referring
to the planting of the country of Israel in 1948, this prophecy was dealing with the
budding of the fig tree, (The New country of Israel). This happened with the signing
of the armistice of peace in the spring of 1949.

This discovery made me realize that a generation from 1949 would take us to 2019.
I personally believe the countdown of a generation started in 1949. I may be wrong,
but I am holding to my view that the Rapture will happen half way into the Great
Tribulation, during the feast of trumpets in September of 2019. I am not saying I
know the day or the hour of the Lord's return. In fact, until we see the forming of
a global government and the revealing of the antichrist, we cannot even be sure of
the year. If I am reading the signs correctly, for which Christ told us to watch, then I
believe we will see things falling together rapidly in the next year ending in 2015 and
going into 2016. Then in order for the Rapture to have a timing that would place
the Saints on the earth for forty two months of War on the Saints, leading up to the
Rapture, this would require that the Great Tribulation start by the end of March of
2016.

There are many prophetic teachers currently saying, "If the Lord does not return
during this Shemitttah cycle that ends September 13, 2015, then the Lord would not

come until another seven year cycle passes." They are basically saying we can extend the events to a later time. These teachers say that Israel did not control Jerusalem until the Six Day War in 1967, and they dismiss the last generation starting in 1949 as I have already established. When you study the scriptures I outline in the introduction of my book, the scriptures establish that God would plant Israel in their own land, and this happened in 1948. I am not going to wait around and see if others are right or wrong. If we wait and see if the global economies are going to collapse at the end of 2015 or early 2016, then we will be caught ill prepared for the years of tribulation ahead.

Based on these conclusions, I will now outline a blow-by-blow scenario of what I feel could be the order of events which could start coming together in the next few months and years. And, once the first domino falls, I believe we will see a rapid series of events come together that will lead us into the Great Tribulation. Please bear in mind, I am not saying this is "Thus saith the Lord." There will be instances where I can establish that certain events will happen based on God's Word, but it is the timing that is hard to nail down. Some events may happen at the same time and some events may happen in an order different from what I am laying out. The purpose of this timeline is to give us a picture to help us visualize what is coming and help us to see how fast things can come together.

CONNECTING THE DOTS

Now that I have laid out several studies that relate to the End-Times, I will share my connecting of the dots. It reminds me of a TV game show called Wheel of Fortune. The way this game is played is, your contestants take turns trying to uncover the clues to a sentence or phrase. Once a certain number of letters are turned over, the meaning of the sentence starts to come into focus. When it is a player's turn, this player can guess what is being said. The one who gets it right first is the winner. We are now seeing many clues to the End-Times being revealed. In fact, I believe that we have had more End-Times clarity revealed to us in the last three years then what we have seen revealed in the last twenty to thirty years. I may not be putting all the pieces of the puzzle together totally spot accurate. I may be off to a degree, but my point is, I see the End-Time events coming together very rapidly. Yet, we will never know the day or the hour of the Lord's Return. But no one who is listening to the Spirit of God can dispute that we are seeing End-Times mysteries revealed.

It is very interesting reading, all the to do out there, concerning the coming "Jade–Helm-15", martial law exercises that will be taking place this year in many major cities. These will be martial law practice drills taking place from July 15, to September 15, 2015. A well connected friend of mine made some contacts to people he knows that are in the know, and he was told that these exercises are being done in preparation for rapid response to coming ISIS attacks in America. When life in America is disrupted by these coming terrorist attacks, we will need a well-organized response, and it will include martial law. I wish I could trust our government, but much has happened to cause me to doubt their supposed good intentions. When martial law is launched, all bets and promises are off the table. Martial law allows our government to do as it pleases. One day of martial law and the constitution is gone.

What I also find interesting is the fact that these exercises will be ongoing until two days after the end of the coming Shemittah cycle. I can't help but think that a future economic collapse will be a planned event, and I cannot think of a better time to pull the plug on the economy than during the end of this coming seven year cycle that already has investors on edge. Many believe the stock market has been held up artificially by the Federal Reserve banks pumping funds into the stock market every time it takes a big dip. Imagine what would happen if during a big dip in the stock market this September, during the time of nervousness, if those who have been propping up the markets were to divest all at once. What kind of a chain reaction would this cause? During a time of economic collapse, would our cities need martial law to maintain law and order? I believe they would.

I read an article on the internet that outlined some of the things that would happen once wide spread martial law comes to America.**"The first thing that you need to know is that the U.S. Constitution would be "suspended". In other words, you would suddenly have no rights at all. There would be no freedom of speech, no freedom of religion, no freedom of the press, no freedom of assembly, and you could be arrested at any time for any reason whatsoever. For the duration of the "emergency", the military would be in control. There would be troops in the streets, a curfew would almost certainly be imposed, and armed checkpoints would be set up. If the "emergency" lasted long enough, we would probably see authorities go house to house confiscating firearms, ammunition, and food supplies. And perhaps most troubling of all, "dissidents" and "subversives" would likely be rounded up and imprisoned."**

POSSIBLE SCENARIO OF EVENTS AND TIMELINE

I am writing this scenario in April of 2015, it seems things are calm but is it the calm, before the storm? There is much infighting in the Middle East. I don't see this as a significant war developing. When the dust settles, then the real events will unfold. What we need to closely watch is the nuclear negotiations with America and Iran. It really seems America is prepared to accept a treaty with a country that cannot be trusted to keep its word and a country that is determined to develop the nuclear capability to destroy Israel. I believe this truth will leave Israel with no choice but to take action against Iran sometime in the months ahead. There is no doubt in my mind that when Israel makes its move, it will be acting alone and will alienate itself from all world sympathy, This will embolden its enemies to retaliate without having to worry that Israel's past allies, especially the United States, will come to their aid.

As we approach the summer of 2015, Many Christians know this is a monumental year with the fourth blood moon approaching, September 28th. But a greater worry is what will happen when we get to the close of this seven year Shemittah cycle ending September 13th? Seven years before, we saw a great crash of the stock market to the very ending day of that cycle. Even Wall Street investors are now nervously watching this coming end to a series of seven, seven year cycles.

It is the first week of August 2015 and a couple of terrorist events happened in America. Not as big as what happened on 911, but many lives are lost, and it creates a great sense of fear in our country. In July our country started doing martial law exercises in many major cities in America. Many fear these martial law practice drills as some plan by our government to establish some sort of dictatorship. On the positive side, these drills are to have a working plan ready to go, to put down any ISIS and terrorist attacks that could and will happen in our country. It is at this time when we are hit by these terrorists that we will see martial law put in place as needed.

On the negative side, once martial law is declared this gives our government the right to suspend the constitution, and if our government has evil intent it will be very hard to impossible to stop.

The race riots that have been simmering for months in a few America cities are festering and start to spread to other cities. Some states are mobilizing the National Guard to help maintain order. As these riots drag on and get out of control, you can be sure that martial law will be used to bring things under control.

Around the first week of September 2015, a great Earthquake hits America. Some prophets are saying this earthquake event will be triggered by a large comet hitting the earth. This would trigger major earthquakes all over the planet. I am praying that we will not see two such events before the Rapture. This event could affect any part of America, possibly in a place we would least expect it. It could trigger a great quake in the Northwest.

It is a 9.2 quake and brings the greatest destruction from a natural disaster ever seen in recorded history. It was predicted that the 520 floating bridge would go out. As it turns out, almost every major bridge in the Northwest collapsed, leaving no easy way to evacuate the survivors. Many tall buildings either collapsed, or fell over on their sides.

The Cascadia fault runs 800 miles from northern California to Vancouver Island in

Canada. This fault is about 60 miles off shore of the west coast. When this subduction fault gave way, it created a great tidal wave that came into the Northwest coast. The devastation was catastrophic, so much so that the loss of life is almost impossible to calculate. It will take weeks to make a count of the losses, and weeks to evacuate the survivors.

Every major TV network has cancelled all programming, giving full coverage to the devastation of this quake. If this earthquake were not in itself bad enough, it has triggered an entire chain of other catastrophic events, including large earthquakes to the north, occurring in Alaska, and large earthquakes to the south down into California. Great tidal waves brought great destruction to countries in all directions.

The economic losses are again almost inconceivable. Great companies such as Boeing Aircraft, Microsoft, Google, Starbucks and many other high-tech companies are devastated. This disaster will have far-reaching repercussions. The stock market goes into a tail spin within hours of the earthquake, and the markets are closed for forty-eight hours, only to go into another tail spin when they attempt to resume business. In fact, no effort seems to calm the markets. The utter chaos that hits the northwest begins spreading to other parts of the country as food shortages strike certain areas, which then triggers civil unrest in some major cities across America.

When it seems things can't get any worse, with our nation teetering on the edge of one of the greatest periods of panic ever, our enemies concealed within our own borders rise up, taking advantage of our crippled condition. We are then attacked with a number of terrorist events in our larger cities. ISIS terrorists are instilling fear throughout America. Both small town America and our cities are being hit with the most heinous crimes against innocent Americans.

Our electrical grid has come under attack in random parts of our country. This forces our government to place many of our cities under some form of marital law. Many of our troops and even much of our naval fleet is called home during this time of great trial on our American soil.

So many things have happened in just a week. As it was feared, the end of the Shemittah cycle that arrived September 13th ushered in a great panic on Wall Street, and every measure was taken to stop this crash from developing into a full blown economic collapse. It was to no avail. It appears that the prophetic words of David Wilkerson were accurate as we see them come to pass before our eyes.

"Soon, very soon, an economic nightmare will explode into reality. What frightful news it will be! *"O thou that dwellest upon many waters, abundant in treasures, thine end is come, and the measure of thy coveteousness, (Jeremiah 51:13)"* America is about to face a time of mass hysteria, as banks close and financial institutions crumble and our economy spins totally out of control." "Scoff if you choose, but the underlying fears about a collapse will soon become a tragic reality. Numerous cracks will appear in our fragile prosperity, and soon even the most pessimistic will know in their hearts that a total collapse is certain. Senators and congressmen will sit in stunned silence as they realize no one can stop the tailspin into chaos. Business, political, and economic leaders will be terrorized by its sudden-ness and its far-reaching effects. *"Son of man, when the land sinneth against me by trespassing grievously, then will I stretch out mine hand upon it, and will break the staff of the bread thereof, and will send famine upon it, and will cut off man and beast from it. (Ezekiel 14:13)"* Davis Wilkerson's book, <u>Set the Trumpet to Thy Mouth</u>, pages 14,15

October and November continue to see America's economy spiral out of control. The crash on Wall Street triggers markets to crash around the world. Martial law is being instituted not only in many major cities in America but in counties around the world. UN troops are heading up the new Rules of Law that are been instituted around the world. In America, our Constitution has been suspended by executive order. The Presidential Election of 2016 has been suspended, and the current president will stay in office. The hand writing was on the wall; the church must form smaller cells and go underground. Many pastors and Christian leaders have been rounded up and sent to re-education centers. It is a sad day, and now it is too late. Most realize we should have seen this coming and prepared for these times.

It is now the first of November 2015, a time when most businesses would be gearing up for the Christmas season. It is now evident this will not be a season to be jolly. This year's Christmas will look like a throwback to the time of the Great Depression, when gifts were either made by hand or when re-gifting what each has to share with friends and family was common. The economy of our country is desperately struggling to stay afloat. Innumerable numbers of businesses are closing their doors daily, food is in short supply, and all Americans are living under some form of food rationing while the Government is trying to salvage a dying economy.

All at once it is reported that hostilities are escalating in the Middle East. America is struggling with its own problems at home, and the enemies of Israel are poised to take advantage of this situation. The ISIS situation in the Middle East has leveled out, and America abandoned its position in Iraq when civil unrest erupted within our borders.

Russia has been arming Iran with S-300 Missiles, creating an Iron Dome that is almost impossible to penetrate. With war imminent in the Middle East, Israel realizes that in order to survive it must make the first move. Israel launches bombing runs to take out Iran's nuclear sites and makes an effort to take out the S-300 missile sites and other military instillations. It is now evident that a full blown war is unfolding in the Middle East.

Those with prophetic understanding realize this is the start of the Psalm 83 War. Tanks accompanied by a great army are seen massing on the borders of Israel, poised to invade the land of God's people. Syria and Iran, along with the most brutal, radical terrorists from ISIS, who now control much territory, along with Egypt and other Muslim countries, are combining their forces for a dramatic move that will wipe Israel off the map. Chants and cries echo throughout the streets of every city in the Middle East, "Death to every Jew!"

As this war is unfolding, it is causing global panic. Stock markets around the globe are collapsing. Global food panics and hoarding of food have triggered global food riots. Currencies are collapsing throughout the entire world. In fact, what is taking place is unlike any event ever anticipated in history! Martial law is being implemented in major cities around America, almost like a great fishing net that is wrapping its control around every major population area in America.

With martial law, our government is shutting down the internet and all communication. Those who are enforcing martial law are going house to house and are confiscating stored food and firearms. With the suspension of the constitution, they say they have the right to disarm Americans, to protect those who are protecting the people. With the suspension of the internet and all phone communication, it makes it difficult for groups to stand up against all that is happening. Some organized groups had anticipated a communications blackout and decided on a predetermined event to alert them that it was time to bug out to their Group Location.

With the collapse of currencies, the collapse of the food infrastructure follows. Within days, families around the world are running out of food, and panic is turning every city into total mayhem. Global starvation is happening, and it does not seem there is anything that can be done about it. Our leaders in Washington are dumbfounded, and with everything spinning out of control, it seems there is nothing that can be done to stop the disintegration of our country. Sadly, many leaders are copping out, and the number of suicides among the leaders in Washington and around the world escalates daily.

At this time, the Leaders of the G-20 Nations are meeting in Europe with other leaders from around the world seeking to find a global solution to this growing global collapse. After much wrangling back and forth over a two week period, a consensus agreement is finally reached. During the two weeks while these agreements for a global solution were being worked out, it was estimated that fifty million people died of both starvation and death by anarchy in cities around the world. The mobs in the streets will kill for a loaf of bread.

It is now the end of January, when it is announced that a global agreement has been worked out. In 24 hours, there will be an international reset of currencies and every nation will come under a new One World currency and a new One World Government. Almost every nation on the globe has signed off on this plan that will bring us out of this crisis. **(The only hold-out is the countries of the Middle East and Israel, as they are too tied up in the breakout of War, to be part of these negotiations. It is hoped that a separate peace and plan can bring them into the Global agreement at a later date.)** This means that every nation will give up its own constitution and sign on to a new One World Government constitution. The plan is calling for a new ten region global government that will be run by ten appointed leaders to head up each of these ten regions. New monetary rules will be phased in during the weeks ahead. It has been said that without this plan, 75% percent of the world's population would die in just a year.

A full blown war has now erupted in the Middle East. Israel is being attacked, not by boots on the ground, but by intense missile fire. Israel's defenses are being overwhelmed, and the Iron Dome cannot protect the cities of Israel from such high numbers of missiles being fired upon them from so many directions. A missile attack strategy is being used just as was used frequently during World War II--*bomb the cities first to weaken the resolve of your enemy, and then launch a land invasion.* Israel realizes that the land invasion will be coming soon, and the numbers of boots on the ground from their enemies will be too overwhelming for the army of Israel to repel. They are backed up against a wall and must make the decision soon whether or not to launch the Sampson Option.

Israel has no choice. The Russian armed S-300 missiles have been very effective in protecting Iran's nuclear sites. Israel must launch the Sampson Option without delay or else they will not survive. Already the loss of life in Israel is unimaginable. As a result, they launch every fighter Jet and bomber in its arsenal. Some jets will be for escorts, some will be decoys, and the bomb payloads will consist of a combination of nuclear war heads and huge fire bombs. Because of the challenge to penetrate the protection of the S-300 missiles, a number of Israeli pilots are taking the Sampson Option personal and are volunteering to go on suicide missions to take out the enemy. For their love of Israel and their God they are willing to lay down their lives.

They are being armed with conventional bombs and nuclear bombs that will be triggered above their enemy's missile sites before Iran can use its Iron Dome to take them out. Knowing that the S-300 missiles will take out most of Israel's jets before they can get close to their targets, Israel has formed a strategy for the pilots who are prepared to die for their country. They are hardening the bombs that are loaded into the jets. Even if the jets are blown out of the sky the missiles will stay intact. The jets will approach their targets from very high altitudes and when they are over the target the pilots will dive bomb at supersonic speed. The nuclear bombs will be set to go off when they hit a preset altitude. The effect of these bombs going off over the target area will fry the circuits of all electronics with the EMP effect and the heat of the blast will penetrate deep into the earth and any buried installations will be cooked and destroyed.

The planes are now in the air, and Israel's enemies are prepared to take them out with their Iron Dome defenses, consisting of a variety of Russian anti-aircraft missiles, and the most effective S-300 missiles. Many of Israel's planes are taken out. On this day many a brave Israeli jet pilot and bomber crew gave their lives for their country. They knew this would be a suicide mission. This day reminds me of when Sampson pushed on the pillars. He was willing to sacrifice his life to take out the oppressors of this people. Their deaths were not in vain, two nuclear armed jets hit their targets. Damascus is hit dead center; a great mushroom cloud rises above the horizon. When a second nuclear armed jet strikes its target in Iran, it is believed that Iran's nuclear development facilities have been taken out. Many jets with firebombs have hit their mark as well, striking many cities throughout the numerous Muslim countries that were attacking Israel. Israel has suffered great losses, but the damage they inflicted upon their enemies has worked, and the Muslim countries are crying for a truce. The rising mushroom clouds and the rising smoke from the cities of the Arab countries were too much for the enemies of Israel to bear.

It is now February 2016, and many of the features of the New One World Government have been put in place, including a new digital global currency. Things are being instituted so fast that many begin to realize this plan was thought out and planned for well in advance of the global crisis, and many Americans are not at all happy about all that has been taking place.

For Americans, giving up their freedoms and their constitution is a hard pill to swallow. In one of the ten new regional governments, a lone gunman has taken it upon himself to express his unhappiness with his country being sold into global slavery. Because he has held a position in the government, he has the clearance necessary to get close to the head of his regional government. He is therefore able to fatally wound one of the ten heads of this New World Government. When this leader is wounded in vital organs of his body, this wounded leader is not expected to live.

When it is announced that this leader has died, within a few minutes, the very thing Christians have feared has now happened! This leader of one of the ten regions of this New One World Government has just come back to life! Too many, it appears to be a miracle of God, but God's people know it is a miracle and lying wonder that was predicted would come at the arrival of the antichrist. This Leader who was dead, but now lives, announces to the world that God has not only healed him, but has sent him to bring peace to the world. He announces that God has given him a plan that will solve the worst rivalry on earth--a plan that will bring peace to the Middle East! Many see the timing of this miracle that has brought this leader back to life as happening at the most perfect time. A devastating war has just happened in the Middle East and the Muslim nations are open to peace after being hit with two nuclear bombs and the many large fire bombs that have devastated many of their cities.

This world leader, who was one of the ten heads of this newly formed One World Government, has now taken control to head up the new One World Government. It is now the end of March of 2016, he has arranged to meet with the leaders in the Middle East in order to propose a seven year peace agreement (to this region of the world). This proposed peace treaty will provide the Middle East and Israel with special privileges not offered to the other regions of the world. For instance, this region will not be required to take the Mark of the Beast on their body. As a result, these enticements will seal the deal.

What is interesting about what is offered at the peace treaty to the Middle East is that it is seven years long. This is the event that will mark the beginning of the seven year Great Tribulation. Daniel 9:27, *"He will confirm a covenant with many for one 'seven', but in the middle of that seven he will put an end to sacrifice and offering. And one who causes desolation will place abominations on a wing of the temple, until the end that is decreed is poured out on him,"* I believe this peace treaty was set at seven years because it is satan's intention to defeat God's plans and rule the world for all eternity at the end of this seven year period of so called peace.

When this peace is announced on the global news media, many rejoice that peace has finally come to this broken, depraved world. However, the Christians throughout the world see this announcement in a totally different light. For them, it is the beginning of the Great Tribulation and a time called, "War on the Saints". It is March of 2016 and the Great Tribulation has begun.

During these last several months, we have witnessed life in America unravel as we could never have imagined. There has been a lot of repenting going on; the sad truth is that America has fallen so far from its Christian Heritage that we have passed the point of no return. God must judge America. Part of that judgment will come from the antichrist who has just come to power, and much of God's judgment will come from the many instruments of judgment that the Bible reveals God used against Israel when they turned their backs on Him and went into wanton sin.

Just as Israel saw famine, destruction, invasion and captivity come to their nation. America, a country that was founded as a covenant nation similar to Israel, is now seeing these same judgments coming to America.

The judgment of famine started a few years ago as massive droughts affected many farm belt states. It seems other than seeing price increases we were able to avoid major famine in our land as we made up for poor crops with the importing of our food from other countries.

September of 2015 with the collapse of the stock market and eventual collapse of our dollar has brought to fulfilment a prophecy in the Bible, "A quart of wheat or a loaf of bread for a day's wages". America is truly seeing the judgment of famine coming to our land. This is resulting in unimagined starvation in our cities. The fifty million Americans previously on food stamps are rioting in the cities and towns across America. Many cities are ablaze from angry mobs rioting and fighting to find their next meal. With martial law in place, the so called peace keepers are waging all-out war in many cities. The peace keepers have been authorized to shoot to kill. Many civilians are trying to flee to the country, but with road blocks in place, the peace keepers of martial law are rounding up all who don't have proper travel documents and sending them off to detention centers.

As the new monetary system of the anti-christ is being implemented, most are seeing this system as a god-send, a system to restore order and bring food back into our stores. For informed Christians this is not a god-send, this system comes from the pit of hell, and Christians must refuse to take part. This is setting up a major rift between the Christians and the new system of government. At first the implanted debit system for buying and selling was voluntary; you had a choice of having the debit chip implanted in your right hand or the forehead. At first, you could opt to have a debit card issued. Once the majority of Americans took the implant, then the voluntary debit cards were turned off.

One last call was made requiring all Americans to either take the implant or be labeled enemies of the state. A great round up of Christians was launched. Once you were arrested for bucking the system, you would be sent off to what were called re-education centers, otherwise known as detention centers. Here you were placed on a meager diet and educated about the New World Order. You would be taught about a new global religion and given a chance to renounce your misplaced faith in Christ or face being sent to a slave camp or die by beheading.

In America's weakened condition, Russia and China launch an invasion. The third phase of God's judgment is underway. China is launching its invasion on the West Coast with much of its army coming up from the south. Russia is launching its invasion from the East Coast and also invading from the north coming down through Canada. The United Nations peace keepers are warned to leave America or face the consequences. America was already defeated before our enemies touched foot on our shores. With rampant starvation, the will to resist this invasion is all but gone. In certain sections of the country, mostly out west, patriot groups are putting up a valiant fight to resist the invasion of their country. It seems that both Russia and China just wanted to take advantage of the situation to insure that America never rises up to super power status again. China takes control of all land on the west side of the Mississippi and Russia takes control of east of the Mississippi and Alaska.

Americans have to accept being ruled by foreigners now, similar to when Rome ruled over Israel. Both Christians and non-Christians are now in a state of captivity similar to what the Jews went through two thousand years ago. The positive spin on this is the great revival that is happening all over America. The underground church is coming to the surface and winning many to the Lord. The system of the beast was not fully implemented before the invasion, and those who had not taken the mark of the beast are now turning to God.

We are now in the third year of the Great Tribulation, and now that America is no longer in control of anything, Russia sets its sights on Israel and the oil fields of the Middle East. Russia is now sending its troops to the Middle East to combine forces with the Arab countries that have been waiting for this day when with the help of their Russian allies it will be the mutually assured destruction of Israel. The War of Gog and Magog is about to happen.

Israel has been enjoying a period of peace for over three years now. Their armies have been in a stand down state for much of this time of peace. Israel is now under the leadership of a more liberal leadership, and they are not prepared for war. Ezekiel 38:10, 11 (NIV) *"This is what the Sovereign Lord says: On that day thoughts will come into your mind and you will devise an evil scheme. You will say, "I will invade a land of unwalled villages; I will attack a peaceful and unsuspecting people -- all of them living without walls and without gates and bars."*

Israel realizes that she has no allies to come to her aid. The new leadership in Israel has dismantled most of Israel's defenses, making Israel a land of unwalled cities. Israel is calling out to God unlike any time in recent history. Will God hear the cries of his people, the Jews?

Ezekiel 38:14-16,(NIV) *"Therefore, son of man, prophecy and say to Gog: 'This is what the Sovereign Lord says: In that day, when my people Israel are living in safety, will you not take notice of it? You will come from your place in the **far north**, you and many nations with you, all of them riding on horses, a mighty army. You will advance against my people Israel like a cloud that covers the land. In days to come, O Gog, I will bring you against my land, so that the nations may know me when I show myself holy through you before their eyes."*

Notice the verse above says that the army of Gog is **coming from the far north**. If you will look at a globe, you will see that Turkey is just to the north of Israel, but **Russia is the land to the far north** of Israel. If you look at the globe, you will see Moscow is directly north of Jerusalem.

The war of all wars is breaking out in Israel. Israel has few jets to launch and a small army to defend its country. They call out to God knowing that God is their only hope.

Ezekiel 38:18-23 (NIV) *"This is what the Sovereign Lord says: Are you not the one I spoke of in former days by my servants the prophets of Israel? At that time they prophesied for years that I would bring you against them. This is what will happen in that day: When Gog attacks the land of Israel, my hot anger will be aroused, declares the Sovereign Lord. In my zeal and fiery wrath I declare that at that time **there shall be a great earthquake in the land of Israel**. The fish of the sea, the birds of the air, the beasts of the field, every creature that moves along the ground, and all the people on the face of the earth will tremble at my presence. The mountains will be overturned, the cliffs will crumble and every wall will fall to the ground. I will summon a sword against Gog on all my mountains, declares the Sovereign Lord. **Every man's sword will be against his brother. I will execute judgment upon him with plague and bloodshed; I will pour down torrents of rain, hailstones and burning sulfur on him and on his troops and on the many nations with him. And so I will show my greatness and my holiness, and I will make myself known in the sight of many nations. Then they*** *will know that I am the Lord."*

Israel has seen a great victory on this day. The armies that rose up against them have been greatly defeated. The children of Israel truly know that God brought them a great victory. The 144,000 specially marked Jews from the twelve tribes of Israel have been moving among the Jews and telling them about the coming Messiah, Jesus, and as God shows his power and holiness to his children and the world, millions have turned to God and accepted Jesus as their messiah.

At this time the Sixth Seal is opened. Revelation 6:12-13 (NIV) *"I watched as he opened the sixth seal. **There was a great earthquake.** The sun turned black like sackcloth made of goat hair, the whole moon turned blood red. And the stars in the sky fell to earth, as late figs drop from a fig tree when shaken by a strong wind."*

A great asteroid has hit the South Atlantic, and a tidal wave of epic proportion is hitting both South America and North America. The impact of the meteor shakes the earth to its very core, triggering mega earthquakes around the world. Many volcanoes erupt during this time, sending ash around the globe, the sun goes dark, and the moon does not give its light. The loss of life is in the tens of millions. Again, this is another event of God's judgment that is causing many to turn to God and at the same time, causing many to curse God.

The Great Tribulation has labored on for over three years; it is now the time of The Feast of Trumpets in September of 2019. The saints have been defeated as the Bible warned. In spite of the blood of God's martyrs, millions have come to Christ. It is at the time of a great earthquake that the sun goes dark and the moon does not give its light that we will see the sign of the Son of Man coming in the clouds to gather his saints on that great and terrible Day of the Lord!

Joel 2:31 (NIV) *"The sun will be turned to darkness and the moon to blood before the coming of the great and dreadful day of the Lord."*

Luke 21:25-27 (NIV) *"There will be signs in the sun, moon and stars. On the earth, nations will be in anguish and perplexity at the roaring and tossing of the sea. Men will faint from terror, apprehensive of what is coming on the earth, for the heavenly bodies will be shaken. **At that time they will see the Son of Man coming in a cloud with power and great glory.**"*

Matthew 24:29-31 (NIV) *"Immediately after the distress of those days, the sun will be darkened and the moon will not give its light.* **The stars will fall from the sky, and the heavenly bodies will be shaken. At that time the sign of the Son of Man will appear in the sky, and the nations of the earth will mourn. They will see the Son of Man coming on the clouds of the sky, with power and great glory. And he will send his angels with a loud trumpet call and they will gather his elect from the four winds and from one end of the heavens to the other."*

Wow! That great and dreadful day has arrived. The saints are being called home to the place God has prepared for his elect. It is a great day for the Believers. When you read the verse in Joel 2:31, above, it says it is a great and dreadful day. Yes, it is a great day for the saints who are going home, but for the unrepentant it is the day of God's wrath. Read what Revelation 6:15-17 has to say about how the unrepentant will react on this day. Revelation 6:15-17 (NIV) *"Then the kings of the earth, the princes, the mighty, and every slave and every free man his in caves and among the rocks of the mountains. They called to the mountains and the rocks, "Fall on us and hide us from the face of him who sits on the throne and from the wrath of the Lamb!* **For the great day of their wrath has come, and who can stand?"**

CONCLUDING COMMENTS

When I was at Morningside for a July event in 2014, I was having lunch with members of the Morningside staff when Kevin expressed his concern that if things didn't happen by the end of 2015, what would this do to our ministries? We discussed it for a while, and when I arrived home, I messaged Kevin on face book with a more detailed response.

The message was as follows:

Kevin, I sensed your concern for what would happen if next year nothing happens. I have an answer for that concern. If five major prophetic teachers are saying or strongly hinting that the rapture is next year, if they are all wrong and if all the signs that are coming together and the blood moons are totally meaningless, if next year the economy goes into a full recovery, if calming global events were to put the church at ease and the church no longer saw a need to prepare for the End-Times, this would greatly affect the support of our ministries. (Kevin's response) "Exactly". But if ALL THESE SIGNS are pointing to what I see coming , The Lord's coming, and if Jim Bakker was raised up for such an hour as this to warn and prepare the church, then we don't have a thing to worry about, because God does not make mistakes. His timing is always perfect.

I believe David Wilkerson was prophesying about Jim Bakker's ministry thirty years ago when he wrote these words in his book, <u>Set the Trumpet to Thy Mouth</u>. Page 17, *"He will comfort their hearts, and as they see these frightful things coming upon the nation and the world, they will be at peace, saying, "God warned us! We are prepared! We knew it all along, and we are not afraid. Our blessed Savior will go with us through it all." This period we are in right now is so packed with the signs of Christ's return. The question I have to ask is, "If Christ told us to watch for these signs, and these signs are happening, why would Jesus have instructed us to watch for them, if they would come and go and nothing would happen?"*

This is the first time in my life that I have seen so many prophetic voices on the same page. I can list five major prophetic teachers and preachers who are either coming right out and saying the Rapture will be in 2015. Some are saying the Great Tribulation has to start in the year following the end of the coming Shemittah cycle, which could mean the Great Tribulation could start in March of 2016 as I have estimated. I do not agree that the Rapture will happen in September of 2015. I believe we will see the beginning of an economic collapse at around that time that will spiral out of control and bring us to the beginning of the Great Tribulation in the spring of 2016.

What we are seeing here is not the lone voice, such as what happened in 1988 when the leader of a sect said there were 88 reasons for Jesus coming in 1988. NO! We have a consensus! Yet most of the church is sleeping through all that is happening because they have been taught that we are to occupy till Jesus comes and we will not see hard times. The Rapture will take us out of here. What a great deception. My heart cries for those who have been so deceived. I fear that millions of souls who have been led to Christ in many a Gospel effort will be lost in the great falling away that Paul referred to in 2 Thess. 2:1-3.(KJV) *"Now we beseech you brethren, by the coming of our Lord Jesus Christ, and by our gathering together unto him, That ye be not soon shaken in mind, or be troubled, neither by spirit, nor by word, nor by letter as from us, as that the day of Christ is at hand. Let no one deceive you by any means: for that day shall not come, except there come a falling away first, and that man of sin be revealed, the son of perdition."*

— CHAPTER TWENTY —

HOW TO PREPARE FOR
THE LAST DAYS

If this study makes sense to you, you know we are fast approaching the coming of the Lord, and we will be going through part of the Great Tribulation. It begs the question, "What can we do to prepare for this time?" I will outline a few important steps we can take to prepare for what is coming soon.

1. Have you accepted Jesus Christ as your Savior?

If your answer is "yes," then the question is, "Are you living the Christian life to your full potential?" During these last days, God wants to use us to our fullest potential, and we must press in to seek God with all our hearts. Do some soul searching. This is where we have to really be honest with ourselves; we cannot hide anything from God. Do you have habits and sins that would be displeasing to God and hinder Him from using you?

As I bring this study to a close, I have felt the Holy Spirit leading me to include a study on the parable of the ten virgins. Jesus told this parable during His ministry on earth. It is found in Matthew 25:1-13; Jesus was teaching His disciples when they asked Him questions recorded in Matthew 24:3: *As Jesus was sitting on the Mount of Olives, the disciples came to him privately. "Tell us," they said, "when will this happen, and what will be the sign of your coming and the end of the age?"* Jesus went on to teach His disciples about His coming in Matthew 24 (much of it is in what I call plain-speak). When Jesus taught His disciples as recorded in chapter twenty-five, He spoke in parables. Jesus' disciples asked Him questions written in Matthew 13:10-11: *"Why do you speak to the people in parables?"* This was his reply, *"The knowledge of the secrets of the kingdom of heaven has been given to you, but not to them."* Jesus went on to say, *"There are those who have become calloused, and the truths of God's word are hidden from them."*

I have given this brief explanation on what a parable is because many parables are difficult to understand and not always explained in the Bible. I believe the parable of the ten virgins holds many insights concerning what will be happening at the time of Christ's return for His bride. I will write out the whole parable and give a brief running commentary on some of the message I believe God wants us to understand as we approach the time of Christ's return for His bride.

Matthew 25:1-13 says, *At that time the kingdom of heaven will be like ten virgins who took their lamps and went out to meet the bridegroom. Five of them were foolish and five were wise. The foolish ones took their lamps but did not take any oil with them. The wise, however, took oil in jars along with their lamps. The bridegroom was a long time in coming, and they all became drowsy and fell asleep. At midnight the cry rang out: "Here's the bridegroom! Come out to meet him!" Then all the virgins woke up and trimmed their lamps. The foolish ones said to the wise, "Give us some of your oil; our lamps are going out." "No," they replied, "there may not be enough for both us and you. Instead, go to those who sell oil and buy some for yourselves." But while they were on their way to buy oil, the bridegroom arrived. The virgins who were ready went in with him to the wedding banquet. And the door was shut. Later the others also came. "Sir! Sir!" they said. "Open the door for us!" But he replied, "I tell you the truth, I don't know you." Therefore keep watch, because you do not know the day or the hour.*

To start off, I did a study on the significance of the number ten. According to Jewish custom, if you have ten Jews living together, you have a congregation, and you can build a synagogue. This truth indicates to me that Jesus was talking about the church as well as a Jewish synagogue. With this in mind, you realize Jesus was saying at the time of the end, when the church is waiting for His coming, many in the church will have similar traits to the ten virgins. There is much significance to the fact they were carrying lamps that needed oil to be ready for the bridegroom's return. The lamps were the vessels that held the oil. When you study the Bible, you learn the oil is symbolic of the Holy Spirit, and we are the vessels in which the Holy Spirit lives.

This parable says the five foolish virgins did not even have any oil. As Christians, the oil of the Holy Spirit is what gives us our power and strength to live the Christian life. I believe that those believers who do not have any oil are not taking their walk with God seriously. They may be going to church, but they are really just going through the motions.

When the Bible says the bridegroom was a long time in coming, I believe it is saying Christ's return has not happened as soon as many expected. I believe, after having done this whole study on the end times, that eighty to ninety percent of American Christians, who have been taught Christ is coming before the antichrist arrives followed by the seven-year tribulation, will be in for a big surprise. I believe the strongest message from this parable is for those who are not taking their walk with God seriously and will be too weak to make it to the end.

Job in the Old Testament story went through the greatest tribulation any man has ever had to suffer. His wife even told him to just curse God and die. Many a man in his day would not have stayed true to God, but Job's walk and faith in God were stronger than any storm or trial that came his way. I believe many Christians going through the coming tribulations of the last days will only make it because they will have an inner strength from the Spirit of God, similar to what Job had. This strength of the Spirit can only be developed by spending time with God in His Word and in prayer. Just showing up at church once a week will not develop the strength of spirit we will need to weather the storms ahead. My last closing thought may raise some eyebrows, but I will speak my mind, for I believe what I am about to say needs to be said. At the end of the parable when the five foolish virgins went on their way to find the oil they needed and later came back wanting to enter the marriage supper, Jesus said, *"I tell you the truth, I don't know you."* **As I was studying this, I wondered what could the five foolish virgins have done that was so bad that they would be totally rejected. What this parable is saying is many people in the church will not make it into the kingdom of God. In fact, it shows that fifty percent will not make it. This is serious. What can this possibly mean?**

As I have studied and prayed over this, I have come up with only one answer. The Bible talks about a sin that is unpardonable. It is referred to as blasphemy against the Holy Spirit. I have heard teaching that considers taking one's own life is also unpardonable. Well, I believe in the last days there is another unpardonable sin, and that is to take the mark of the beast. I believe, in the last days, when we are going through the tribulation before the wrath of God begins, this portion of the last days will be a time of testing for Christians unlike anything we have ever seen here in America. I believe the weight of scripture shows the church will have to make the choice of whether or not to accept the antichrist's system. We will be amply warned not to take the mark of the beast, but I believe many churches are full of weak Christians, and many of these will say, "God would not expect them to go hungry and die." I believe they could be easily deceived into believing the antichrist is their savior and go along with his system. The bottom line is, unless we are full of the Spirit of God and have the strength of the Spirit that will carry us through these times of trials and tribulations that lie ahead, we could end up being like the foolish virgins who do not make it into the marriage supper of the Lamb. I am listing a few Scripture references below that go along with what I am saying in this study on the ten virgins. I encourage you to look them up and see if what I am saying is plausible.

God warns the saints not to take the mark of the beast... Revelation 14:9-12

Why the Lord delays His coming... 2 Peter 3:9

God warns saints to be patient... Revelation 13:9-10

War on saints to last three and one-half years... Daniel 7:25

If you have not accepted Jesus as your Lord and Savior, these easy steps will put you in right standing with God.

1. Admit you are a sinner and repent.

Romans 3:10: *As it is written: there is no one righteous, not even one.*

Romans 3:23: *For all have sinned and fall short of the glory of God.*

Luke 5:32: *I have not come to call the righteous, but sinners to repentance.*

2. Believe in the Lord Jesus Christ.

John 3:16: *For God so loved the world that he gave his one and only Son, that whosoever believes in him shall not perish but have eternal life.*

3. Confess or declare that Jesus is the Lord of your life.

Romans 10:9: *That if you confess with your mouth, "Jesus is Lord," and believe in your heart that God raised him from the dead, you shall be saved.*

THE SINNER'S PRAYER

If you would like God to forgive all your sins and make Jesus Christ the Lord of your life, then stop here and say this prayer to God. (Prayer is simply talking to God.)

Dear Heavenly Father, I know I am a sinner. I believe Jesus Christ died on the cross for me. Please forgive me of all my sins. Jesus, please come into my heart and wash my sins away. Please be the Lord of my life and help me to live for you every day. I ask this in Jesus' name. Amen.

The Bible says when a sinner repents and makes Jesus his Lord, the angels in heaven rejoice.

A word of warning is advised at this point. As we read in the story of the ten virgins, not all who call themselves Christians will make it to heaven. Knowing about Jesus and the plan of salvation is no guarantee of making it to heaven. When we arrive in heaven, the greatest surprise will be seeing people we did not think would make it. And just as surprising will be the absence of those we thought would be there. The Bible says Jesus knocks on the door of our hearts and wants to come in and live with us. The important thing to realize is God wants our hearts, not just our minds. Head knowledge about salvation does not save us, but sincerely allowing God to forgive and wash our sins away will allow God to give you a new heart. When your heart is changed, people will notice you have been changed and made into a new person in Christ. This is called being "Born Again."

I would like to share a story from a recent conversation I had with a young man who believes we really are close to the Lord's return. He told me he would never take the mark of the beast. Yet he believes it's acceptable for him to live with his girlfriend and go out and get drunk from time to time. He has what I call "designer faith." It is NOT based on the pure Word of God, but it is based on what seems good to him. What a shame it would be for someone to go through the Tribulation of the last days and refuse to take the mark of the beast and then still not make it into the Kingdom of Heaven because they did not have a true Born Again experience, based on the Word of God.

As a new believer, your next step would be for you to find a network of believers to help you grow in the Lord. Finding a good church is a good place to start.

2. Is your financial house in order?

This question requires taking steps to streamline your budget and get out of debt, if at all possible. Even Christians have been wasting money and living beyond their means. Based on my study of God's Word, I believe the beginning of the Great Tribulation could be only three to seven years away. When I started this study two years ago, I realized I had assets I could use to help me get out of debt. I went through my credit card bills and looked for recurring monthly bills I could cut from my budget. I personally eliminated three hundred dollars a month through this process. A lot more can be said in this category, but the bottom line is, as we approach the Lord's coming, we will witness the world and society being turned upside down as we know it. The opportunities to witness to the backsliders and the lost will be tremendous. Those who get their financial house in order will be in the best position to reach out to the lost during these times.

Under the subject of finances, I cannot believe how many financial advisors are telling people to put their resources into gold and silver. I do not believe we will ever see gold and silver become the medium of exchange in America or the world. How do you split a gold coin to buy food? If you think about it, the thing that really drives up the value of precious metals is fear. The fear that the value of our currency will collapse and become worthless. This did not even happen during the Great Depression. Now I am not saying this could not happen. In fact, I believe we are heading towards a global economic collapse, and this event will lead to the formation of a one-world government. I believe this event must happen before the antichrist can rise to power. So, as a Christian, I want to know what God's Word has to say about my investments. Ezekiel 7:19 says, *They shall cast their silver in the streets and their gold shall not be able to deliver them in the day of the wrath of Lord. They shall not satisfy their souls, neither fill their bowels.* Then read Zephaniah 1:18: *Neither their silver, nor their gold, will be able to save them on the day of the Lord's wrath.*

Think about this, as we approach the Lord's coming and the global famines that will take place as described in the opening of the seals of Revelation 6, people who have prepared and have food will not want your gold for their food. As Ezekiel 7:19 says, *..they shall not satisfy their souls, neither fill their bowels...* Bowels are your belly. To me, God's Word is saying it is wiser to have food for your belly than to have gold. You could even say during these coming hard times that food will be gold.

The other day I was reading headlines on the internet. One headline from a financial advisor, Paul Mladjenovic, had a title that caught my attention. When I opened the link, it said he wanted everyone to consider three simple things to gain greater financial peace of mind:

1. Diversify away from paper assets.

2. Accumulate essentials

3. Refocus your portfolio with emphasis on "Human Need."

His second item, coming from a non-Christian perspective, really caught my attention. He said, "Accumulate essentials." He went on to say, "As odd as this may sound for some of you, consider starting a pantry or otherwise consider stocking up on essentials such as non-perishable foods, extra water, etc. NO, I am not asking you to become a survivalist or a hermit. I consider this to be just another form of diversification. The world is too precarious right now and is quite vulnerable to disruptions. Severe inflation is not far off. Potential problems can come from a variety of expected and unexpected venues. What do you think will have greater value a few years from now, a dollar or a can of soup?" I think this is sound advice for anyone. I could not have said it better.

3. What pastors can do to prepare their church.

As pastors, you have an important responsibility to teach your flock to be ready for the last days. I am not just talking about having food pantries stocked, but you must provide leadership and hope to your people. If you fall short in this area or you wait until it's too late to prepare, your people will blame you. When the Titanic was sinking, many people were in a state of panic because the ship was not prepared for its last day.

As the pastor of a church, you should consider starting home cell Bible studies or cell groups. I believe as persecution grows against the church and Christians, we will need to go underground. Already under our newly elected president, there is talk of eliminating churches' tax-exempt status and eliminating tax deductions for giving to churches and charities. If our country and the world go into a time of global economic collapse as we approach the Lord's coming, it is easy to see the high tax burden being assessed on churches will cause many to go bankrupt, forcing churches to move into homes. Also, home cells can be very effective in bringing the lost to a saving knowledge of Christ. When things start falling apart in our society and our economy collapses, and when the government is not there to meet every need the people have, it will be the close friendships that will develop in the small group settings that will make your Christian friends closer than a brother who will be there when you are in need.

I believe pastors hold a unique responsibility to help prepare their flock for what is to come. Pastors should realize the church will be in for horrendous hard times before the Lord returns. I believe churches should lead by example and have a food pantry for the needy. They should encourage their people to use a portion of their resources to lay aside essentials for the hard times ahead. Proverbs 21:20 states, *In the house of the wise are stores of choice food and oil, but the foolish man devours all he has.*

If what I say in this book makes sense, but you take no action to warn and prepare your church, it's no different than not having read this message at all. Once the truth of this book becomes evident to all, it will be too late to get ready.

I believe in the years ahead leading up to the return of Christ for His bride, the church, or better yet the saints in the churches, will be responsible to preach the gospel to their lost or backslidden family, friends, and neighbors. We should have extra Bibles. I believe God's Word says there will be a famine of the Word of God in the last days, and we should be prepared while there are no limits on how many

Bibles, hymnals, and songbooks we can have.

4. Food storage and gardening.

So much can be said under this subject. The Bible clearly predicts food will be scarce in the last days, and many will die of famine and starvation. I believe many Christians, who have been told the Rapture will come before the Great Tribulation starts, will turn bitter towards God and the church. I believe they will be part of a great falling away. The Bible also says there will be a great revival in the last days as well.

Esau gave up his birthright for a bowl of soup, and I am afraid many Christians who fall away in the last days will be the ones unprepared for a time of Great Tribulation. When they are offered an opportunity to buy into the system of the antichrist for food, they will succumb. Many Christians in America do not believe we will see famine on our shores. If this is what you think, you will be in for a big surprise. We are more dependent on our food coming from foreign lands now than anytime in American history. Not only does our food come from places like Canada, Mexico, and South America, but many of the local farms that produce the food for the local market have been turned into housing developments or Wal-Marts.

I believe we need to learn how to grow food in our own gardens. Stored food will run out, but if you learn to grow your own food, you will have food for your daily needs. Most people have not learned how to raise their own food. We are too dependent on stocked shelves in our grocery stores. If you do not know how to garden, do not wait to learn. Start practicing now. **Do not wait until it is too late to buy garden tools, seeds, and other garden supplies. Remember: learning how to can your crops and having sufficient canning supplies on hand is an important part of having a garden.**

We should look at the Mormons. They have been taught to prepare for hard times. They are told they should have at least a year's worth of food stored for unexpected calamities, whether it is losing a job or widespread hard times.

Today, with all the natural disasters and economic turmoil in this country and around the world, the Red Cross is recommending that we have seven days of food and water on hand in case of an emergency. If what you are reading in this study makes sense to you, then I hope you realize that seven days of food and water will not cut it. How much preparation is necessary? This is something we need to seek God about while we pray for His wisdom and guidance.

Some Christians say the Bible says to "take no thought for tomorrow." Stop and think about this. There have been extraordinary times in history when these words did not apply. Before the flood, God prompted Noah to prepare. Read Hebrews 11:7: *By faith Noah, when warned about things not yet seen, in holy fear built an ark to save his family.* God showed Joseph that Egypt was to prepare during good times for a seven-year famine to come. There was a time in the New Testament when the Christians had things in common during hard times, but how can Christians share if they do not have anything to share?

Wouldn't you agree that the coming of the Lord, with the catastrophic events leading up to His return, will be extraordinary times? Today, we are witnessing economic earthquakes that are shaking and taking down countries around the world. Millions are losing their homes to foreclosure. Many are losing all they have worked years to accumulate. I know Christians who are up to their ears in debt, trying to hold onto multiple assets and homes that are more than they can afford. Many are holding on tightly, hoping some bailout will rescue them. I am praying we will see an economic turn-around, and if this happens, I pray the church will realize we have been seeing the birth pains leading up to the coming of the Lord and recognize time is short. We need to take the short time we have to consolidate our debts and pay off our homes, if possible. Turn off the television and turn God's Word on in our lives. Let God show you what you need to do with the short time we have before His coming.

I want to encourage the readers of this book to consider obtaining a food and preparedness insurance policy. If you buy a home, there may be less than one in a thousand odds your home will burn down, but you are required by the bank to have a fire insurance policy. If you buy a car and drive, even though the chances of having an accident are less than one in a thousand, you are required to have an auto insurance policy. Now, if you have studied along with me and agree, we are seeing unprecedented times and cataclysmic events that are sending clouds of uncertainty around the world. You must realize before the world or America will be willing to agree to join a one-world government, America will have to experience economic and social collapse. The will of the world to resist change will be broken. If you believe as I do that the odds of these things happening before the Lord's return are at least fifty-fifty, why not acquire a preparedness insurance policy? I hope your response will not be what I heard from one pastor, "Why store food or have a garden? Others will only steal it from you anyway." It is a good thing Noah or Joseph did not have that attitude.

5. How to organize a group or Team

When things fall apart in America, I believe the church will have to go underground. We are already seeing intense persecution of Jews and Christians around the world. This will come to America as well. Look at the model of the early Christian church after the time of Christ's crucifixion. The church was house to house, and these groups had all things common. It was this coming together as groups that gave them the resources and strength to survive. It was not just from the sharing of food and the numbers to protect them, but with the greater numbers in their groups, they had greater power in prayer. Remember the house group praying for Peter's release from prison, and God sent angels to release him?

So how do we organize a group for these last days? It would be a lot easier if the pastors of our churches would see what is coming and organize their churches into cell groups and help to facilitate the needed task of preparing for the days ahead. If Pastors would take this responsibility, it would not splinter the church. It would strengthen them for the days ahead.

In light of the fact that we will be on our own at this time, I will share my thoughts and encourage you to remain faithful to your local church. When things start to fall apart you can be in a position to help your local church to follow the model you have learned.

The first stage in preparing for a group is to prepare for your family and loved ones. 1 Timothy 5:8 gives us a strong admonition to do this. *"If anyone does not provide for his relatives, and especially for his immediate family, he has denied the Faith and is worse than an unbeliever."* It is a sad truth, but at this time most Christians do not see how close we are to the Lord's coming; this includes your family. This necessitates that we do all within our power and means to prepare and store up the needed food and resources to help our loved ones through this time of coming tribulation.

Once you have prepared for your inner circle, it is time to think about the needs of others outside of your family. This time that is coming will literally turn our world upside down. I believe the events that will be coming soon will not only wake up a sleeping church, but it will cause great numbers of backslidden and unbelievers to come to the Lord. I see a great harvest opportunity for those who are prepared for these coming days. Those in the church who are unprepared will not be able to help others, as they will not even be able to help themselves and their families. I hate to make this analogy, but many in the church who are ill prepared for these days will be like the foolish virgins who had no oil on the eve of the Lord's Return.

The expanding of your circle of preparation needs to include resources to help widows, orphans and unsaved neighbors. Realize that during this time many children could be abandoned at your door. If we ask the question, "What would Jesus do?" We know what he would say, "We cannot say no to these in need." I believe that as we share in these days, that even though our food will have to feed more than we expected, God will multiply the food in our pot as we trust him to help us to help others. An important point to always keep in mind as we go through the tough times ahead, "It is not our goal to just make it to the Rapture", No! It is our goal to be here to lead others to Christ and help bring them with us into eternity.

What I have just laid out is the completion of your first stage in preparing your group. You have prepared for your family and others. Now you need to look for other like-minded families to team up with to create a group that will give you the spiritual, physical, and material resources to go through these times.

Each family group will have some strengths and weaknesses. The way I can best describe this is to share the strengths of three family groups.

1. This group has great hands on skills. They have a large piece of property in the country; they have a big garden and know what to can what they grow. What they don't have is a lot of money to put away storage food for the time of poor crops or crop failure due to unforeseen inclement weather.

2. This second group have financial resources to buy long term food storage, but they live in an urban area and they are not able to grow a garden nor have the know-how to raise their own food, to replenish and supplement what they have stored. This family will probably be run over by urban gangs going house to house looking for anyone who has food. They will not only take your food but they could bring severe harm to your family and loved ones.

3. This third group is led by a man with military and security skills, maybe a real Rambo type. He focused on having the supplies to defend his home and family but he did not have the foresight or skills to be able to provide the food he would need for the long term days ahead. Many who share his way of thinking, think they can go out and shoot wild game and continue to feed their families. The sad truth is that wild game will become scarce in a matter of weeks once large numbers of hungry hunters head for the woods. This was proven during the great depression.

Now, when these three families come together as a team, the weakness in one family is made up for by the strength of the other families. For reasons of group security It may be necessary to be vigilant on a 24/7 basis. When you only have a small group you are out there like sheep to be taken by the wolves that are looking for those who are weak. This group scenario does not address all the needs of a group. Having a spiritual leader among you is so important. Some family groups may be stronger in more than one area.

The last point I need to address concerns those in your group who will challenge your group leadership and authority. None of us are perfect, we all have weak areas in our lives in which we need God's grace and help. During these days, as we are working together to finish the race God has set before us, we will need wisdom that comes from above in order to be able to deal with the many different people living close together. Everyone will need to do their share to the utmost of their ability. You can't expect the elderly to carry the same load as the young. But you cannot let someone who is lazy, a complainer, a backbiter or other negative personality traits ruin the dynamics and the peace of your group. Use wisdom in choosing your group and realize a team government of sorts will need to be prepared to administer discipline. It may be necessary to give someone who will not change negative behavior a grab and go bag and told to go. This should be a last resort, as this person or group could lead others back to you to endanger your whole group.

6. For how long should we be prepared?

If you have read my book from the beginning, then you know that I firmly believe we will go through three and a half years of the seven years of what I call the Great Tribulation. Others refer to this time period as Daniel's Seventieth Week. I have shown in my book why I believe in what is called a Mid-Tribulation Rapture. What I will do now is again make my case as to why, from scripture, I see God's elect going through three and a half years of this period of time.

I also must point out that we will also see a period of Birth Pains leading up to the beginning of these seven years that will appear to some as if we are already in the seven years of Tribulation. It is hard to calculate how long the period of Birth Pains will last because, for some Christians, in parts of the world, the Birth Pains have already started. Consider what is going on in the Middle East right now to Christians in countries like Iran. It must appear to them that we are already in the seven year Great Tribulation. Christians are being beheaded, and some are being crucified for Christ right now. Children are being told to recant their faith in Jesus or be beheaded. These children are choosing Jesus.

I fear for the Church in America. We are so spoiled in our thinking, saying, God would never allow us to suffer before the Rapture takes us home. How will these American Christians react when disaster strikes? How will we react when our economy crumbles and there is no longer food in the stores? Are we strong enough to stand up to the threats of death as the Children in Iran and other countries are?

I am going to lay out a little Bible study now that will help you to see why I believe we need to prepare to go through three and a half years, plus whatever time of Birth Pains we will see before the countdown begins.

This first verse is found in Revelation13:5-7(NIV). **It talks about a coming war on the Saints that will last for forty-two months.** *"The beast was given a mouth to utter proud words and blasphemies and to exercise his authority for **Forty-Two Months**. He opened his mouth to blaspheme God, and to slander his name and his dwelling place* *and those who live in heaven. He was given power to make war against the saints and to conquer them. And he was given authority over every tribe, people, language and nation."*

My second verse is found in Daniel 7:25. Again, this passage talks about the saints being under the thumb of the anti-christ for a period of three and a half years. My translation calls this period of time, Time, times and half a time. Other translations call this time period three and a half years. *"He will speak against the Most High and oppress his saints and try to change the set times and the laws. The saints will be handed over to him for a **time, times and half a time**",* **(again three and a half years).**

Daniel, chapter seven is a very important chapter, as it talks about the war on the saints. It then talks about God's deliverance, which we know is the rapture, and it talks about Jesus coming in the clouds to lead his people to the Throne.

For further study along with reading Daniel 7:25, read Daniel 7:21,22 , then read Daniel 7:13. If you will look at these three verses in Daniel chapter seven, you will notice they are in reverse order. It talks about Jesus coming in the clouds first, but we know that Jesus coming in the clouds is the Rapture that comes after the deliverance that is spoken of in Daniel 7:13.

My next verse is found in Daniel 9:27. This verse explains that the antichrist will make a covenant with the Jews and the Muslim nations for seven years. Then it goes on to say that he (the antichrist) will break this covenant in the Middle,**(three and a half years)**, and then it says his time will last until God's judgment falls on him. If you will read Matthew chapter 24, you will see the sequence of the Rapture following the time of the antichrist desecrating the temple. Daniel 9:27,(NIV) *"He will confirm a covenant with many for one 'seven', but in the middle of that seven he will put an end to sacrifice and offering. And the one who causes desolation will place abomination on a wing of the temple, until the end that is decreed is poured out on him."* Now, if you read Matthew 24:15, you will see that Jesus actually spoke of this event that is recorded in Daniel 9:27. Matt 24:15,(NIV) *"So when you see standing in the holy place, 'the abomination that causes desolation,' spoken of through the prophet Daniel – Let the reader understand."*

My conclusion to why I see God's elect going through three and a half years of this seven year tribulation period before the rapture comes from a study from Daniel chapter 12 and Matthew chapter 24. Both of these books of the Bible are referring to an event that you will recognize as the same event. As you study these two books that are talking about this coming time, you will see a time period of three and a half years is attached to this event.

Daniel 12:1b-2 a, (NIV) *"There will be a time of distress such as has not happened from the beginning of nations until then. But at that time your people – everyone whose name is found written in the book – will be delivered. Multitudes who sleep in the dust of the earth will awake:"* Notice that this time of distress happens at the time of the Rapture.

Now we will look at what Jesus describes in Matthew 24 as a time of distress that he also said would happen before the Rapture. Matthew 24:21 (NIV), *"For then there will be great distress, unequaled from the beginning of the world until now – and never to be equaled again."*

Both of these verses are describing an event that is yet to happen. Now I will bring us back to Daniel 12 where Daniel asks the Lord, How long will this time of distress last until the Rapture? Daniel 12:6b-7 (NIV) ***"How long will it be before these astonishing things are fulfilled?"*** *The man clothed in linen who was above the waters of the river, lifted his left hand toward heaven, and I heard him swear by him who lives forever, saying."* **It will be for a time, times and half a time.** *When the power of the holy people has been finally broken, all these things will be completed."* **Many translations of the Bible call "a time, times and half a time", Three and a half years.**

In conclusion, I will now show you from Matthew chapter 24, Jesus is explaining to his disciples what they will see as the signs of his coming. **I will show you that Jesus said that after this same time of distress that Daniel was told would last for three and a half years,** *Jesus tells his disciples that after this time of distress he will come in the clouds to take us home to heaven.*

I am writing out parts of these verses that show the sequence of what I am saying, you can read all of Matthew 24 to see the full picture of what is happening. Matthew 24:29a,30 and 31,(NIV), *"Immediately after the distress of those days, "The sun will be darkened, and the moon will not give its light; (30,31) "At that time the sign of the Son of Man will appear in the sky, and all the nations of the earth will mourn. They will see the sign of the Son of Man coming on the clouds of the sky, with power and great glory. And he will send his angels with a loud trumpet call, and they will gather his elect from the four winds, from one end of the heavens to the other."*

I believe that if you have read these verses with an open heart to learn the truth, and if after reading this, you would pray for the Holy Spirit to bear witness with your spirit and reveal to you the truth, I believe you will know that we will go through three and a half years of this time of distress that is spoken in God's Word.

In Closing

I would like to encourage you to start buying extra food items on a weekly basis. I find that, if I shop the sales, when I see certain canned goods at a good price, I will buy ten instead of two. With frugal buying, you will discover you can accumulate quite a pantry without expanding your food budget. I recently figured out that for $300 you can buy enough food for one person for a year at a box store such as Costco. I'm talking about food that will store well for years, like rice, beans, oatmeal, and other items to compliment a simple diet that will keep you alive on a low budget. If you have the financial resources, you should consider buying food that is packaged to last for twenty to thirty years or more. Again there are creative ways to find the money you need to make this type of investment. Maybe it is time to sell the boat, the motorcycle or some other cherished item that you will not need when your way of life has been turned upside down. Below I will list some sources for long term food. Realize that your grocery store is a good source, as well as the discount box stores. I have read studies that have shown that regular canned goods stored in a cool place are still good to eat after thirty years with very little taste and nutrient loss.

Jim Bakker Ministries. They sell food packages that come in large buckets and even larger tote storage boxes. These storage food packages are freeze dried and dehydrated products that will last for twenty to thirty years. The Bakkers have just had their food packages upgraded to improved recipes and new menu items that make there offerings the best value per serving that can be found. You can contact them at 417-779-9000. Their internet address is www.jimbakkershow.com/shop

Ready Made Resources. This company is probably the biggest resource for both long term food and preparedness products that you could find. They sell food packages that will be balanced with dehydrated, freeze dried and whole grains, for long term food storage. They are distributors for Mountain House freeze dried- storage foods. They are offering great value packages. They specialize in personal and home security items. They are specialized consultants for night vision and communications. Free phone consulting in all areas of preparing for their customers. The owner, Robert Griswold is a leading authority on preparing and is very much committed to helping Christians prepare for hard times ahead. Robert Griswold also does retreat and preperation consulting. You can reach this company at 800-627-3809 or on the internet at www.readymaderesources.com. When you order, if you will mention my name, Ready Made Resources will make a donation to my ministry.

SUN OVEN The Ultimate Solar Appliance! Bake, boil or steam food naturally and helps the environment. Cooks at 360° to 400° powered by the sun. Ideal for use in the event of a power failure. Pays for itself quickly by keeping the house cool in the summer when you keep the cooking heat outside. Can also be used as a solar dehydrator and to boil or pasteurize water. I personally recommend having more then one Sun Oven so you can cook for a larger group and save your cooking fuel resources. I have worked out a group discount without your having to do a group buy. Save $80.00 on the All American Sun Oven with accessories. Go to www.sunoven.com/shorey-coupon, or call 1-800-408-7919, and use discount code: "Shorey"

— CHAPTER TWENTY ONE —

CLOSING THOUGHTS ABOUT THE LORD'S RETURN

The Bible says the weapons of our warfare are powerful through God for the pulling down of strongholds. In the last days, and I am talking about now, God is raising up an army. This army must not shrink back from the task ahead. God's army will be fully equipped with God's most powerful weapons, but if we shrink back, God is not pleased. If we do not appropriate the weapons God has made available, we will not be prepared for what lies ahead.

I remember as a teenager visiting the Winchester Gun Museum in New Haven, Connecticut. I was so intrigued to see the Gatlin gun. I still have a picture I took of this awesome weapon. The weapon display gave some background information I have never forgotten. It said this model of Gatlin gun was made available to General Custer. This gun could shoot two hundred rounds a minute, and when General Custer received word he should take it with him to Little Big Horn, his response was "It would just slow me down." So he went charging out to meet the enemy, and when he found himself surrounded, he must have thought, "I have two hundred Indians a minute more than I can handle. Why didn't I bring that gun?" Well, it was too late for him at that point.

The Bible says the weapons of our warfare are powerful for the pulling down of strongholds. There is a weapon in the arsenal of God like the Gatlin gun, and it is often left behind. This weapon is prayer and fasting. I would like to share a couple of stories of how I learned about how prayer and fasting can greatly benefit your life.

Back in the early seventies when I was saved, I was working in a logging camp for most of the year, then I would attend college in the winters. Before I attended Bible college, I was going to college at the University of Alaska in Fairbanks. While going to school, I attended Fairbanks First Assembly of God. I received some good teaching on prayer and fasting, and I started taking time to fast and pray while I was attending school. At that time, I did not have many struggles, but I sensed God was doing good things in my life. I transferred to Northwest Bible College. After a few years in attendance there, I became concerned because I had not met the woman of my life. So before going back to college for my third year, I started fasting and praying seriously for God to bring that special person into my life. When I went back to Northwest College in 1977, I met Shawnette Rasmussen, who would later become my wife.

When I look back, I can see God's hand powerfully involved in bringing us together. Shawnette was six years younger than me. I did not really want to pursue a girl this young, but God kept bringing her across my path. Before long, I had to ask God if He was trying to tell me something. I remember thinking that I needed to keep an open mind as I did not want to miss God's will. God gave me many confirmations that it was okay to pursue this neat, cute girl. Before long, I had an opportunity to meet her grandparents, who drove down from Canada to visit her. They invited us to drive up for Thanksgiving, and God gave me special favor with them. When her parents got together with her grandparents for Christmas, Shawnette's grandparents could not quit talking about me. I met her parents when they dropped Shawnette off at college after Christmas break. Again, God gave me favor with her dad.

Our marriage has been good, and I would not trade Shawnette for any girl in the world. I am totally convinced that Shawnette came into my life because I fasted and prayed. When I did my part to let God know that I wanted His best for my life, then He made all the arrangements to bring the most perfect girl my way.

You would think that I would have learned a great lesson here, but the truth is I hardly fasted after seeing God answering my requests from prayer and fasting. I believe I was just too comfortable. During the last two to three years, I have rediscovered the power of prayer and fasting. As we have been seeing our country enter a period of economic hardship, I have been up against a wall financially several times. But for the last three years, as I have fasted and prayed for my needs and have sought God for His will in my life, God has come through every time. During this process of rediscovering the power of prayer and fasting, it is almost like I have rediscovered how great and loving our God is and how much He wants to have a close relationship with us individually. In these last days, we will have trying times. We need to seek God like we never have before. As we press into God, we will discover how great and loving our heavenly Father really is and how much He wants to protect us and meet our every need. We must never lose sight of God's love for us. John 3:16: *For God so loved the world that he gave his one and only Son, that whosoever believes in him shall not perish but have eternal life.*

Imagine this: God is giving His church a last chance to finish the Great Commission and preach the gospel to the millions who will be seeing hard times. As we are approaching the Great Tribulation, there will be many lost and confused souls who will want to know where to turn. Remember when 911 hit, and the churches were full for a week or two? When the Great Tribulation gets started, and the seals start to pop open, the global events that will be taking place will make 911 and the Twin Towers look like a picnic. When 911 hit, our churches filled up for two weeks and then emptied again. When the coming economic collapse happens, it will be like 911 again, but it won't go away in two weeks.

Try to imagine the church being raptured before any of this happens. On the following Sunday, the churches fill up to overflowing, just as they did after 911. All these millions will fill up our churches to get answers, and they will be open to hear the gospel. What will they find? All the pastors have been raptured and only the returning backsliders and lukewarm Christians are left to lead these millions to the Lord (the lukewarm Christians who skipped out of Sunday School and have not studied their Bibles and do not have the answers.) So, we have two scenarios here. We can hold to a pre-tribulation rapture view and believe the saints, involved in the "war on the saints" described in the book of Revelation, will be the ones the Bible depicts as the triumphant church. This church will be made up of all the lukewarm Christians and repentant backsliders who were left behind but now are on fire for God. Those people would end up becoming the church, tried by fire, for which Christ is coming back. Or the second option: the Rapture is a mid-tribulation rapture, and we are prepared to help our unprepared family, friends, and neighbors by ministering to the needs of the lost and hungry, so that many will be saved, for we are still here and not yet raptured.

As I have said, I would rather see a pre-tribulation rapture. It would be so much easier for me and all of us Christians. Wait a minute; does God's Word not say God is unwilling that any should perish? If the Rapture is a pre-tribulation event, and it were to happen tonight while you were sleeping, what would it be like to stand before Christ, the one who gave His life that all could be saved? You have just entered the glorious gates of heaven; you have no doubt your eternity is secure. What would you do if Jesus were to ask you, "Did you do all you could to tell others about me before you left?" If Jesus could give you a choice to stay in heaven or go back and have a part in the greatest evangelistic opportunity in history, what would your choice be?

I was recently watching a movie called *Schindler's List* about a German business man named Oscar Schindler who organized and ran his factories with cheap Jewish labor. When he started, his motives were purely based on greed. As the war went on, he developed a love for the Jewish people, and he used all his wealth and influence to bribe the Nazi officials and save his workers from the death camps. When the day came that the war was over and the Jewish people were set free, those whose lives he saved wanted to give him a gift. They pulled out their teeth which had gold fillings and made a ring for Oscar Schindler. He cried, "I could have saved more." When we get to heaven, it will be the same. Those whose lives you had a part in getting to heaven will be your best friends for eternity. We will also cry, knowing we could have helped more people get to heaven.

I believe the church must wake up to the facts that they will not have a future secured by their retirement plans, their only hope is in Christ, and they are in the final countdown. This awakening will lead to the greatest revival the world has ever seen. As the revelation of Christ's coming sinks in, it will finally hit home that only what is done for Christ will last.

I am afraid that the church of today is not ready for what is before us. When prophetic events soon begin to unfold and the timing of the Rapture does not happen as we have been taught, this error will lead to great confusion. Many believers will rise to the occasion as Jesus' disciples did when given a choice by Christ to leave Him. They said, "ONLY YOU HAVE THE WORDS OF ETERNAL LIFE." On the other hand, many in the church will feel God has abandoned them to suffer on the earth during this time, and their bitterness will cause many to turn away from Christ.

I was recently visiting a pastor and talking to him about my book. Before we parted, he told a story he had heard from a pastor friend who shared my view of a mid-tribulation rapture. This pastor shared this story about a tribe in Northern Africa that had two churches, each teaching a different position concerning the coming of the Lord.

One of the missionaries to this tribe taught that the Lord was coming soon, and they did not have to worry about going through a time of great tribulation. They would all be raptured out before things became very bad. The second missionary taught those in his church that we would see a period of Great Tribulation before the Lord returns. Some may even die, but God's grace would carry them through any trials or tribulations they would face.

This area came under attack by terrorists. Many died from both churches. The church that was taught not to worry about trials and tribulation was devastated. Many left the church and lost their faith in God. The church that was taught that they would have to face trials and tribulations came out stronger in their faith than they were before. I am afraid for the church in America which has been taught that before things get bad, we are "out of here." Please pray with me that the message of this book will travel rapidly and that its readers would have an open heart to receive its message.

If I am correct in this study that the church is to go through the first half of the Great Tribulation, we need to realize God does not want His church to suffer through part of the Great Tribulation for no reason. No! God wants His church to be a <u>victorious</u> church and to show Satan His church will not retreat with its tail tucked in. No! We will rise to the occasion and do exploits for God, and in the end, it will be Satan who will lose. I believe we will be the victorious church God will use to reach out and snatch the lost out of Satan's grasp. Every time we lead a lost soul to Christ, it is like we have punched Satan in the nose. The salvation of those lost souls will make it worth any suffering we have to endure. Sure, we will have casualties, but we will win the war!

I was watching the movie *Titanic* the other day, and this spiritual thought about the last days came to me. I watched the minister on board moving among those who were not able to get on a lifeboat; these were people who knew they were facing certain death. The minister was not looking for a way onto a lifeboat because he knew he had a lifeboat in Christ Jesus. At the end of the movie, reportedly, most of the lifeboats were only half full, and the fortunate ones who were in lifeboats could have gone back and helped those who were in the water drowning. This inaction led to a lifetime of guilt.

In closing, as we approach the last of the last days, do we want to head for home with our lifeboat half full? Our reward is secure, so why should we be in such a hurry to head for home?

May we be ready for His Coming!

John Shorey

Appendix

Much of what is contained in this appendix is a blue print for survival

John Shorey's Ten Reasons Why We Should Prepare for the End-Times.

After creating my list, I realized I left out the most important reason of all to prepare.

Whether the timing of the rapture is Pre-trib or Mid-trib, Global events must happen to cause the nations of the world to give up their independence and join a One World Government. This event will probably be a global economic collapse. This event will cause great hardship before the One World Government is fully in place to set the stage for the antichrist to arrive. This time period, where the stage is being set for the beginning of the Great Tribulation to start, will be a time of great trial and hardship. Even if you believe we will be raptured sooner than later, you need to be prepared for this period of tribulation we will go through before the Great Tribulation even starts.

1. America must be diminished as a world super power for prophecy to be fulfilled.

2. Iran will soon have Nuke capability, and the antichrist must show up to broker a peace treaty

3. Recent elections show that America may never see the recovery and happy days of the past.

4. America is on course to crash our economy.

5. Events in Syria are pointing to the Psalms 83 War.

6. Political and natural events are points that the signs of The Lord's coming are here.

7. Many prophetic voices are giving warnings that we are in the Window of the Lord's Return.

8. I care for my family and want to provide for their safety.

9. I want to be positioned to minister to the needs of my friends, family and neighbors for the last harvest.

10. If I wait until everyone recognizes we need to prepare, it will be too late.

<u>Tips for protecting electronics from an EMP event</u>

It is becoming increasingly clear that we have enemy's that would like to see America destroyed. Terrorist's plots are being discovered and stopped monthly if not weekly in our country. One real threat that could become a reality is an EMP attack on our Land. EMP stands for Electro Magnetic Pulse. This is basically an Electric wave pulse that is given off after exploding a nuclear device in the upper atmosphere or the same effect is giving off from explosions from the sun called CME, (Coronial Mass Ejections).

The electrical waves given off from these events, basically, short circuits the delicate electronics that most appliances, radios, vehicles of transportation and most anything electrical that is exposed to these electrical waves. There are some exceptions to this, such as autos made before 1980, old tube radios and other electronic devices that don't have sensitive circuits. Think of these electrical pulses as something similar to radio waves. Radio waves will penetrate most buildings and materials. This is why few things will be safe from these damaging electrical pulses. The good news is, these electrical waves do not penetrate all materials.

It is possible to build buildings or a room in a building that is EMP proof. You can also buy or build EMP proof containers to store important electrical Items. I am going to focus this article on containers and ways to protect smaller items from the effect of an EMP event.

If money is available, there are premade EMP containers that will virtually protect its contents from a strike by lightening. These EMP proof containers that are big enough to store a small generator and radios and other important electronic devices may be purchased from Jim Bakker Ministries. Another more economical solution for protecting small electronic items is to use a metal garbage can, with a tight lid. Whether you are using a small container or an EMP proof building to protect your electronics, you are basically trying to prevent these EMP pulse waves from getting to your items of protection. There is a way to test if your protection container will do its job and that is to test your container with an FM radio. EMP waves are very similar to FM radio waves. If the radio waves will not penetrate your EMP protective container, then neither will the damaging waves of an EMP event.

If you have ever had to replace the onboard computer board for your automobile, you will see it comes shipped in a Mylar bag. This metallic bag is used to protect the sensitive circuits of this computer board from getting short circuited from even static electricity. You can purchase Mylar bags in many sizes and any electrical devices that you seal in these bags will be protected. One problem we have with modern automobiles that have sensitive circuits is the fact that they are so big; it is hard to keep our automobiles in a big enough EMP proof container. One solution to this problems is to buy all the sensitive parts that will be effected by an EMP event and place these parts in protective containers like the suggested Mylar bags. Then when the EMP event strikes you swap out the good parts for the bad.

Another solution for protecting electronic gear is to take an old Microwave oven and cut off the electric cord. This oven is designed to prevent harmful electrical waves from leaving the oven. It will also work in reverse and prevent harmful electrical waves from entering the oven.

I will conclude this discussion with some last suggestions. Some of these should work in theory, but you should test them out with a FM radio. I believe if you take Aluminum foil and tightly wrap what you want to protect, it should be fine. A metal building if properly grounded from roof to walls and walls to ground should also give some level of protection. These electrical waves coming from a Coronial Mass Ejection will seek a ground to the earth. If you can properly ground a metal building, you can guide these damaging electrical waves to a safe ground in the earth. A last solution to protect important gear is to have backup Items of those items that you would lose to an EMP event and bury them in any sort of waterproof container.

Six Enemies to Food Storage

Survival Basics: The Six Enemies of Food Storage

By Gaye Levy http://www.backdoorsurvival.com

When it comes to stockpiling survival preps, two items are always near the top my list: food and land to grow food. Those, in my opinion, are the two most valuable commodities to have if the world and society goes to heck. As I say that, I realize that the land portion of that equation may be unattainable for many. On the other hand, almost everyone can acquire food and a place to store it.

By now you have read over and over again ad nauseam that during a disaster or a SHFT disruptive event, the grocery store shelves will be barren within a day or two. In addition, there is a strong likelihood that amenities such as electricity and refrigeration will no longer be available. That's why having food, and an extensive knowledge of food storage techniques, is so important to long term survival.

Since the beginning of Backdoor Survival, I have explored many areas of preparedness, from basic preps, to more extensive studies of self-sufficiency and the psychological aspects of survival. Beyond all else, however, I have taken a keen interest in food and food storage.

With the rapid escalation of food prices, I want to reintroduce you to the six enemies of food storage. They are important to understand and, even if they are sometimes unavoidable, the six enemies are good to keep in mind as you invest in food for your prepper pantry.

The Six Enemies of Food Storage

Storing food for the long-term is a daunting task. For the short-term, you can usually find a spare shelf or two in your kitchen cabinets and call it a day. Beyond the short-term, things start to get more complicated. The reason is that most food products have a shelf life which is pretty much limited by some common factors, referred to as the Six Enemies of Food Storage:

Temperature

Oxygen

Moisture

Light

Pests

Time

As you will see, each of these factors are interrelated in such a way that there is a domino effect with all of the tiles falling upon each other and ultimately affecting your stored items in a cumulative fashion. I will briefly address each one so that this becomes clear.

Temperature: Long-term food storage is best achieved by maintaining cool, constant temperatures. Ideally, temperatures between 40 degrees and 70 degrees Fahrenheit are best for long-term storage. Anything warmer or cooler results in loss of color, nutrition, texture and taste. A common rule of thumb is that for every 18 degree Fahrenheit increase in temperature (10 degrees Celsius), your food's shelf life is cut in half.

The second factor when it comes to temperature is consistency. So if you have a location where the temperature is 40 degrees one day and 70 the next, there is going to be some loss in quality and shelf life. Let me put this another way. If you have stored your food in a garage where the temperature fluctuates between summer and winter, the shelf life will be based upon the highest temperature not the lowest.

Oxygen: Many food nutrients can oxidize in the presence of oxygen. This creates rancidity and off flavors. In addition, bacteria and microorganisms (larvae and bugs) thrive in an oxygen-rich environment. Fortunately, the use of oxygen absorbers can suck out the oxygen in your food containers, leaving only product and nitrogen (which is not harmful).

Moisture: Moisture comes in many forms, but the most typical are humidity and condensation. When stored food becomes moist or even slightly damp, molds and bacteria begin to grow, causing spoilage. If this food is consumed, illness will occur. In addition, moisture can cause packaging to break down, exposing the food to further degradation.

The ideal level of humidity for your stored food is 15% or less. I live in Washington State where the humidity is typically 60% or 70% or more. The way around the humidity and moisture issue is proper packaging. And with packaging, there are lots of choices including Mylar bags, food grade buckets with or without gamma seals, vacuum seal bags (such as the Food saver), Mason or canning jars and more. What you decide to use to package your food will dictate how much light your food is exposed to (remember those dominoes?)

Light: The easiest way to explain how light affects your stored food is to equate light to energy. When the energy of light zaps your food, it transfers some of that energy to the food itself, degrading its nutritional value, taste and appearance. This is especially true when it comes to the fat soluble vitamins such as Vitamins A, D and E as well as proteins.

Pests: Pests are another problem. Moisture and humidity provide a breeding ground for bugs and larvae of all types. Pests come in many forms. From bugs to rodents, pests are not only a nuisance, but also a major factor to eliminate when storing food for the long-term.

It is important to be aware of the pests that are particular to your geographical climate and further, that you set a barrier between your food and the critters. In addition to a physical barrier, the use of oxygen absorbers will eliminate the oxygen (air) that most pests need to survive.

Time: Over time, food will degrade in nutritional value, appearance and taste. Time is the final enemy of food storage. And while there are many items that have an extended shelf life of 20 or 30 years, unless they are properly packaged and stored, the optimal shelf life will be considerably less. If you really do desire products with a 30 year shelf life, I suggest you look at some of the commercially packaged alternatives at Ready Made Resources, and others. These days you can even find products packaged for 20 or 30 year storage at Wal-Mart and Costco online.

Resources to Mitigate the Enemies of Food Storage

Once you understand the six enemies of food storage, the challenge is to learn to store food in such a way that these issues are mitigated. The easiest and most manageable method for storing food for the long-term is to use Mylar bags, food grade buckets, and mason jars (if kept in a dark place) in conjunction with the use of oxygen absorbers.

You will find that once you get started, it is pretty easy to package up bulk food items yourself and while you may not be able to avoid fluctuations in temperature, your food will still be viable for longer than those items left in their original store packaging.

The Final Word

The intent of this article is to give you a top level overview of the considerations you need to keep in mind as you begin to acquire food products for long term storage.

I know from your many emails and comments that resolving some of these food storage woes will be difficult if not impossible. Still, knowing what they are will help you be better prepared, and if nothing else, encourage you to set up an active food rotation program. And that, in my opinion, is not a bad thing.

John Shorey's, List of the most neglected prep items

1. Extra Bibles and Devotional materials.

2. General first aid supplies

3. Prescriptions

4. Antibiotics

5. Vitamins

6. Water filters

7. Canned meats

8. A surplus of beans and rice

9. Enough sauces to go with beans, rice and pasta

10. Personal hygiene items

11. Abundance of toilet paper

12. All types of soaps

13. Extra socks and underwear

14. Extra shoes and work shoes

15. Fire extinguishers

16. Extra fuel for autos, heat, cooking and other uses

17. Misc. batteries

18. Extra food for sharing

19. Plenty of spices

20. Enough garden tools

21. Extra garden hoses

22. Abundance of garden seeds

23. Fertilizers

24. Items for pest control

25. General tool kit

26. Tools for cutting firewood

27. Tools and training and protection

28. Lanterns and fuel

29. Extra blankets and sleeping bags

30. Water storage

31. Black plastic for windows

32. Duct tape 33. Barb wire, chicken wire and fence supplies

The 100 Plus Most Important Things to Store for the Last Days

You could also call this "The Top 100 Things you should start stocking up on." Even if you don't need more than 2 (you should always have 2 of everything) each item on this list will be great for bartering.

1. Generators

2. Water Filters/Purifiers

3. Portable Toilets

4. Seasoned Firewood.

5. Lamp Oil, Wicks, Lamps, Lanterns

6. Camp Stove Fuel – Impossible to stockpile too much.

7. Guns, Ammunition, Pepper Spray, Knives, Clubs, Bats & Slingshots.

8. Hand-can openers, & hand egg beaters, whisks.

9. Honey/Syrups/white, brown sugar

10. Rice – Beans – Wheat

11. Vegetable Oil (for cooking) Without it food burns/must be boiled)

12. Charcoal, Lighter Fluid

13. Water Containers

14. Mini Heater head (Without this item, propane won't heat a room.)

15. Grain Grinder (Non-electric)

16. Propane Cylinders (Urgent: Definite shortages will occur.

17. Survival Guide Book.

18. Lantern Mantles

19. Baby Supplies: Diapers/formula. ointments/aspirin, etc.

20. Washboards, Mop Bucket w/wringer (for Laundry)

21. Propane Cook stoves

22. Vitamins

23. Propane Cylinder Handle-Holder

24. Feminine Hygiene/Haircare/Skin products.

25. Thermal underwear / Polypropylene

26. Bow saws, axes and hatchets, Wedges (also, honing oil)

27. Aluminum Foil Reg. & Heavy Duty

28. Gasoline stored with fuel stabilizer

29. Garbage Bags

30. Toilet Paper, Kleenex, Paper Towels

31. Milk – Powdered & Condensed

32. Garden Seeds (Non-Hybrid)

33. Clothes pins/line/hangers

34. Coleman's Pump Repair Kit

35. Tuna Fish (in oil)

36. Fire Extinguishers (or..large box of Baking Soda in every room)

37. First aid kits

38. Batteries

39. Garlic, spices & vinegar, baking supplies

40. Big Dogs (and plenty of dog food)

41. Flour, yeast & salt

42. Matches

43. Writing paper/pads/pencils, solar calculators

44. Insulated ice chests

45. Work boots, belts, jeans & durable shirts

46. Flashlights, Light sticks, torches, Lanterns

47. Journals, Diaries & Scrapbooks

48. Garbage cans Plastic

49. Hygiene: Shampoo, Toothbrush/paste, Mouthwash, floss

50. Cast iron cookware

51. Fishing supplies/tools

52. Mosquito coils/repellent sprays/creams

53. Duct Tape

54. Tarps/stakes/twine/nails/rope/spikes

55. Candles

56. Laundry Detergent (liquid)

57. Backpacks, Duffel Bags

58. Garden tools & supplies

59. Scissors, fabrics & sewing supplies

60. Canned Fruits, Veggies, Soups, stews, etc.

61. Bleach

62. Canning supplies, (Jars/lids/wax)

63. Knives & Sharpening tools: files, stones, steel

64. Bicycles…Tires/tubes/pumps/chains, etc

65. Sleeping Bags & blankets/pillows/mats

66. Carbon Monoxide Alarm (battery powered)

67. Games, Cards, Dice

68. Rat poison, MOUSE PRUFE II, Roach Killer

69. Mousetraps, Ant traps & cockroach magnets

70. Paper plates/cups/utensils (stock up, folks)

71. Baby wipes, oils, waterless & Antibacterial soap

72. Rain gear, rubberized boots, etc.

73. Shaving and hygiene supplies

74. Hand pumps & siphons

75. Soysauce, vinegar, bullions/gravy/soupbase

76. Boy Scout Handbook

77. Chocolate/Cocoa/Tang/Punch

78. "Survival-in-a-Can"

79. Woolen clothing, scarves/ear-muffs/mittens

80. Reading glasses

81. Window Insulation Kit

82. Crackers, saltines, pretzels, Trail mix/Jerky

83. Popcorn, Peanut Butter, Nuts

84. Socks, Underwear, T-shirts, etc. (extras)

85. Lumber (all types) and plywood to cover windows

86. Wagons & carts (for transport to and from)

87. Cots & Inflatable mattress's

88. Gloves: Work/warming/gardening, etc.

89. Lantern Hangers

90. Screen Patches, glue, nails, screws,, nuts & bolts

91. Teas

92. Coffee

93. CB Radios and other Radios

94. Extra Bibles

95. Paraffin wax

96. Glue, nails, nuts, bolts, screws, etc.

97. Chewing gum/candies

98. Atomizers (for cooling/bathing)

99. Hats & cotton neckerchiefs

100. Goats/chickens

101. Chicken wire and fence supplies

102. Plumbing supplies

103. Extra blankets and sleeping bags

104. Night vision scope

105. Potassium Iodine

106. Outdoor motion sensors, (Dakota Alert)

107. Puzzles and Board Games

108. Good reading material

109. Canned Meats and Fish

110. Solar Power system

120 Most Important Tips for Preppers

Our world is becoming increasingly unstable, and millions of Americans are feverishly preparing for what they consider to be "the end of the world as we know it". In fact, it is estimated that there are now approximately 3 million "preppers" in the United States. But for people that have never done much prepping before, getting started can be both confusing and intimidating. In fact, I get more questions about prepping than anything else. People are constantly asking me how they can prepare for the difficult times that are coming. Well, in this article I have compiled 120 powerful pieces of advice for preppers. No two situations are exactly the same. Almost every prepper approaches preparation differently, but there are some basic principles that apply to almost everyone. Without a doubt, a lot of people that are not preparing now are going to regret it in the years ahead. The global financial system is falling apart, the United States and Europe are absolutely drowning in debt, earthquakes and volcanic eruptions are becoming more frequent, signs of social decay are everywhere, and war could erupt in the Middle East at any time. Actually, it is absolutely amazing that there are so many people out there that still believe that "prepping" is not necessary.

When people ask me what they can do to prepare, there is usually one tip that I give above everything else. It is not very "sexy", but it is absolutely foundational. During the last recession, millions of people lost their jobs, and because a lot of them had no financial cushion, many of them also lost their homes. For the next couple of years, my number one tip is to build up an emergency fund. If you are a prepper, and you are living month to month, then you are in a very vulnerable position.

What is going to happen to all of your preparations if something goes wrong and you suddenly lose your home to foreclosure? I recommend that everyone have an emergency fund that will be able to cover all bills and expenses for **at least** six months.

Yes, cash is continually losing value. But during any economic downturn it is absolutely essential that you be able to continue to pay your bills. Having a cash reserve is the smart thing to do.

So what else can people do to start prepping for the tough times that are on the horizon? A good place to start is by focusing on the five basics....

1) Food

2) Water

3) Shelter

4) Energy

5) Self-Defense

If you have those five areas totally covered you will be in pretty good shape.

The following are some more things to consider as you are prepping....

*Do not post pictures of money or gold or your preps on Facebook. If you do, you might get some unwelcome visitors to your home.

*Make sure that your preparations are not against the law. If you have any doubt about this, make sure that you do not go on national television and tell all of America what you are doing.

*In the event of a major disaster, there will likely be hordes of "non-preppers" running around looking to take away the things that all of the preppers have been storing up. This is something for which you will need to be prepared for.

The following are 6 excellent privacy tips for preppers that come from an article by an anonymous author:

1. **Trust no one that you do not personally know.** Even the little old lady down the

road will rat on you if she is hungry when the SHTF.

2. **Keep your prepping to yourself.** Again, do not tell anyone you are prepping. If they know you have stores of food, where do you think they will think of first when the SHTF? Oh and don't forget, the Department of Homeland Security thinks people with stockpiles of food and weapons are potential domestic terrorist.

3. **Don't share any prepping articles on Facebook or other social media.** Don't draw attention to yourself by posting prepping articles or discussing the topic on the website. You may think you are educating your friends, but in reality you are just letting them know of your actions and plans.

4. **Make sure boxes are not labeled with the company name if you order emergency supplies.** Most companies will publish this in their ordering information. You don't want to tip off the UPS driver that you just received a year's worth of freeze dried food.

5. **Do not tell anyone what you are up to.** You don't know how hard it is for me not to tell people I meet that I was almost on the National Geographic TV show. That would be a disaster.

6. **Be alert to what others are saying.** I was sitting in my dental hygienist chair a week ago, and she told me about another customer that was storing food. She thought he might be prepping, and she said if it ever got bad, she knew where to find some food. I just acknowledged the statement and let it rest.

10 things that you can start doing right now to get yourself into a better position for the chaos that is coming....

1 - Get Out Of Debt

2 - Find New Sources Of Income

3 - Reduce Your Expenses

4 - Learn To Grow Your Own Food

5 - Make Sure You Have A Reliable Water Supply

6 - Buy Land

7 - Get off The Grid

8 - Store Non-Perishable Supplies

9 - Develop Stronger Relationships

10 - Get Educated And Stay Flexible

Norse Prepper shared 11 questions that all preppers should be asking themselves....

1. What am I preparing for?

2. Am I going to bug in or bug out?

3. Can I defend my family, property and preps?

4. Do I have enough to feed my family until order is restored?

5. How will I heat my home?

6. How will I keep clean?

7. How will I provide light and electricity?

8. How will I keep up on information and communicate with the outside world?

9. What do I have to offer others?

10. How will I fight off boredom?

11. How do I pay for all of this?

Many people do not realize this, but you can grow herbs that have tremendous healing properties

Things to consider in the event of a major economic collapse:....

#1 Food Shortages Can Actually Happen.

#2 Medicine Is one of the first things that becomes scarce during an economic collapse.

#3 When an Economy Collapses, So Might the Power Grid.

#4 During An Economic Collapse You Cannot Even Take Water For Granted.

#5 During An Economic Crisis Your Credit Cards And Debit Cards May Stop Working.

#6 Crime, Rioting and Looting Become Commonplace During An Economic Collapse.

#7 During A Financial Meltdown Many Average Citizens Will Start Bartering.

#8 Suicides Spike During an Economic Collapse.

#9 Your Currency May Rapidly Lose Value During An Economic Crisis.

#10 When Things Hit The Fan The Government Will Not Save You.

"20 Things You Will Need To Survive When The Economy Collapses And The Next Great Depression Begins"

#1) Storable Food

#2) Clean Water

#3) Shelters

#4) Warm Clothing

#5) An Axe

#6) Lighters or Matches

#7) Hiking Boots or Comfortable Shoes

#8) A Flashlight and/or Lantern

#9) A Radio

#10) Communication Equipment

#11) A Swiss Army Knife

#12) Personal Hygiene Items

#13) A First Aid Kit and Other Medical Supplies

#14) Extra Gasoline (But Be Very Careful How You Store It)

#15) A Sewing Kit

#16) Self-Defense Equipment

#17) A Compass

#18) A Hiking Backpack

#19) A Community

#20) A Backup Plan

Additional items to add to that list....

1. A K-Bar Fighting Knife

2. Salt

3. Extra Batteries

4. Medicine

5. A Camp Stove

6. Propane

7. Pet Food

8. Heirloom Seeds

9. Tools

10. An LED Headlamp

11. Candles

12. Clorox

13. Calcium Hypochlorite

14. Ziploc Bags

15. Maps Of Your Area

16. Binoculars

17. Sleeping Bags

18. Rifle For Hunting

19. Extra Socks

20. Gloves

21. Gold and Silver Coins For Bartering

The factors to consider when choosing a location for a survival retreat....

1. Property Placement

2. Community Network

3. Defensibility

4. Water Availability

5. Food Production

6. Proximity to National Forest

7. Secondary Retreat Locations

Survival Mom once shared the top ten survival tips that nobody wants to talk about

1. Duct taping your windows will not save you from radiation poisoning.

2. You may have to dig a latrine (more than one time).

3. You may not receive any government benefits or payment from your place of employment during a disaster.

4. It is possible that you may be sick or in the hospital during a disaster.

5. Your pets may not survive.

6. It is likely that your cell phone will not work.

7. No one is coming to help you.

8. Insurance doesn't cover everything, if there is an insurance company left.

9. There will not be enough food and water for everyone.

10. If it is the end of the world, the previous nine tips will not matter!!!

Off Grid Survival recently posted a list of four powerful <u>traits that most survivors have in common....</u>

1. Survivors stay Calm in the face of Danger

2. Survivalists are Experts at Improvisation

3. Survivors are D.I.Y Experts

4. Survivors are Great Leaders

But if you choose simply to have blind faith in the system and you choose to stick your head in the sand, you might find that "ignorance is bliss" for a little while but when the stuff hits the fan it is going to be incredibly painful for you.

Previous generations understood that it was wise to store up supplies in the good years in order to make things easier in the lean years.

Unfortunately, most people these days have never been through truly hard times so they have no idea what they are like.

Just because the world has enjoyed a tremendous amount of prosperity for the last several decades does not mean that things will always be this way.

Wake up, take a look at the storm on the horizon and get prepared while you still can.

If you choose not to prepare now, you will regret it later.
<u>Most of the lists above were found on the internet</u>

<u>Three Years In Hell...</u>

Coming to a neighborhood near you.

The story below is not for the faint of heart. I had serious second thoughts about putting this story in my book. In the end, the lessons to be learned outweighed the course reality of what is contained in this story. If you believe that the rapture will take you home to heaven before things get really bad, then you don't need to read this story. You can keep going to happy church, where your pastor preaches feel good sermons and does not warn you of the hard times of Great Tribulation.

If you believe, as I do, that the Church will go through rough times leading up to the forming of a one world government, with this happening before the Great Tribulation even starts, then when this one world government is formed, the antichrist will rise to power and shortly thereafter the church will go through 3 ½ years of war on the saints as taught in Daniel and the book of Revelation, if this is you, then you should read this, as it could be a good illustration of what is to come. You may even learn some tips of things you can do to prepare for these hard times to come. Please remember that this story has no Christian perspective. **John Shorey**

The following story has been translated more than once to reach us in our language. This story came out of war torn Bosnia. Some things may have been lost in the translation, some things toned down a bit and *some things, especially the terror of war, are never lost in translation:*

the actual author to this story is unknown.

I am from Bosnia. You know, between 1992 and 1995, it was hell. For one year, I lived and survived in a city with 6,000 people without water, electricity, gasoline, medical help, civil defense, distribution service, any kind of traditional service or centralized rule. Our city was blockaded by the army; and for one year, life in the city turned into total crap. We had no army, no police. We only had armed groups; those armed protected their homes and families.

When it all started, some of us were better prepared. But most of the neighbors' families had enough food only for a few days. Some had pistols; a few had AK-47s or shotguns.

After a month or two, gangs started operating, destroying everything. Hospitals, for example, turned into slaughterhouses. There was no more police. About 80 percent of the hospital staff were gone. I got lucky. My family at the time was fairly large (15 people in a large house with six pistols and three AK47's). and we survived , most of us, at least.

The Americans dropped MREs every 10 days to help blockaded cities. This was never enough. Some — very few — had gardens. It took three months for the first rumors to spread of men dying from hunger and cold. We removed all the doors, the window frames from abandoned houses, ripped up the floors and burned the furniture for heat. Many died from diseases, especially from the water (two from my own family). We drank mostly rainwater, ate pigeons and even rats.

Money soon became worthless. We returned to an exchange. For a tin can of *tushonka* (think Soviet spam), you could have a woman. (It is hard to speak of it, but it is true.) Most of the women who sold themselves were desperate mothers.

Arms, ammunition, candles, lighters, antibiotics, gasoline, batteries and food. We fought for these things like animals. In these situations, it all changes. Men become monsters. It was disgusting. Strength was in numbers. A man living alone getting killed and robbed would be just a matter of time, even if he was armed.

Today, my family is well-prepared, I am well-armed. I have experience. It does not matter what will happen: an earthquake, a war, a tsunami, aliens, terrorists, economic collapse, uprising. The important part is that something will happen.

Here's my experience: You can't make it on your own. Don't stay apart from your family; prepare together, choose reliable friends.

1. How to move safely in a city

The city was divided into communities along streets. Our street (15 to 20 homes) had patrols, five armed men every week to watch for gangs and for our enemies.

All the exchanges occurred in the street. About 5 kilometers away was an entire street for trading, all well-organized; but going there was too dangerous because of the snipers. You could also get robbed by bandits. I only went there twice, when I needed something really rare. Nobody used automobiles in the city: The streets were blocked by wreckage and by abandoned cars. Gasoline was very expensive. If one needed to go somewhere that was done at night. Never travel alone or in groups that were too big — always two to three men. All armed, travel swift, in the shadows, cross streets through ruins, not along open streets.

There were many gangs 10 to 15 men strong, some as large as 50 men. But there were also many normal men, like you and me, fathers and grandfathers, who killed and robbed. There were no "good" and "bad" men. Most were in the middle and ready for the worst.

2. What about wood? Your home city is surrounded by woods; why did you burn doors and furniture?

There were not that many woods around the city. It was very beautiful — restaurants, cinemas, schools, even an airport. Every tree in the city and in the city park was cut down for fuel in the first two months.

Without electricity for cooking and heat, we burned anything that burned. Furniture, doors, flooring: That wood burns swiftly. We had no suburbs or suburban farms. The enemy was in the suburbs. We were surrounded. Even in the city you never knew who was the enemy at any given point.

3. What knowledge was useful to you in that period?

To imagine the situation a bit better, you should know it was practically a return to the Stone Age. For example, I had a container of cooking gas. But I did not use it for heat. That would be too expensive! I attached a nozzle to it, (I made it myself) and used it to fill lighters. Lighters were precious. If a man brought an empty lighter, I would fill it; and he would give me a tin of food or a candle.

I was a paramedic. In these conditions, my knowledge was my wealth. Be curious and skilled. In these conditions, the ability to fix things is more valuable than gold. Items and supplies will inevitably run out, but your skills will keep you fed. I wish to say this: Learn to fix things, shoes or people. My neighbor, for example, knew how to make kerosene for lamps. He never went hungry.

4. If you had three months to prepare now, what would you do?

Three months? I would run away from the country? (joking)

Today, I know everything can collapse really fast. I have a stockpile of food, hygiene items, batteries — enough to last me for six months. I live in a very secure flat and own a home with a shelter in a village 5 kilometers away. Another six-month supply there, too. That's a small village; most people there are well-prepared. The war had taught them.

I have four weapons and 2,000 rounds for each. I have a garden and have learned gardening. Also, I have a good instinct. You know, when everyone around you keeps telling you it'll all be fine, but I know it will all collapse.

I have strength to do what I need to protect my family. Because when it all collapses, you must be ready to do to take drastic measures to protect your family.

Surviving on your own is practically impossible. (That's what I think.) Even when you're armed and ready, if you're alone, you'll die. I have seen that happen many times. Families and groups, well-prepared, with skills and knowledge in various fields: That's much better.

5. What should you stockpile?

That depends. Those who plan to live by theft, all they need is weapons and ammo. You must plan a defense from these who will come to get what you have prepared. You will need more food, fuel, good water, (have water filters),hygiene items, batteries, little trading items (knives, ammo, lighters, flints, soap).

Many people died from insufficient hygiene. You'll need simple items in great amounts. For example, garbage bags, lots of them, and toilet paper. Non-reusable dishes and cups: You'll need lots of them. I know that because we didn't have any at all.

As for me, a supply of hygiene items is perhaps more important than food. You can shoot a pigeon. You can find a plant to eat. You can't find or shoot any disinfectant. Disinfectant, detergents, bleach, soap, gloves, masks. First aid skills for washing wounds and burns. Perhaps you will find a doctor and will not be able to pay him. Learn to use antibiotics. It's good to have a stockpile of them.

You should choose the simplest weapons. I carry a Glock 45. I like it, but it's a rare gun here. So I have two other pistols for backup. I don't like Kalashnikov's AK 47's, but again, same story. Everyone has them; so do I.

You must own small, unnoticeable items. For example, a generator is good, but 1,000 BIC lighters are better. A generator will attract attention if there's any trouble, but 1,000 lighters are compact, cheap and can always be traded.

We usually collected rainwater into four large barrels and then boiled it. There was a small river, but the water in it became very dirty very fast. It's also important to have containers for water: barrels and buckets.

6. Were gold and silver useful?

Yes. I personally traded all the gold in the house for ammunition. Sometimes, we got our hands on money: dollars and Deutschmarks. We bought some things for them, but this was rare and prices were astronomical. For example, a can of beans cost $30 to $40. The local money quickly became worthless. Everything we needed we traded for through barter. Food and ammo was like gold.

7. Was salt expensive?

Yes, but coffee and cigarettes were even more expensive. I had lots of alcohol and traded it without problems. Alcohol consumption grew over 10 times as compared to peacetime. Perhaps today, it's more useful to keep a stock of cigarettes, lighters and batteries. They take up less space.

At this time, I was not a survivalist. We had no time to prepare — several days before the SHTF, The politicians kept repeating over the TV that everything was going according to plan, there's no reason to be concerned. When the sky fell on our heads, we took what we could.

8. Was it difficult to purchase firearms? What did you trade for arms and ammunition?

After the war, we had guns in every house. The police confiscated lots of guns at the beginning of the war. But most of them we hid. Now I have one legal gun that I have a license for. Under the law, that's called a temporary collection. If there is unrest, the government will seize all the registered guns. Never forget that.

You know, there are many people who have one legal gun, but also illegal guns if that one gets seized. If you have good trade goods, you might be able to get a gun in a tough situation. But remember, the most difficult time is the first days, and perhaps you won't have enough time to find a weapon to protect your family. To be disarmed in a time of chaos and panic is a bad idea.

In my case, there was a man who needed a car battery for his radio. He had shotguns. I traded the battery for both of them. Sometimes, I traded ammunition for food, and a few weeks later traded food for ammunition. Never did the trade at home, never in great amounts.

Few people knew how much and what I keep at home. The most important thing is to keep as many things as possible in terms of space and money. Eventually, you'll understand what is more valuable.

Note: I'll always value weapons and ammunition the most. Second? Maybe gas masks and filters.

9. What about security?

Our defenses were very primitive. Again, we weren't ready, and we used what we could. The windows were shattered, and the roofs in a horrible state after the bombings. The windows were blocked — some with sandbags, others with rocks.

I blocked the fence gate with wreckage and garbage, and used a ladder to get across the wall. When I came home, I asked someone inside to pass over the ladder. We had a fellow on our street that completely barricaded himself in his house. He broke a hole in the wall, creating a passage for himself into the ruins of the neighbor's house — a sort of secret entrance.

Maybe this would seem strange, but the most protected houses were looted and destroyed first. In my area of the city, there were beautiful houses with walls, dogs, alarms and barred windows. People attacked them first. Some held out; others didn't. It all depended how many hands and guns they had inside.

I think defense is very important, but it must be carried out unobtrusively. If you are in a city and the SHTF comes, you need a simple, non-flashy place, with lots of guns and ammo. How much ammo? As much as possible.

Make your house as unattractive as you can. Right now, I own a steel door, but that's just against the first wave of chaos. After that passes, I will leave the city to rejoin a larger group of people, my friends and family.

There were some situations during the war. There's no need for details, but we always had superior firepower and a brick wall on our side. We also constantly kept someone watching the streets. Quality organization is paramount in case of gang attacks.

Shooting was constantly heard in the city. Our perimeter was defended primitively. All the exits were barricaded and had little firing slits. Inside we had at least five family members ready for battle at any time and one man in the street, hidden in a shelter. We stayed home through the day to avoid sniper fire. At first, the weak perish, then the rest fight.

During the day, the streets were practically empty due to sniper fire. Defenses were oriented toward short-range combat alone. Many died if they went out to gather information, for example. It's important to remember we had no information, no radio, no TV — only rumors and nothing else.

There was no organized army; every man fought. We had no choice. Everybody was armed, ready to defend themselves. You should not wear quality items in the city; someone will murder you and take them. Don't even carry a "pretty" long arm, it will attract attention.

Let me tell you something: If SHTF starts tomorrow, I'll be humble. I'll look like everyone else, desperate and fearful. Maybe I'll even shout and cry a little bit. Pretty clothing is excluded altogether. I will not go out in my new tactical outfit to shout: "I have come! You're doomed, bad guys!" No, I'll stay aside, well-armed, well-prepared, waiting and evaluating my possibilities, with my best friend or brother. Super-defenses, super-guns are meaningless. If people think they should steal your things, that you're profitable, they will. It's only a question of time and the amount of guns and hands.

10. How was the situation with toilets?

We used shovels and a patch of earth near the house. Does it seem dirty? It was. We washed with rainwater or in the river, but most of the time the latter was too dangerous. We had no toilet paper; and if we had any, I would have traded it away. It was a "dirty" business. Let me give you a piece of advice: You need guns and ammo first — and second, everything else. Literally *everything*! All depends on the space and money you have.

If you forget something, there will always be someone to trade with for it. But if you forget weapons and ammo, there will be no access to trading for you.

I don't think big families are extra mouths. Big families means both, more guns and strength — and from there, everyone prepares on his own.

11. How did people treat the sick and the injured?

Most injuries were from gunfire. Without a specialist and without equipment, if an injured man found a doctor somewhere, he had about a 30 percent chance of survival.

It isn't the movie. People died. Many died from infections of superficial wounds. I had antibiotics for three to four uses — for the family, of course.

People died foolishly quite often. Simple diarrhea will kill you in a few days without medicine, with limited amounts of water.

There were many skin diseases and food poisonings... nothing to it. Many used local plants and pure alcohol — enough for the short-term, but useless in the long term. Hygiene is very important, as well as having as much medicine as possible — especially antibiotics.

<u>Words from God's prophets</u>

I have been hearing messages from God's prophetic voices and I believe as I assemble these Words from God's Prophets, It will become clear that time is running out.

John Shorey's Dream in May 2013.

May 11th Dream of a coming Northwest Earthquake

Dear Friends,

I had a dream on May 11, 2013. This dream has caused me much concern, my wanting to know if this is a revelation from God. God has called me into the prophetic and as a watchman on the wall. I have seen God confirming his call on my life with many signs and wonders. God called me to write a book on His soon return, but I have witnessed an incredible lack of interest in Christ's coming. Many pastors will no longer preach on this subject.

I labored several days over whether I should send this message to my Facebook friends and the contacts from the sale of my book. I have decided that God has not given me light to hide it under a bushel. Some of my friends will pass this off lightly, some will defriend me. I am willing to accept any criticism from man, in my efforts to be obedient to God. Below I will explain and share this dream.

It is now Tuesday evening May 14th. On Saturday, May 11th I woke up from just having a dream that was not like my normal dreams, I could remember every detail and conversation concerning this dream. In this dream, I was with people I knew from the Northwest Seattle area. It was about an earthquake that was about to hit the Northwest. It had not yet happened, but we were discussing it as if it had already happened. In the dream we knew this quake was of the same magnitude as the earthquake that hit Alaska in 1964 which is said to have been a magnitude 9.2. Like I said, we were discussing it as if it had happened but it had not yet happened. It was like I was warning the people I knew, but they would not take it seriously. However, they seemed to know it was going to happen.

I feel it will happen soon, because in the dream we were talking as if we knew it were about to happen. I am also praying that if it has to happen that it will happen on a weekend when office buildings are not occupied. I prayed for three days that God would let me know if this dream was really going to happen, I even asked if God would give this dream to me a second time, but this did not happen. This morning as I was praying, I continued to ask for God to confirm if this dream were from him. I then went to my office to read my Bible. As I was reading my Bible, I just happened to be reading from the book of Psalms and this verse jumped out at me.

Psalms 18:6-7 "In my distress I called to the Lord: I cried to my God for help. From his temple he heard my voice; my cry came before him, into his ears. The earth trembled and quaked, and the foundations of the mountains shook; they trembled because he was angry."

This verse from Psalms was the answer to my prayers. Yes this dream was from God.

It has dawned on me that this dream has a very interesting parallel to Christ's return. My Christian friends and the church in general know that Jesus is coming soon; they talk about His coming as if it was happening very soon, but they are not taking it seriously. They are not preparing for this event.

TD Hale's Dreams, Tell the Future of America

The following is a transcript of an interview with Pastor TD Hale from Calvary Christian Center in Galipolis, Ohio. In the interview, Pastor Hale describes the details of two dreams that he received from the Lord. The first dream was on December 28, 2011. The second dream was the very next night. The interview was conducted on March 27, 2012 by Rick Wiles, and was broadcast on Truenews.com.

TRANSCRIPT OF THE FIRST DREAM

With the situation that we see going on in America, with the president and the administration certainly there are warning signs coming up. On December 28, 2011, I had been seeking the Lord for a word to give to our assembly. I went to bed that night just like any other night. The Lord just really dealt with me in the middle of the night concerning things that were coming. I certainly was shocked when I saw what I saw. In the dream I began to see myself going across America. I was floating, suspended in the air going across America. I had no fear about what I was seeing. Then all of a sudden I began to see bombs had landed everywhere. The land was totally destroyed. It looked like things were totally just wiped off, grass, trees, everything. Everything was gone, burned. There was nothing left. There was nothing **on the trees. There was just total disaster. I don't know if it was** everywhere but it was everywhere that I could see, from the point I was at.

When I saw this I saw people standing around their homes and things that were left, holding onto each other. I saw people that laid dead, and I **heard the cries of the people saying, "This should never have happened,** this should **never have happened."** It was like they just kept saying it over and over again, "This should never have happened, oh Lord, this should never have happened."

You could tell that life had changed. There was no food. There was no water. I could see babies crying, grownups, men all crying, holding onto their families. They were begging God for mercy. As I moved along I saw people running, looking for their loved ones who were missing and they were completely, completely out of their minds. Insanity had taken over. I could see people slinging themselves off of bridges, committing suicide. It was just so vivid what I could see.

Then I came over a big city that looked like Columbus, Ohio. That is when all of a sudden I saw mass hysteria, riots and all kinds of things breaking out in the streets of the city. There were windows being busted. There were people just grabbing things left and right. But when I saw it, I did not see them grabbing things like TVs and electronics. They were grabbing food. They were grabbing chips. They were grabbing water. They were grabbing anything they could get in their hands to sustain their lives. It was all about survival. I could tell that this was different from riots that we have seen in the past.

They had come into the stores by the thousands, as many as could come in. I saw them pushing shelves over and pushing electronics aside. They were trying to grab the food, the bread, and the cases of water. They were seeking everything they could get for survival. The rioters were fighting among themselves. I saw one man grab a gun out of his pocket and shoot another man right in the head.

The next part of the dream was the most startling for me. As I left that place, I was going like at the speed of light. I found myself standing on the backside of the White House. As I stood there I looked up. I heard a **voice say, "Look up to the Truman balcony." I knew what a balcony was**, but I did not know the balcony had a name. I did not know that there was a Truman balcony until I later shared this with a friend who told me there is a balcony by that name at the White House. In my mind, I believe the Lord identified that to let me know that my dream was from the Lord. I saw the president of United States, President Obama, standing on the balcony and I saw in his hands a shotgun. All of a sudden, to my left hand side I heard a loud scream, real loud. When I turned my head to see where the scream was coming from I saw flying high in the air was a majestic eagle flying in the air around Washington DC. I knew that scream. I knew it was an eagle.

I saw all of a sudden the president of United States point that shotgun and shot that eagle dead and it fell to the ground. When it did I looked back up at him and he just had a smile on his face like a smirk. And **these were the words I heard in the dream, "I've done it and I won't have to deal with this in my administration."**

Then there was dead silence. Then I heard **a voice say "Tell the people** that this is my will, that this is my hand, this is the hand of the Almighty both upon the generation of the righteous and the cursed. The righteous will find their way and will know what to do. The cursed will wander around **with no compass because the cup is full.**" **There will be people running around saying we don't understand why these things are** happening, but people need to understand that God has everything under control. The Lord let me know that this is his will. This is his hand upon the righteous and the cursed and we have to accept that.

It amazes me how people have their heads buried in the sand when God is sending so many warnings to people through all kinds of His servants and yet they still will not believe. It is just like in the Bible (with ancient Israel). God sent the prophets and warned them there is going to come **destruction, there's going to come trouble, the nations are going to come in and take over. But the people said, "No that's not going to happen, God is not going to let that happen. God won't do something like that."** But then it did happen. Then the people went back to God and apologized to him and said we are sorry, but it was too late.

It is like people have fallen asleep. They don't have a prayer life. They constantly just go on as if nothing is going to happen. They act like life is going to continue on as it is, like America is going to continue on as it is, and there is no urgency. They have their heads buried in the sand, but **God is saying** "it is time to wake up. Things are getting ready to happen. **It is going to move at a fast rate. It is time to get a prayer life back."**

At that point in the dream I knew we were coming to a showdown between good versus evil. I saw people gathering in their homes and there were prayer meetings. People were praying in the spirit. Then I **heard the Lord say, "Tell my servants and my handmaidens a special** anointing will reside on you in the last days. Hold not back your voices but speak your hearts for out of them come the issues of life. Pick up the mantle of prayer and cover yourselves in a secret place of prayer. Your eyes will be anointed with a special anointing. There will be others who will be blinded to my word. All things will be revealed in their due course. There will be a supernatural wave of the spirit that will come over this **generation very soon."**

The final voices are in the land to speak one last time. Yet through the ministries of tapes and DVDs and books that people would have in their possession that God will give them that spiritual food to sustain them **during these times that are coming upon us. The Lord said, "There are harsh days coming." All of a sudden, things**

changed in the dream and I began to hear a voice, the voice of God. I saw in front of me a very old antique table. I knew there had been documents signed on this table, special documents. I am hesitant to say this but I saw a voting ballot laying there on the table. As I looked at the ballot I saw two names on it. **I saw the President's name and I saw Mitt Romney's name on it.** Then all of a sudden I looked and I saw the president of United States name check marked. I knew then what that meant. I looked at the ballot and I **saw written on the ballot, "This is the will of the Lord."** Then I woke up.

America's days are numbered. The handwriting is on the wall. I am telling my church to be prepared and to get their house in order. I am telling them that whatever they need to do for their families do it quickly.

TRANSCRIPT OF THE SECOND DREAM

The very next night I had a second dream in which I saw the American people going into slavery. In this dream I came upon a wooded area where I saw some people that were camping. They were not camping like we normally think. They were hiding. They were all standing by their tents. There were two tents. The people looked tattered. They looked like they had not taken a bath in ages. There were gallon jugs of water and **they were trying to light a fire but they didn't want to bring attention to themselves**. But they had already been found out.

I saw some federal officials coming up around and they took these families. They handcuffed the adults and took them to the cars, and they took their children with them. I also saw two elderly people and they took them and put them in the car. I saw the federal agents and they said **"We are from the United States government and you are under arrest."**

I knew that these people had been running to get away from being arrested. They took these people to some kind of a processing place. I was standing in front of this building where I watched them being taken in and processed. To me, it was like I was looking at the days of Hitler again. The building looked like it had been modernized and updated and painted, but it looked tattered and things were very run down. I knew they were old military bases that had been shut down. I saw them take the people inside where they were being processed. I even saw them being fingerprinted.

I saw rail cars that came up beside this place. I did not go into the rail cars so I did not see inside them. That frightened me. It really disturbed me. I knew America was in trouble when I saw that. I knew we were headed down a path that was not going to be turned around. I felt like I had entered into a death camp. What I saw literally sickened me. I knew that America was about to change.

Dr. Jonathan Hansen prophecy letter

On Mar 23, 2015, at 9:42 AM, "Jonathan Hansen"

<dr.jhansen@hotmail.com> wrote:

"America, America, awake out of your slumber; I will shake you, I will shake you with a shake that has never shaken you before." You flaunted yourselves above the world; you flaunted yourselves above your neighbor and your neighbors: brother against brother, kingdom against kingdom, people against people, Christian against Christian in your ungodly attempt to self-glorify yourselves. Both in the church and throughout America your leaders religiously, politically and economically are vain, corrupt and amoral. You are fast losing the salt, the purity that has held you together; that has made you great, if not the greatest of all nations. But, I will bring you down; like the wind brings down the tree, so I will bring you down. You will not escape my wrath; for it is an expression of my love, my deep love that will do all it can to get your attention before my eternal wrath, to remove all those who do not and will not love thy neighbor, will fall. Some say, many say, 'Oh, we will escape. It will not happen to us; for we are your elect; we are God's chosen.' But, I say, you have blinded yourselves with your own vanity. My elect are not the people, the church in America; but my elect are the people of the world that are called by my name and do my will on earth as it is done in heaven. Not people with a false tongue of divination of thy heart, but of divination of my will. For you are a thankless, godless, amoral generation that has been raised by the philosophies of the heathen and I will challenge your philosophies till you hate me and my people. My people will not escape your wrath -- the wrath of the world as some falsely teach; for only the world's wrath will open their eyes clearly to what I am saying so they are prepared to meet me. I am coming quickly for a people, a church without spot or wrinkle; a blood washed, blood soaked

people who are really called Christian; not the hypocritical, self-righteous, self-taught, self-educated fool who propitiates his own dogma today. I will tear down the haughty; the mighty religious leader in my kingdom, in my church who has deceived my people with your ever babbling rhetoric that has filled the pulpits across America. Instead of my church being one, you have become institutionalized where my true servants are not even welcomed because you're protecting your own man-made philosophies and your own selfish interests. You think the people are yours, but I tell you they are mine and your man-made denominational institutions will fail; for I am shaking and calling the very elect to follow me, not you. Awake, awake, oh Jerusalem; for the King of Glory is about to appear and only the true elect, the glorified elect, will live in that New Jerusalem that I am preparing. America, your religious leaders are vain and corrupt; your church leaders are vain and corrupt; your political leaders are vain and corrupt; your relatives are vain and corrupt; your neighbors are vain and corrupt. A generation of heathen, those that appear to many as the elect -- my chosen, yet, I have not accepted them because I can see their heart. They are imitations of the genuine; a pearl in the rough. But don't give up; for I will wash you and prepare you through the fire of my love, not the world's wrath, but my love. As a father chastens his children, so I will chasten you and tear down your sand castles, your delusions of grandeur, until you can see the kingdom again."

John Newpher wrote: On Monday, October 13, 2014

It is 10:45 pm and He has awakened me to write this eye opening word.

HEAR ME MY CHILDREN !!!!

THAT DAY IS TODAY ....HARKEN TO ME AND HEAR AND SEE MY WORDS TO YOU IN ACTION.

I HAVE SENT THE PROPHETS I HAVE CHOSEN AHEAD AS I DID IN THE OLD TESTAMENT.

AND YET !!!! AS THE CHILDREN OF ISRAEL .. YOU DO NOT LISTEN. WHY I ASK?

MY WORD SAYS THAT "HE WHO HAS EARS LET HIM HEAR" I WOULD SAY THAT HE WHO HAS EYES LET HIM SEE !!! AND YET ! THESE ARE MY

SERVANTS WHOM I HAVE BEEN ISSUING WARNINGS AS THEY "HAVE EARS". THEY ARE LISTENING AND ARE HEARING FROM....ME....SAITH THE LORD. I AM... HAS CALLED THEM FORTH FOR SUCH A TIME AS THIS AS...I AM ...IN CONTROL OF THIS WORLD.

I WILL UNLEASH A DESTRUCTION AS YOU HAVE NEVER SEEN AND YOU WILL NEVER SEE AGAIN.YOU ARE NOW SEEING THE BEGINNING OF THE END. "I AM" THE ALPHA THE OMEGA THE BEGINNING AND THE END...

YEA ! I HAVE SENT MANY WARNINGS AND SIGNS...BUT.... YOU DID NOT HEED THEM.YOU PRAY AND SEEK MY FACE AND ...YET... YOU DO NOT HUMBLE YOURSELF BEFORE MY THRONE ! YOU JUST GO THRU THESE DAYS AS THO THERE IS ..NOT...A...THING AT HAND ALMOST LIKE YOU ARE BLIND....YOU ARE !!

YOU ARE AND HAVE BEEN DECEIVED BY THE ENEMY...SOMETHING IS AND WILL BE HAPPENING !!

"YOU" ARGUE THE SCRIPTURES AS TO GIVE FOUNDATION TO WHAT "YOU" BELIEVE. ALSO "YOU" ARRANGE THEM WITHOUT ..SEEKING ...ME SO I MAY SPEAK TO YOU.YOU LISTEN TO OTHERS WHO WILL TICKLE YOUR EARS.....SO BE IT !

LISTEN TO THESE WHO WILL DO LITTLE TO WARN YOU OF THE THINGS AHEAD AND ...YOU WILL .... BE DECEIVED AS MY WORD SAYS !

YOU HAVE ENTERED INTO THE TIME MY SERVANTS WHO HAVE BEEN SPEAKING AND WRITING TO YOU ABOUT WHEN THINGS WILL NOT TURN AROUND AS THE WORLD SAYS AND BELIEVES. THEY ARE NOT OF THIS WORLD BUT THEY ARE FROM THE SPIRITUAL WORLD AS I HAVE CHOSEN THEM BY MY HAND SAITH THE LORD!

YOU HAVE SEEN SOME OF THESE AS WARNINGS IN THE PAST MY CHILDREN.

THE TIMES YOU ARE IN ...NOW... ARE NOT WARNINGS SO DO NOT THINK THAT THEY WILL CHANGE.....I HAVE BEGUN TO MOVE IN MY

JUDGEMENT SAITH THE LORD.

SIN IS SO PREVALENT AND OPENLY ACCEPTED BY THIS COLD WORLD. THIS WORLD IS FOCUSED ON THEMSELVES AND NOT SERVING OTHERS WITH MY WORDS. THIS WORLD DOES NOT RECEIVE ME AS THE GREAT ....I AM..... AND THEY DO NOT LOOK TO ME AS THE WAY THE TRUTH OR THE LIFE AS I HAD SENT FORTH THRU MY WORD.IT IS A WORLD OF DECEPTION...GREED...AND SO UNFAITHFUL AGAINST MY WORDS WHICH ARE UNHEEDED.

HOWEVER, MY REMNANT IS THERE AND I WILL MOVE THRU THEM AS THEY HAVE HEARD AND UNDERSTAND THE TIMES YOU ARE IN AS ...I AM ..IS SPEAKING TO THEM AND THRU THEM IN THE SPIRIT AS TO WHERE I AM TAKING THEM.

MY WORD TELLS YOU OF ALL THE THINGS THAT ...ARE COMING. THERE WILL BE SMALL HINTS OF THOSE THINGS THAT THE PROPHETS HAVE WRITTEN AND SPOKEN TO THE PEOPLE.THEY ARE COMING !

BUT NOW COMES THE FORCE OF THE TIMES YOU WERE WARNED OF... FINANCES,PESTILENCES,EARTHQUAKES,FIRES AND TURBULENCES. THIS COMING TIME IS VERY DARK....VERY DARK. AS YOU HAVE NEVER EXPERIENCED BEFORE. BUT WHEN IT IS DARK THE LIGHT SHINES BRIGHTLY ! ! IT IS YOUR TIME ! IT IS TIME ! TIME TO LET YOUR LIGHT SHINE. AS PEOPLE SEE THE DARKNESS APPROACHING AND GETTING DARKER THEY WILL SEE THE LIGHT OF THE WORLD ! I AM THE LIGHT OF SALVATION ...THE ONLY WAY....THE ONLY TRUTH....THE ONLY LIFE...LIFE AS YOU KNOW IT IS AND WILL TOTALLY CHANGE IN THE "BLINK OF AN EYE"

SEEK ME ! SEEK ME ! SEEK ME ! YES, NO MAN KNOWS THE DAY AND THE TIME YOU ARE IN LIKE I DO.....I AM.... THE AUTHOR AND FINISHER OF FAITH. AND I CALL OUT TO YOU TO WALK TOTALLY IN THAT FAITH THAT YOU ...SAY.... YOU HAVE. SEEK ME AS NEVER BEFORE MY CHILDREN.DRAW CLOSER TO ME.

This was sent to me Feb. 7th 2015

First Name = Chelsey

John Shorey,

I had a dream that a huge angel had a stainless steel arrow...there was anointing oil on the tip of the arrow. It was the hardest kind of steel and before he put it in his bow I saw the White House in front of me and all that was in the White House was a huge heart... Like a legitimate heart organ. And inside the organ was a 1 dollar bill, a 5 dollar bill, a 10 dollar bill, a 20 dollar bill, a 50 dollar bill and a 100 dollar bill... All stacked in order, the 100 dollar bill being on the very bottom of the stack. And the heart beat was barely beating it was so slow you could tell the heart was about to give out.

Then the angel shot the arrow at the White House and the arrow went through the White House and all the windows broke from the force of the arrow and the wind of heaven, and the arrow went through the heart and the stack of money bills and it caught on fire from the oil on the tip. When that happened the heart beat stopped and this constant screeching noise was released from the heart after it was hit. It was so loud I covered my ears and my ears eventually bled. This sound was a spiritual sound, pitches I've never heard before. I looked up at the angel and there was 6 more angels in a circle they were all facing away from the circle and then they all released their arrows and each arrow hit a continent and burned their money, Asia, Africa, South America, Antarctica, Europe and Australia.

Then this huge demon... I think it's the antichrist spirit... It was huge... Came out from the core of the earth and was holding 21, 6's in its hand and put 3, 6's on each arrow. (The hole of the six was around the arrow) and eventually those 6's turned green and became money but they still had the shape of a 6. More demons came and took the 6's off the arrows and broke the 6's like bread and distributed it to the people and they ate it like communion. By then my ears were bleeding real bad and then The Lord spoke to me. He said, " There will be thousands of people who will not hear me because their real God is money. This year I (this word) will be fulfilled and the economy will burn...and a one world government will be established to kick the last days in motion. Warn the people" And then I woke up.

If you believe in the message of this book and would like to share in the ministry of getting this important message out, please consider taking a part by:

- Writing about *The Window of the Lord's Return* on your blog, Twitter, MySpace, and Facebook page.

- Suggesting *The Window of the Lord's Return* to friends and send then to the books website **www.tribulationtruth.com**

- Writing a positive review on www.amazon.com.

- Purchasing additional copies to give away as gifts.

You can order additional copies of the book from my website by going to **www.tribulationtruth.com**. Special bulk quantity discounts are available.

Other teaching aids available at: **www.tribulationtruth.com**.

Recently, I did a series of television tapings where I clearly and visually outlined the highlights from my book. This is vital information I believe you and your family will want to see and share with family and friends. To order this DVD, go to my website: **www.tribulationtruth.com**

SPEAKING SCHEDULE

I am available to share the insights God has directed me to write in this Book. To contact me concerning speaking and preaching engagements, I may be reached through my web site: **www.tribulationtruth.com**.